This book is an impressive collection of the rationale, norms, roles, and procedures involved in a parish council if it is to be faithful to the Conciliar vision of church and helpful to the building up of the parish's community and mission. It is both idealistic and practical, offering ideals toward which we can strive in the Conciliar process and structures for action that help us to deal with our inevitable limitations.

Rev. Philip J. Murnion
Director, National Pastoral Life Center

The *Practical Guide* was an important book when it first appeared in 1979, for it put pastoral councils into the context of the church's history and law. Father Rademacher there blended the skills of a theologian with the experience of a pastor.

The revised edition takes into account the publication of the New Code of Canon Law and many studies on consultation in the church. But *The New Practical Guide for Parish Councils* is more than up-to-date. By inviting the collaboration of Marliss Rogers, Father Rademacher gains the perspective of a lay person, a church professional, and a woman.

Mark F. Fischer
Chairman, Parish and Diocesan Council Network

Foreword by
Most Rev. Rembert G. Weakland, O.S.B.

The New Practical Guide for Parish Councils

William J. Rademacher
with Marliss Rogers

TWENTY-THIRD PUBLICATIONS
Mystic, Connecticut

Acknowledgments

The authors and publisher are indebted to the offices and agencies of several archdioceses and dioceses that have granted permissions to reprint the various documents cited in the text and Notes of each chapter.

Permission was also granted to reproduce portions of *Sharing Wisdom*, by Sr. Mary Benet McKinney, © 1987 by Tabor Publishing, a division of DLM, Inc.

Twenty-Third Publications
P.O. Box 180
185 Willow Street
Mystic CT 06355
(203) 536-2611

ISBN: 0-89622-371-X
Library of Congress Catalog Card Number 88-50662

Edited by Daniel Connors
Designed by William Baker

The Cover Logo was rendered by Geri Guenther and is used with permission of the Parish Council Services Offices, Archdiocese of Denver. It signifies unity of effort in building the Kingdom of God. The circles depict the variety of talents of the people of God working in harmony, sharing responsibility in fulfilling their baptism-confirmation commitment and mission. The key element of the logo is the dove, indicating the source of the council's unity and love as well as the force of all strategy and action.

FOREWORD

It is only natural for Christians to compare the church today to the descriptions of the Acts of the Apostles. What an exciting church then! It seems that the action of the Holy Spirit was not only abundant in quantity but ubiquitous, too. Such a full presence of the Spirit also affected how people reacted to the events of their day. We see them full of courage even when logic would have pointed out the heavy persecution that was to follow such enthusiasm. What seems to strike us most is not just this power of the Spirit in the midst of the faith-community, but that everyone seemed to be drawn into that new life; no one was omitted, no one seemed excluded.

At times one has the impression almost of a certain rashness in the early church. They did not hesitate to say that "They and the Holy Spirit" decided this or that. Such confidence was in marked contrast to their previous timidity, their fear that the Lord would leave them orphans. The source of their strength was an unshakable faith that the Holy Spirit was truly in their midst. They had to listen to that Spirit, but they should not be afraid.

As one reads the accounts that Luke gives in Acts, one sees that the apostles exercised real leadership. They were not afraid to raise sensitive and disturbing issues to the community—What to do about the complaints of the Greeks that their widows were not being adequately cared for? What to do about the very divisive debate over circumcision for the non-Jewish converts—issues that would have tried the faith and hope of any community. But in facing these issues, the apostles sought the advice of all. They recognized the Spirit in all, and they respected the voice of that Spirit.

Luke's description, however, always sounds too easy. There is always unanimity, but does not say how it was arrived at. Paul, for example, describes the first Council of Jerusalem in much less irenic terms. He shows that the debate was animated and heated and the conclusion not understood in the same way by all. In

Luke, the unamity seems exaggerated, but the process is right. Consultation is necessary because of the communal nature of the church and the way in which the Holy Spirit animates the entire body and distributes gifts as the Spirit wishes.

Today, then, we ask the same questions the apostles must have asked at that time: How are we to listen to the Spirit in the church today? How are we to respect the action of the Spirit in each believer? How are we to arrive at that consensus that Luke describes in Acts? These are still vital questions for the church. The dynamics of the post-conciliar church make them urgent questions.

First of all, I believe we need the same trust in the Spirit that animated the first believers. Our Pentecost is no less effective than theirs. We too must be changed from a timid body into one that is courageous. We must not be afraid to trust the Spirit, to be excited about the presence of the Spirit in us, leading us and teasing us onward.

Next, we must not be afraid to tackle the tough issues. Like the apostles, we must face up to those problems that are characteristic of our age. We must not let outside forces split the hierarchy from the laity in this process; but, as we read in the Acts of the Apostles, we must again find that balance of trust and confidence between hierarchy and laity, of listening before deciding, of respecting the roles each possesses.

Lastly, we must continue to seek those forms that will work best in our day. Here we are fortunate in having the decade or more of experience with parish councils, the most promising method devised thus far for such listening and for working out the way to proceed on the local level. We know that often our political culture might intrude; we may enter meetings to debate and not to listen to God's Word and to the Spirit as they arrive to us through others. We forget so often that we are not politicians but people living out a faith. That temptation would be there regardless of the process used and, thus, we must always fight to overcome it. In doing so, we will build a sounder community of faith and be better instruments of the Spirit in the building of God's Kingdom.

I am delighted to see William J. Rademacher's *The Practical Guide for Parish Councils* revised and brought up to date, with the sure-handed assistance of Marliss Rogers. It has been a useful handbook for all of us in the last decade, a book full of wisdom and practical advice. After ten years of experience and experimentation, one can only be joyful and grateful that a new and insightful edition has been prepared.

May it be an instrument for continuing to unlock the action of the Spirit among us today.

Most Reverend Rembert G. Weakland, O.S.B.
Archbishop of Milwaukee

PREFACES

It has been ten years since the first edition of *The Practical Guide for Parish Councils* was published. On the level of theory it was designed to help parishioners apply Vatican II pastoral theology to their parish councils. On the level of practice it was meant to be a "how-to" handbook for the organization and operation of parish councils.

As the church moves into the next decade, it is encouraging to note that parish pastoral councils continue to grow and develop. If this *Guide* is going to be a real guide, it has to keep pace with that growth and, indeed, lead it. For this reason, an updated and enlarged edition of *The Guide* is now offered.

The publication of the new Code of Canon Law has serious implications for the council's structure and decision-making process. At the same time, more and more lay and religious pastoral associates have joined the pastor to form parish pastoral teams. Then, too, many councilors have expressed the hope that *The Guide* would deal more extensively with the whole question of lay spirituality.

Since starting my own parish council in 1964, I have conducted over 250 workshops in over 40 dioceses in the U.S. and Canada. I have been edified by the zeal and dedication of parish councilors across the country. In offering this new edition of *The Guide* I hope I can do my little part to help those councilors as they respond to the Spirit's call for the renewal of their parishes.

As this major revision goes to press, I want to thank Marliss Rogers, my co-worker on this project. Her practical experience in ministering to the parish councils of the Archdiocese of Milwaukee is a precious gift to this book. I also thank her for gently correcting my occasional lapses into sexist language. I pray with her that our words may serve the upbuilding of the church and its parish pastoral councils.

William J. Rademacher

It is satisfying to have an opportunity to share with councilors throughout the country some of the insights and concerns about council ministry that it has been my privilege to experience over the past 15 years. Working with councils in Milwaukee has been both a joy and a challenge. As a team coordinator for councils in the archdiocese, I have dialogued with councilors in many different parishes, large and small, and with their pastors, and responded to all kinds of queries about how councils function. Most councilors sincerely wish to help their councils become more pastoral and prayerful, more centered on parish mission. The importance of good organization for councils and their committees also cannot be underestimated.

I have also had the privilege of serving on the preceeding organization to PADICON (Parish and Diocesan Council Network) on the national level, and to present parish council workshops across the country. All of this experience with councils indicates to me that they remain an important part of parish life.

Councils are bound to continue to change and grow. I strongly believe, however, that some form of parish council is essential to good leadership and to give people in parishes a real voice in the decisions that affect their faith lives. It is my hope and prayer that councils will move ever deeper into discernment of the Lord's will and the common good, and that they will learn to exercise a prophetic ministry for the parish as it moves into the future.

It has been a joy to work with Fr. Rademacher again on this project. I would also like to thank my fellow team coordinator in the office, Fr. Mike Hammer, whose vision for councils has been both steady and creative, and Maureen Fletcher, whose able computer assistance was invaluable.

Marliss Rogers

CONTENTS

CHAPTER 1

CONGRATULATIONS!

The votes are in. You've been elected or discerned to the parish pastoral council. You have mixed feelings. On the one hand, you are excited about the prospect of sharing your talents and experience with the parish council. On the other hand, you wonder what it's all about. "Will it be worth it? What's the next step?"

First, congratulations on responding to the call to serve on the council! You now have a unique opportunity to help build up your council, your parish, your church.

Serving on the council can be a challenging experience. It is a time for giving. A time for receiving. A time for growing. It is a time to be a pioneer in creating a more responsive and more responsible church. It all begins with you in your parish. Your council, just like the parish, is a living organism. It is a unique and often mysterious meeting of the human and the divine. Your very presence affects the human chemistry of the council. Your timely humor reduces tension. Your optimism kindles hope. Your questions open new doors. Your faith strengthens the weak. Your cheerful acceptance of committee work lights a spark in the passive and apathetic. Your attentive listening is healing and compassion for the pain of rejection and loneliness within the Christian community.

The risen Lord, in his own mysterious ways, builds up his church through you. He uses humble elements like water and oil in baptism. He uses simple bread and wine in the eucharist. He uses you in the council. "For where two or three are gathered in my name, there am I in the midst of them" (Matt. 18:20). At times you may not feel up to the task. That's understandable.

However, Paul has a word for you: "But thanks be to God, who in Christ always leads us in triumph and through us spreads the fragrance of knowledge of him everywhere. For we are the aroma of Christ..." (1 Cor. 14-15). "My grace is sufficient for you, for my power is made perfect in weakness" (2 Cor. 12, 9).

The council is a microcosm of the Christian community. It brings together one living cell of the body that is the church. It is a meeting of the mystery of holiness and the mystery of evil. It is a "get-together" of Christian believers who come with different visions, different perspectives, and even different expressions of the faith. They are all graced by the Lord's holiness and, at the same time, flawed by the effects of original sin. Their collaboration on the council is a model for the parish's collaboration in the mission of the church.

Dreamers, Doers, Criticizers

The council also brings together the Dreamers, the Doers, and the Criticizers. Those who are dreamers at heart are poets, artists, or mystics. Responding to intuition, they are full of great ideas. Rich in imagination, they soar high above the nitty-gritty of the organizational details. They have the grand, and sometimes grandiose vision, but they don't know how to put it into practice. They can't come up with any concrete plan of action. For that, they need someone else. Doers are the practical ones. They want to get moving. They get impatient with all the talk about goals, vision, and pastoral priorities. "Let's cut the discussion! Let's get on with the building campaign." The criticizers are skeptical. They question everything. They test and challenge: "It won't work. We tried that before." They are super-cautious. They have no patience for the dreamer and are skeptical of the doer.

Now a good council needs them all—the dreamers, the doers, and the criticizers. It is from the fruitful interaction of all three types that the best parish policies will emerge. Your parish council is not perfect. Like the church itself, it is constantly in need of renewal and reform. It hasn't arrived at the kingdom of heaven yet. It is still searching. It is very much a part of the church's earthly pilgrimage. That means there's lots of room for folks like yourself.

So, once again, welcome to council ministry! May serving on the council be a pleasant and challenging experience. May this book become your friend and guide as you offer your gifts and talents to the upbuilding of the church.

Sharing

1. Each member of the council shares why she or he made a commitment to serve on the council.
2. Discuss how the council is a "microcosm" of the Christian community.
3. Each councilor shares whether he or she is a "doer," a "dreamer," or a "criticizer." How can these personality styles be blended on our council?

CHAPTER 2

COUNCILS
AND THE PEOPLE OF GOD

Vatican II doesn't give us a blueprint about either the theory or the practice of parish pastoral councils, and they are mentioned in the revised Code of Canon Law in only a limited sense. Vatican II does, however, provide us with the broad themes that rightly lead to the formation of parish councils. One such theme is the image or model of the church as the people of God. This model is described at length in the second chapter of *The Constitution on the Church*, entitled, "The People of God." Fr. Avery Dulles, S.J., in his book, *Models of the Church*, explains the historical development of this model in his chapter, "The Church as Mystical Communion."

The bishops of Vatican II chose the title "The People of God" first, because they wanted the church to be seen in its totality according to what is common to all the faithful, and second, because the pastors and the faithful collaborate in the diffusion and sanctification of the whole church.

The themes with special application to parish councils can be quickly summarized: (1) The church is seen as a new people of God, coming into existence because Christ instituted a new covenant in his blood.[1] (2) This people is established as a communion of life, love, and truth. (3) This people is used by Christ as the instrument of salvation for all. (4) This people has the dignity and freedom of the sons and daughters of God. (5) In virtue of baptism, this people is "consecrated...to be a holy priesthood" and "shares in the one priesthood of Christ." (6) It shares in the prophetic office of Christ. (7) It is filled with the Holy Spirit who distributes special graces among the faithful of every rank, making them fit and ready to undertake various tasks and offices for the renewal and building up of the church.[2] (8) This people is a communion of disciples who have the obligation of spreading the faith to the best of their ability.[3] Now let's discuss these eight themes in order.

1) The first point to note in the formation of the people of God is that it is God who chooses this people. Christians do not become God's people by lifting themselves up by their own bootstraps. It's not by their own efforts, however pious, that they acquire a claim on God. Instead they are chosen by the free and gracious will of God. They become God's people when they respond in faith to God's choice, i.e., when, by saying "Yes," they let God make them God's people.

We don't belong to the people of God because we are Mexican, Canadian, German, Polish, Irish, or American, or because we were all "brought up Catholic," or because we all worked so hard together building our parish. We don't belong to the people of God because we pray the rosary and obey the pope, or because we belong to the Knights of Columbus, or even because we go to church on Sunday.

We belong to the people of God because God freely chooses us, because in faith we say "Yes," and finally, because in baptism we become part of that new covenant instituted by the blood of Christ. The people of God comes into existence not through church law, custom, or tradition but through God's free choice.

2) This people is called to be a community. The people of God become one people, not because the laws are the same in every diocese, but because they all respond to one call. They become a communion in "one body, one Spirit...one Lord, one faith, one baptism, one God and Father of us all, who is above all, through all and in all" (Eph. 4:4-6). Because of God's call (vocation) and the people's "Yes," there comes into existence "a communion of life, love, and truth."

The people of God's unity or communion of life, love, and truth consists in the following: (1) oneness in mission, (2) oneness in witness, (3) oneness in prayer and praise, (4) mutual dependence and interdependence conferred by common faith, (5) the bonds of faith being more powerful and more demanding than a table of laws, (6) the brotherhood and sisterhood of faith fashioning or constituting all the structures (such as diocesan and parish councils) within the people of God.

3) This community is called to be a community of salvation. When God chooses us to be the people of God, it is for a purpose. God doesn't choose us so "we can save our souls," or so "we'll get to heaven." God chooses us so we can be instruments of salvation for all. God chooses us not for privilege, but for responsibility, not for security, but for service. God's call is not a once-for-all happening at a particular hour on the clock. God calls us constantly. He calls us to new responsibility and to new service. That is why we need constantly to come together in meetings (even council meetings) to discern God's will, to hear and respond to this call anew.

4) This people is "graced" with Christian dignity and freedom. Because this people belongs to God, it is a free people. It cannot again become enslaved to mere human laws. By Christ's death and resurrection, it has been freed from demonic power, from the stranglehold of evil. It has also been freed from slavery to the law. It cannot be forced to march like an army. Its freedom and dignity must be respected. No one can legislate or pre-program the form of the people's response to God's call to service. It must be the free, internal response of a lover.

It must also be the response of mature, adult, responsible men and women. Paternalism and authoritarianism can have no place within this new people. No one may assault its freedom and dignity and reduce the citizens of the kingdom of God to the status of children even though some people would prefer that. ("Let Father do it. I'm not interested in responsibility.") Laity who passively accept token or "paper" councils demean their own dignity and status as a people of God.

5) This new people, in virtue of one baptism, shares in the one priesthood of Christ. This means that the risen Lord's present saving activity is at work, in some way, through all the baptized,

without regard to sex or ecclesiastical ranking systems. The risen Lord does not have to ask for Father's blessing or permission before he uses a baptized person "as instrument of salvation for all."

As the risen Lord uses water, oil, bread, and wine as instruments of saving grace, so Christ can and does use all the baptized as his anointed instruments and ministers of his own holiness. This means that the baptized participate in the mission of Christ, not the mission of Fr. Joe Smith. It means, further, that the baptized are not "Father's helpers," but like Prisca and Aquila, "fellow workers in Christ Jesus" (Rom. 16:3). "So neither he who plants nor he who waters is anything but only God who gives the growth" (1 Cor. 3:7).

6) All the people of God also share in Christ's prophetic office. The Jesus in the New Testament is more prophet than priest. This does not mean that Jesus spends all his time predicting the future. It means he confronts the value systems of both the religious and secular establishment. When the Jewish religious leaders say: "Stone the woman," Jesus says: "Accept her." When the religious and civil law says: "Do not associate with women, sinners, or Samaritans," Jesus "eats and drinks with them." When society says: "Pay special attention to what you shall eat, drink, and wear," Jesus says: "Do not be anxious saying, 'What shall we eat?' or 'What shall we drink?' or 'What shall we wear?'"

In their prophetic ministry, the baptized people of today share in that same mission whereby the risen lord still confronts the value systems of society. When society says: "First seek your own human fulfillment," the people of God say: "Deny yourself." When society says: "Look first to your own security in stocks, housing, and insurance," the people of God say: "Seek first the kingdom of God." When society practices racial and sexual discrimination, the people of God say: "In the kingdom of God there is neither Jew nor Greek, there is neither slave nor free, there is neither male nor female" (Gal. 3:28).

7) The Spirit equips the people of God for the work of the ministry (Eph. 4:12). The gifts are allotted according to the measure of faith, as the Spirit wills.

The Spirit makes the people of God fit and ready to undertake various tasks and offices for the renewal and upbuilding of the church. This means that the Spirit is constantly active in every believing Christian, acting on the Spirit's terms, not theirs.

This mysterious activity of the Spirit means that Christians don't have to be ordained before they begin to minister in the building up of the church. It also means that most parishes probably have more gifts and talents than they need. These gifts may still need to be discovered, trained, and then supported by the people of God. These gifts also need to be submitted to a process of prayerful discernment to determine if they are truly of the Spirit. For the mystery of evil is also at work within the people of God, and not every movement, inspiration, or religious outburst is of the Spirit.

8) The people of God are all called to be a communion of disciples in the Lord. They are called to follow him in laying down their lives for others. To follow the Lord as a disciple is to become totally identified with his mission in today's world. The word "disciple" is used 250 times in the New Testament. Discipleship is one of the most pervasive themes in the early church. All councilors, therefore, when they gather around the table for their monthly meeting, are first called to be faithful disciples of the Lord.

Since the sisterhood and brotherhood of faith is the first and foremost reality of the people of God, a parish council needs to grow out of, and witness to, that reality. It needs to be a sign of the *basic equality* of all the members rather than a sign of social or religious castes. It needs to witness to unity as a unique and precious value within the Christian community.

While there's always room for healthy conflict, the council is no place for cliques, factionalism, or political partisanship. The council can't be a lay group organized against the rectory or the clergy. The priests, deacons, and religious, in spite of their unique ministries, are members of the council. Like the rest of the councilors, they are first baptized Christians and disciples of the Lord.

The theology of the people of God, which has just been explained, has some practical application for the operation of parish councils. It means that the council is called to rely more on faith, prayer, and the Spirit than on its bylaws and constitution. Voting procedures may be helpful but faith in the Lord and in fellow Christians is primary. Every meeting is meant to be an experience in faith and in community. Since councilors are citizens of the kingdom, they enjoy the freedom and dignity of the sons and daughters of God. They may not be used as rubber stamps. They may not be manipulated by agenda control or by invoking the mystery of secret knowledge, for example, canon law, theology, the "mind" of the bishop, etc.

Even though a pastor could easily take advantage of some passive and ignorant lay persons, he needs to challenge them to assume their full responsibility in serious, and often unpopular, decisions. He may have to pitch some hot potatoes into the lap of the council. It may take more time to reach a decision that way, but a lot of people will become more mature and more responsible in the process. Since the baptized laypersons share in the priestly and prophetic mission of Christ, and not of the pastor, their service on the council can hardly be reduced to advice-giving. When Paul tells us in Eph. 4:11 that Christ equips the saints (i.e., the baptized) for the work of the ministry, he speaks of prophets, evangelists, and teachers. It is evident that the Spirit doesn't limit the baptized to one gift—advice-giving. (More about this in Chapters 5 and 6.)

Just as the prophets Amos and Micah rebuked the old people of God for their sins against justice, so councilors today may be called, in view of their prophetic ministry, to confront the new people of God for their sins against justice. For example, several parish councils in one diocese, after much prayer and reflection, determined that the parishes would become sanctuary sites for Central American refugees. They provide a striking example for the whole church. The recent U.S. bishops' pastoral, *Economic Justice for All*, challenges parish leaders and all Christians to renewed commitment to justice in the economic life of our country. Parish councilors may expect to meet some bitter opposition from some other parish members when they take prophetic stands on issues.

Since the Spirit is in all the baptized according to the measure of faith, councils must have respect and even reverence for the opinions of the most uneducated member of the council. The Spirit's activity is not limited to the learned. On the other hand, Paul tells us the Spirit gives many "natural" gifts. He mentions teaching, helping, administering, serving, and exhorting. Thus, the Spirit can and does act through professional experts who have their "measure of faith" and who give the gift of their specialized training to the upbuilding of the church. The council needs the gifts of the trained teacher, accountant, writer, and communications expert. It also needs to keep a balance between the grass-roots people and the trained experts. The Spirit has made no covenant to work more through one than through the other.

A meeting of the council, therefore, isn't just another meeting. It is an experience in the mystery of being church according to the model of the people of God. Since the people of God is a sharing community, it is called especially to share the Lord's gifts. The next chapter will explore how this sharing of gifts can be carried out.

Notes

1. *Dogmatic Constitution on the Church*, in *Vatican Council II*, p. 359.
2. *Ibid.*, p. 363.
3. *Ibid.*, p. 369.

Sharing
1. If God's call to become a community is ongoing, what does this say about the way we meet?
2. In what ways does our council confront the value systems of today's society? What values underlie council decisions?
3. What gifts are present among our council members? How will we use them in service to the parish and community?

CHAPTER 3

SHARING OUR DIVERSE MINISTRIES

Having gifts that differ...let us use them" (Rom. 12:6).

We live in a world of teamwork. Without the teamwork of a wide variety of skilled technicians, a moon trip would be impossible. Every ship heading out to sea needs a radio operator, an engineer, a mechanic, a navigator, a cook, a captain, etc. Every jet winging into the sky needs a pilot, a copilot, an air traffic controller, etc.

The parish also needs the help of diverse skills, talents and services. In the church we call these services ministries. Some Catholics feel the word ministry is "Protestant." Others feel that it has something to do with ordination and therefore applies mostly to what goes on in the sanctuary.

Ministry is not a Protestant word. Nor is it restricted to ordination or to "churchy" activity. In the New Testament, ministry is any service offered in genuine love for the common good in the name of the Lord. In the early church any significant activity done for the upbuilding of the church was considered ministry. Thus, in Acts 6:3, serving at table is ministry. It is at least possible that this ministry included managing the money table (like operating the cash register) for the daily distribution to the poor. In 2 Cor. 9:12 the collection for "the saints" in Jerusalem is called a ministry. In 1 Cor. 16:15 Stephanas is overseeing a house church. His service is called a "ministry to the saints."

Whether it is preaching the word (Acts 6:4), or washing the feet of the disciples (John 13:15), it is called ministry. In the early church, ministry, in the humble sense of the servant who waits at table, was the word for all loving care for others. The crucial point is not the kind of work being done, but the quality of love that inspires that work.

That ministry is not restricted to ordination is also plain from Pope Paul VI's exhortation, *On Evangelization in the Modern World:*

The laity can also feel themselves called, or be called, to work with their pastors in the service of the ecclesial community, for its growth and life, by exercising a great variety of ministries according to the grace and charisms which the Lord is pleased to give them. It is certain that, side by side with the ordained ministries...the church recognizes the place of nonordained ministries which are able to offer a particular service to the church.[1]

The Spirit gives gifts to all the baptized according to the measure of faith (Rom. 12:3). "Having gifts that differ according to the grace given to us, let us use them...if service, in our serving; he who teaches, in his teaching; he who exhorts, in his exhortation...he who does acts of mercy, with cheerfulness" (Rom. 12:6-8). In 1 Cor. 12:28 Paul lists the ministries of healing, helping, and administering along with the ministry of the apostles and prophets. He doesn't require ordination as a prerequisite to ministry. If Paul were writing today, he certainly would list service on the parish council as a ministry.

In spite of the Bible's broad use of the word ministry, however, not every good deed is ministry. (1) It has to be done in the name of Jesus/Lord (Col. 3:17). Agnostic humanists who feed the hungry and give drink to the thirsty are not doing ministry, for they are not acting in the name of the Lord. They are *still* doing good deeds but not ministry.

2) Ministry needs to be done for the upbuilding of the church, the people of God. That means that whatever is done can't wreck or tear down the church, as would preaching heresy or profaning the sacraments. Ministry needs to witness to the sav-

ing activity of the risen Lord in and through his people.

3) All ministry has a public dimension to it. The church, as a recognizable group of people, is by its very nature public. Strictly private and personal services or love that do not issue into action are not ministry.

4) Ministry is not really reducible to a single external act. It needs to flow from an inner, more or less permanent, commitment to the Lord. And it can't be separated from that inner commitment. It has to be done out of genuine love.

5) All ministry is accountable to the church, the people of God, especially to its leaders. In 1 Cor. 14:28, Paul told the speakers in tongues (one of the ministries listed in 1 Cor. 12:10) to be silent because without an interpreter, their ministry wasn't building up the church. Paul, in virtue of his apostolic authority, made a judgment about their ministry and found it wanting in its upbuilding dimension.

6) Ministry needs to be done in a context of *ordered* relationships. Paul's two images of the body (1 Cor. 12:12-26) and the building of God (1 Cor. 3:9) help us here. If the teeth start biting the fingernails and then the fingers, the brain has to tell the teeth to stop. The teeth are "ministering" out of order. They are "ministering" in the wrong place.

In the same way, in Paul's image of the building of God, if a carpenter, on some early Monday morning, is found nailing in a 2 x 4 in the middle of the living room, someone has to say: "Hey, you're nailing that 2 x 4 in the wrong place." It may be another carpenter (co-worker's correction) or the supervisor (bishop), but someone has to do it. So, too, in the church, a ministering person can't just go around doing his or her own thing. Ministry has to be done in an order of relationships with the other ministries and with the total mission of the church. Otherwise, the minister may indeed be working hard, but nailing the 2 x 4 in the wrong place.

Ministry and the Council

Now how does this explanation of ministry apply to parish pastoral councils? In the first place, it should have some effect on the attitude of the councilor. What motives inspire the ministry of the man or woman who is elected to serve on the council? Bishop Kenneth Untener speaks to this question:

> If parish council service were considered a ministry, the whole process (of elections) would be cast in a new light. A ministry is a gift from God, and candidates for ministry respond because they sense a call from God to use that gift— even when it is not something they particularly feel like doing. (Moses, for example, did not jump at the chance to lead the Israelites...but he was called by God to do so.) That should be the spirit of parish council nominations.[2]

Ministry emphasizes *serving* more than representing. Parishioners sit on the council because God has "gifted" them and called them to serve the whole parish.

> When parish council members see their role as a ministry to the entire parish, they try to build a community rather than a constituency. They are called, as every minister is called, to join in searching out the will of the Father rather than simply representing special interests.[3]

Second, ministry means that those who serve on the council are expected to be *accountable*. They are accountable in the first instance to the council itself. But more especially, they are accountable to the Lord, to the diocesan church, and to the whole parish community. Ministry in the New Testament is not for the minister, but for the upbuilding of the church. For this reason, the church and the parish community can set down certain standards or qualifications for ministry on the council. They can insist that councilors be exemplary Christians, that they have sufficient knowledge, that they truly wish to prepare themselves to serve the whole parish, etc. (More about this in Chapter 9.)

Finally, serving on the council is a *public* ministry. This means, among other things, that some kind of public installation ceremony is entirely appropriate. This ceremony first praises God for the gifts God has given to the church in the person of the councilor. Then it establishes a relationship of support and accountability between the serving councilor and the whole parish community which, by its applause, expresses its support of the councilor's ministry.

Shared Ministries

Now that we know that serving on the council is true ministry, we can proceed to the shared aspect of all ministry.

In the church, there is no "Lone Ranger" ministry. The shared aspect of ministry flows from the fact that the Christian community as such is a sharing community. It shares in the breaking of the bread and in the drinking of the cup. It shares in a "partnership in the gospel" (Phil. 1:5).

Paul calls the Christian community a *koinonia* (1 Cor. 1:9). The literal meaning of this Greek work is partnership. It means "a sharing in." It can also mean "fellowship." In secular Greek, *koinonia* refers to the intimate partnership of the marriage relationship. It indicates the mutual, reciprocal giving and receiving that is the very life of any true partnership. If ministry is going to be truly Christian, it needs to be true to the shared aspect of a sharing Christian community. The meeting of a parish council is a time for that mutual giving and receiving that is a mark of a sharing Christian community.

In the church, therefore, all ministry is to some extent incomplete. In Phil. 2:25 Paul does not hesitate to acknowledge that Epaphroditus ministers to his need. Paul commends Epaphroditus "for...risking his life to complete your service to me" (Phil. 2:30). Paul often refers to Timothy, Titus, Stephanas, and Apollos as his fellow workers. In Phil 4:2 Paul writes: "And I ask you also, true yokefellow, help these women for they have labored side by side with me in the gospel. . . ." In Rom. 16:3 we read: "Greet Prisca and Aquila, my fellow workers in Christ Jesus."

It's okay, therefore, to admit the incompleteness of our ministry. We can say that we can't do everything. The pastor needs the ministry of the accountant. The teacher needs the ministry of the printer. The marriage councilor needs the reconciling ministry of the priest. And the priest who ministers healing to his people, is himself in need of being healed.

Fortunately, we don't need to do everything. We don't need to be omni-competent. Millions of baptized Christians are both able and willing to complete the incompleteness of our ministry. The process whereby one ministry is completed by another is

easily understood from the two Pauline images: the body of
Christ and the building of God. In Rom. 12:4-6 Paul writes: "for
as in one body we have many members, and all the members do
not have the same function, so we, though many, are one body in
Christ, and individual members of one another."

The human body is an interlinkage of many services: the service of the hands helping the feet, the service of the tongue
helping the teeth, the service of the ears helping the eyes, the
service of the heart helping the brain, etc. The service of one
member is, to some extent, incomplete without the service of another. The Pauline body image is a sign that the pluriformity
and the interdependence of various ministries is an essential
part of the life of the church.

We don't need to be housebuilders to understand Paul's second
image, the building of God (1 Cor. 3:9). For Paul, the church is
always in process of being built up because its members, responding to the Lord's grace, are all offering their different skills as
ministries in the church.

Paul's idea is that every Christian has been gifted with
some talent to serve the total upbuilding process. This skill or
talent can rightly be called a ministry. In Paul's upbuilding
process, there is no passive audience. There aren't any bleach-
ers. Everybody is involved. Building a house requires a variety
of builders: carpenters, painters, plumbers, plasterers, electricians, sweepers, etc. Electricians, for example, can't build the
house alone. They need to coordinate their skills with those of
the other builders and all work from one master plan.

So also in the parish. Each parish community needs a variety of ministers: lectors, teachers, religious education coordinators, ministers of eucharist and of music, ministers to the poor
and to the sick, ministers for communications, for health care,
helpers, administrators, accountants, preachers of the Word,
and councilors. None of these ministers can build up the church
alone. All need to relate their ministries to one another so they
will truly be partners in the total upbuilding process. They need
to coordinate ministries by working from one common plan.

In this upbuilding process, parish councils have a threefold

function: (1) they take an inventory of the needs of the parish;
(2) they discern who in the parish has what gift, skill, or ministry; (3) they serve as the coordinating body in relating the
ministries to the needs, and the ministries to one another.

Because each parish has a wide variety of needs, it is plain
that each parish needs a diversity of skills or ministries. At
the same time, if the parish is going to be true to its call to be a
sharing community, all these ministries need constantly to be in
a sharing relationship with one another. They need to support
one another in a concrete, positive way. As a husband is supportive of his wife and vice versa, so each minister is supportive of
the other ministries. That's how the church gets built up.

It hardly needs saying that Paul doesn't view the church as
a coming together of distinct classes: priests, deacons, laity,
brothers, sisters, etc. He doesn't believe in a caste system. His
church gets built up on the basis of different functions: evangelists, pastors, teachers, healers, prophets, administrators, etc.

Parish councils, therefore, do not primarily represent various
classes of people: youth, senior citizens, clergy, laity, religious,
minority groups, etc. Councilors don't come to a meeting primarily to represent, or lobby for, a particular class or faction in the
parish. They come because they have a function, a ministry, to
offer for the whole parish. The councilor may be a youth or a
senior citizen, a black or a white, but the function, the ministry,
is more important than either age or skin color, for neither age
nor skin by itself builds up the church.

Finally, Paul doesn't measure the value of a ministry by any
kind of ecclesiastical ranking system. Whatever ministry
builds up the church the most is the most valuable. Thus, lay
ministries could be more valuable than priestly ministries because they build up the church more. On Paul's scale, the ministry of Mother Teresa of Calcutta is probably more valuable
than that of many priests and bishops. In the final analysis
only God knows whose ministry is the more valuable.

The council is, of course, not concerned about ranking any ministries. It is more concerned with activating all the people of the
parish to share and develop their diverse ministries. The council

serves as an enabler for all the ministries in the whole parish.

Councilors, therefore, have to resist the temptation to do everything themselves. Before Vatican II, the priest did everything. Now, in some parishes, the council does everything. That means the number of ministers has increased from one to about 15. That's not much progress. It means that the council hasn't understood that its first ministry is to enable and facilitate the diverse ministries in the rest of the parish. Councilors should not give the impression that the Spirit has favored them with gifts, but bypassed everybody else. They need to help the people develop their own untapped gifts.

The council will be a leaven for all the gifts of the parish if it takes to heart the advice of St. Ignatius of Antioch (c. 107) writing to the church of the Smyrnaeans: "Labor with one another, struggle together, rise up together as God's stewards and assessors and servants."[4] The meetings of the council may be a time to get some business done. But more important, they are a time to share, support, complete, coordinate, and evaluate the various ministries that build up the parish.

Now we need to understand how these ministries relate to the parish council and its functions. Thus, Chapter 4.

Notes

1. New York: Daughters of St. Paul Press, 1976, p. 48.

2. Bishop Kenneth Untener, *The Michigan Catholic* (Editorial), March 18, 1977.

3. *Ibid.*

4. *The Apostolic Fathers*, Kirsopp Lake, Trans. (Cambridge: Harvard University Press, 1970), p. 275.

Sharing

1. How did the early church view ministry? What were some of the ministries Paul mentions in his letters?

2. Why is it so important that ministry be exercised within a context of ordered relationships?

3. To whom is the ministry of parish councils accountable? Why?

CHAPTER 4

THE PARISH COUNCIL:
ITS PURPOSES AND FUNCTIONS

Many parish pastoral councils were organized after the Second Vatican Council. In general, they have been part of the postconciliar movement toward shared responsibility and shared ministry. They are so many little models of the church as a communion of the people of God. They witness to the basic equality of all the baptized. The revised Code of Canon Law provides for the formation of parish councils in Canon 536, #1:

> In every parish in the diocese, a Pastoral Council shall be established, if the diocesan Bishop, after consulting with the Council of Presbyters, so decides. The pastor presides over the Pastoral Council. The Pastoral Council is composed of members of the congregation together with those on the parish staff who have pastoral care by reason of their office. The Pastoral Council assists in promoting pastoral action in the parish.

But even if Vatican II had not recommended the formation of councils and they were not provided for in Canon Law, there are many reasons why they make a lot of sense.

1) Parish councils help to discern the needs of the parish and the community. Since councilors ideally represent all the parishioners, they have their finger on the pulse of the parish. They can report what they feel. They can sense the gap between the demands of the Gospel proclaimed in the pulpit and the actual Christian life in the world. Parish councils often conduct open forums to learn more about the needs and concerns of people

in the local community. They hold weekend workshops where they have brainstorm sessions concerning the needs of the parish.

For example, one council, while brainstorming for parish needs, discovered that it had no programs for its senior citizens and no committee to welcome new parishioners. In another parish, the council's worship committee discovered that the lectors were poorly prepared to read the Scriptures on Sunday. There were no criteria for selecting lectors. There was no training program. In another parish, the extraordinary ministers of the eucharist were all white and male even though many women and Mexicans were active in the parish. The Christian service committee learned that no one was visiting the sick at a local convalescent home. Also, no one was doing anything about a serious drug problem at a nearby high school.

2) Parish councils help to set goals and priorities to respond to the needs of the parish and the community. For instance, one council decided to make adult education its top priority, and to create a position for a full-time adult education coordinator. Another council decided to collaborate with a neighboring parish on providing a meal program for the community.

3) Councils discover all kinds of new talents in the parish. They go through the parish census and compile a list of all the skills and talents of the people. Then they invite the educator to serve on the education committee, the accountant to serve on the finance committee, the writer to serve on the communications committee, etc. They recruit lectors, teachers, ministers of music and of the eucharist. Often they find out that they have more than enough gifts and resources to respond to the parish's needs.

4) Councils are effective organs for dialogue within the Christian community. At council meetings, the liturgist talks to the pastor, the director of religious education talks to the principal of the school, the teenager talks to the senior citizen. Besides, most council meetings are open to all parishioners who want to express their opinions. And, many councils conduct an open forum twice a year so everyone in the parish can come and have a voice in parish development.

5) Councils are a living sign of the partnership every Chris-

tian community is called to be. They are a sign of the basic equality of all the baptized in Christ. By inviting many diverse people to work together, councils bring about a greater unity. They eliminate overlapping and competitive activities. Parish societies see themselves as partners in the larger parish plan. So they don't waste a lot of time defending their own turf against someone else.

Councils are also training schools for new and diverse lay ministries. As the number of sisters and priests continues to decrease in the years ahead, the church will rely more and more on lay ministers. Sometimes they will be paid; other times they will be volunteers. Lay persons will be appointed administrators of parishes, institutions, and missions. They will assume more responsible roles in preparing the people for baptism and marriage and in the pastoral care of the sick. The parish councils, with their growing emphasis on spiritual development, will produce a pool of highly motivated and knowledgeable lay ministers who will be ready and willing to serve when the time comes. The so-called vocation shortage may be God's way of reminding the church of the biblical truth that all the baptized have a vocation to minister.

6) Councils bring together a variety of ministers—priests, deacons, sisters, brothers, laymen, and laywomen. Every council meeting is a reminder that everybody, no matter what his or her talent, belongs to one and the same church.

7) Councils are called to make the Gospel known. Vatican II tells us that the purpose of councils is: "to assist the Church's apostolic work, whether in the field of evangelization and sanctification or in the fields of charity, social relations and the rest."[1] They are called to witness to the biblical mandate: "But seek first his kingdom and his righteousness and all these things shall be yours as well" (Matt. 6:33). Councils are formed to make sure the parish gives top priority to the apostolic, missionary, and spiritual needs of the parish.

8) Councils, while they are definitely not lay organizations, are, nevertheless, one good way of implementing Vatican II's teaching on the role of the laity in the church. "According to

their abilities the laity ought to cooperate in all the apostolic and missionary enterprises of their ecclesial family."[2] "The apostolate of the laity is a sharing in the salvific mission of the church. Through baptism and confirmation all are appointed to this apostolate by the Lord himself."[3]

9) Councils are the natural vehicle for renewing the parish. Every parish, like the church itself, is constantly in need of renewal. And parish councils are rightly concerned about fostering that process of renewal. But such renewal begins with the individual councilor when he or she commits to a life of service to Christ. Councils are not an end unto themselves. They serve the Spirit who comes to renew the face of the earth and the church.

10) Councils are a precious opportunity for adult education in the faith. They become a learning experience when they tackle specific pastoral problems. As the councilors wrestle with each new problem, they tap the riches of their faith in a wide variety of ways. They call on resource persons who are well versed in liturgy, theology, religious education, etc. They read up on their faith and so fill in the gaps between their catechism days and their present adult life.

11) Council meetings provide an excellent opportunity for shared prayer and for growth in the spiritual life. Councils read the Scriptures together and then share their reflections on its meaning for their lives. The council is small enough to provide all its members a rich experience in a common sharing in the faith and prayer life of one another.

12) Councils foster a climate of mutual support and accountability. Everyone who ministers in a parish (laypersons, sisters, brothers, deacons, priests) is accountable to God, to the gospel, and to Christian community. Councils generate many questions: What priorities determine the parish budget? Who was supposed to talk to the public school board about renting its classrooms? Who was going to call the diocesan office of education? The council meeting is a public forum where the Lord's servants render an account of their stewardship to one another and, at the same time, receive one another's support for their ministries.

13) Councils broaden the members' vision. When they discuss

the annual budget, councilors have to reflect on the broad vision of the church. During the course of the year they also learn to work with neighboring parishes, both Catholic and Protestant. Then too, diocesan offices frequently invite councils to offer suggestions regarding the pastoral policies of the diocese. Thus, councils learn to work with diocesan offices and departments. In this way, councilors gain a deeper understanding of the relationship between the parish and the diocesan church.

14) Councils provide their members an opportunity to share in participative decision making in a Christian context. Members are encouraged to share in discussions and so to make some contribution to the final decision. Since North American Catholics have been conditioned by the democratic process, they are very much at home in a parish council.

Of course, the parish council is not a democracy. Nor is it a legislative assembly, corporation board, or "organization of organizations." It is primarily a faith community, a communion of disciples, gathered together to discern the will of God for a specific parish. It is a brotherhood and sisterhood listening to God's word and then responding in faith and obedience to that word. The parish council is a unique form of shared responsibility that brings the parishioners into the decision-reaching process of the church at an adult, responsible level. It is one of the fruits of Pope John XXIII's New Pentecost, a catalyst for parish renewal as the church approaches the 21st century.

What a Council Is and Does

We've talked about the broad foundations for parish councils. Now it's time to get down to business and explain what a council is, what it does, and finally, how to start one.

A parish council is an organism of shared ministry that plans and coordinates the overall policy of the parish in order to carry out the mission of Christ in the church. It is a consultative body of leaders within the boundaries of the doctrine, liturgy, and laws of the church.

The Archdiocese of Milwaukee describes the parish council as possessing seven essential characteristics:[4]

1) A parish council is *prayerful*. Its members are to be persons of prayer; that is, they see the value of private prayer for their own personal growth in holiness as well as the value of community prayer for growth in Christ's community of faith and love. The council thus spends time together in prayer and retreat experiences for the purpose of drawing together in love and trust, to heal divisions, and for the discernment of God's will for the community.

2) A parish council is *pastoral*. It strives to discern the movement of the Holy Spirit among God's people in the parish for the purpose of investigating and weighing matters that bear on pastoral activities affecting the lives of parishioners, and to formulate in behalf of the parish practical conclusions regarding them. The council decides what specific actions or programs the parish should adopt to perform its *spiritual* mission, that of making the Gospel known and of helping people in their spiritual journeying. Only then can it determine what resources (people, facilities, money) it needs to carry out those actions or programs, and how to provide such resources.

3) A parish council is *representative*. It is a representative body rather than a body of representatives. A council member is not the representative for a particular neighborhood, age bracket, special interest group or organization: each councilor ministers to the entire parish community. Thus, the council represents in a holistic sense all areas of parish life: old and young, men and women, laity, clergy and religious, people with divergent viewpoints and ethnic/cultural backgrounds. All work together in an atmosphere and spirit of trust and openness, merging their expertise, insights, and experiences to further the mission of Jesus among all people. The priests of the parish and a sufficient number of lay persons, with their respective gifts and talents, are to be members of the council. Any religious attached to the parish may also be appropriately represented. Parish trustees, by virtue of their special position with the parish corporation, are to be ex-officio members. Eligibility requirements for council membership are to be reasonable; some form of elective process in which the entire parish is

involved seems necessary. All members of the council are voting members.

4) A parish council is *discerning*. Its members participate effectively in the policy formulating process for the parish by bringing together the needs and the hopes of the parishioners and of the entire community (neighborhoods) in which they live. Through a prayerful consensus/discernment process, it merges the insights, the diverse experiences, the expertise and the faith of the councilors in order to provide vision and direction for the parish community. That vision finds expression in the priorities established and the broad policies adopted.

Three principles are to be observed in this connection:

a) Only policy decisions are to be made by the parish council; day-to-day administrative decisions are made by the parish staff.

b) The council's decisions are to be consistent with faith and morals, civil and church law, and archdiocesan policies.

c) The pastor/pastoral team ratifies the decisions of the Council through his/their presence at meetings and full participation in the consensus/discernment process. It is within this process that consultation takes place.

d) Since the pastor/pastoral team is accountable to the diocesan bishop for the parish, and as part of the presbyterate is responsible for the spiritual life of each parishioner, councilors must be open to reconsideration of a decision in light of this responsibility.

5) A parish council is *prophetic*. As a result of experiencing the fullness of God's Word, it brings a broader, more challenging vision to parish life. It strives to move outward to tackle some of the bigger issues within the church and in the world, seeking to be a credible sign of concern for justice, peace, reconciliation, and practical love, bearing witness to all that the reign of God is already unfolding. It is a group of people who are not afraid to challenge and take risks; who support, affirm, and share their convictions of faith with one another as they strive to build more trusting relationships in the continual process of building up the Body of Christ. Council membership

calls people to be sensitive to the anguish and pain of others and to respond in healing, reconciling ways.

6) A parish council is *enabling*. It strives to recognize and acknowledge the giftedness in God's people and to enable each person's unique giftedness to surface, to be shared and organized for the upbuilding of the community to faith, and finally to be celebrated. It seeks to help persons discover that for which they were created, and monitors the ongoing renewal of parish life. To aid the council in this challenging task, the council works with standing committees which correspond to the church's mission of proclamation, worship, service, and community: Worship/Spiritual Life; Christian Education Formation; Human Concerns/Works of Justice; and Parish Renewal. An Administrative Services committee (finance, buildings and grounds) is established to support the parish mission. Other committees or sub-committees may be established as required.

7) A parish council is *collaborative*. Its members are to be visionary and concerned with appropriate sharing. As a "cell of the diocese," the parish seeks to collaborate with other parishes to carry out the church's mission. The parish council, as a community of stewards, is responsible for leading the parish in seeing to it that the resources of the parish are used not only for the parish community to which they belong, but for the common good of all the members of the church. The council seeks ways to promote this collaboration in mission and ministry, in harmony with archdiocesan policies.

The council works to promote unity in diversity—keeping the parish together by enabling people to think, pray, work, and play together. At the same time that it unites, it respects the diversity of the community by encouraging each person to bring forth his/her special competence in ministry and service to others.

The function of the parish pastoral council, in the Diocese of Nashville, is described in their guidelines in this way:

> The function of the Parish Pastoral Council, as representatives of the community, is to know the individuals of the community; to gather thoughts, feelings and ideas from the community; and to process this data into parish

policy. These policies become the stimuli for programs to be designed and carried out by the pastoral staff and those delegated by the pastor. In its role as a coordinating and unifying structure, the council works with the pastor and administrative staff as well as the community to fulfill parish needs and to achieve true unity.[5]

Drawing on these descriptions, we could compose a list of parish council functions:

1) To pray together, to nurture faith and reflect on the gospel

2) To be a sign of a truly Christian community before the church and the world

3) To provide servant leadership and direction for the parish by enabling parish people to share responsibility for parish life

4) To engage families in parish planning and overall policies for parish ministry and mission

5) To serve as a permanent, but flexible, structure for constructive dialogue among priests, staff members, religious, and laity of the parish and with the bishop and his representatives so that they can work in close collaboration in fulfilling Christ's saving mission.

6) To assure through its committees a continuous and integrated survey of both spiritual and temporal needs of the parish, community, and diocese and after setting priorities, to provide for the development and implementation of programs aimed at meeting these needs

7) To coordinate parish activities with the regional or deanery councils and with the diocesan pastoral council

8) To identify, support, and maximize the gifts and talents of all the members of the parish and provide for the training of lay ministries

9) To be stewards of all parish resources and gifts: personnel, facilities, and monies

10) To develop a parish mission statement in accordance with the mission of the church

Now that we know what a parish council is and what it does, what is the best way to begin one?

Careful Foundation

In starting a parish council it is best to make haste slowly. It may take nine months to a year to do the job well. It just doesn't pay to skip any essential steps. The step-by-step procedure goes something like this:

1) The pastor appoints a steering committee. He is careful to select members who represent a variety of viewpoints and experiences. The committee includes old and young, joiners and non-joiners, new and old-timers, men and women. In this way, the steering committee will already be a preview of what the council should be.

2) The steering committee begins to pray together, and asks the parish to join them, for the success of their efforts. The pastor explains the process of consensus decision making and then the committee begins to practice it. In this way, the steering committee gets initiated into a process that should become the normal procedure once the council gets going.

3) The steering committee launches a program of self-education. The members read at least two documents of Vatican II, for example, *The Dogmatic Constitution on the Church* and *The Decree on the Laity.* They also familiarize themselves with the canons relating to parish councils and finance councils, as well as any diocesan norms or guidelines. Then they form discussion groups. They study the nature of the church, the diocese, and the parish. They explore the role of the pastor and staff in relation to the council. The priests and sisters teach and learn with the rest of the committee.

4) The committee launches an educational program for the parish. They gather a good supply of materials. (See appendix.)

The educational program may include the following:

a) series of homilies on shared responsibilities and council ministries

b) bulletin inserts describing council ministries in creative images

c) a slide presentation on shared responsibilities and parish councils during all the Sunday Masses

d) open parish forums for parishioners conducted by the steering committee

e) open discussion during meetings of all existing parish organizations

f) neighborhood discussions in various sections of the parish conducted by the steering committee members

g) outside speakers, including priests and laity from other councils, as well as experts on group dynamics

h) parish survey of special talents, ministries, interests.

5) The steering committee develops a set of interim guidelines for the future parish council. The committee may collect copies of other council guidelines, perhaps from a diocesan office or from neighboring parishes. At this stage guidelines are broad, flexible, and temporary—just enough to give the parishioners an idea about what the parish council will be like. They may eventually become a part of a constitution, but that step is a long way down the road. The committee, however, does have to decide how many will serve on the council.

The steering committee may also decide which committees the council should have, and begin to determine the responsibilities and membership of the committees. (In fact, some parishes form committees before parish councils.)

At this stage, the committee will have to determine how the parish organizations will fit into the picture. The committee may survey the parish to find out how many parishioners are still active in each organization. Then it consults the various organizations to get their ideas on how they might best fit into the council structure. After dialoguing with the officers, the committee decides how its parish organizations will relate to the council. In recent years, in order to avoid becoming an "organization of organizations," councils have provided for parish organizations and societies to relate directly to committees.

6) The steering committee sets up the procedures for the first elections. It will determine voting eligibility, qualifications of candidates, list of nominees, and, finally, the form of the ballot. The committee will also decide whether elections will take place by mail or after Sunday liturgy.

Some steering committees may decide to choose membership through a process of prayerful discernment, which involves an initial calling forth of possible candidates by the entire parish. Other steering committees print a special bulletin insert with pictures and biographical data of each candidate. Sometimes the pastor or the chairperson on the steering committee introduces each candidate to the people before the Sunday Masses. Coffee and doughnuts after the Masses provide another opportunity to meet the candidates. (More about this in Chapter 9.) In some parishes, the steering committee prepares a special liturgy for election Sunday. The Scripture readings, homily, and prayer of the faithful concentrate on the "diverse ministries given by the Spirit for the upbuilding of the church."

Of course, the key factor in starting a council is communication at all levels. Open and honest dialogue with everyone is crucial. It takes time, but it is worth it. Communication can make the difference between success or failure.

We have discussed what a parish council is, what it does, and how it gets started. Before we explore the ministry of the pastor, it may be useful to reflect on the meaning of consultation in the church.

Notes

1. *Decree on the Apostolate of Lay People,* in *Vatican Council II,* Austin Flannery, O.P. ed. (Northport, N.Y.: Costello Publishing Co., 1975), p. 791. (Henceforth all reference to Vatican II documents will be to the Flannery edition.)

2. *Ibid.,* p. 778.

3. *Dogmatic Constitution on the Church,* in *Vatican Council II,* p. 390.

4. *Living the Spirit,* Archdiocese of Milwaukee.

5. *Called to Serve with Vision,* Diocese of Nashville.

Sharing

1. Discuss one or two of the 12 purposes of parish councils. How do these ideas compare with your council's expressed purposes?
2. Discuss some of the "essential characteristics." At which characteristic does your council excel? Which does it lack?
3. Which of the council functions is most important? Why?

CHAPTER 5

CONSULTATION IN THE CHURCH

The new Code of Canon Law was promulgated by Pope John Paul II in January 1983. In announcing the new Code the pope said:"...The church has been accustomed to reform and renew the laws of canonical discipline so that...they may be better adapted to the saving mission"[1] of the divine founder. In emphasizing the newness of the Code, the pope called attention to the Vatican II

> doctrine according to which all members of the people of God, in a way suited to each of them, participate in the threefold priestly, prophetic and kingly office of the Christ, to which doctrine is also linked that which concerns the duties and rights of the faithful and particularly of the laity.[2]

Reactions to the new Code were mixed. That portion of the people of God participating in the ministry of parish councils was not exactly overjoyed to discover that from now on the parish council "possesses a consultative vote only" (Canon 536). Some councilors had hoped the new Code would say nothing about parish councils so that this new organism could be shaped more freely in response to the American Catholic experience. Others had hoped the new Code would mandate the formation of parish councils in every diocese. They were not pleased to learn that a parish council is to be established in each parish only if the diocesan bishop "judges it opportune" (canon 536). Many Catholics, no doubt, could agree with Fr. John Lynch, writing in the *Jurist:* "It is surprising that the new law does not take a more positive stand toward the formation of parish councils."[3] Vatican II had insisted rather forcefully that: "The laity should develop the habit of working in the parish in close union with their priests."[4]

Since the publication of the new code there has been considerable discussion about the meaning of the phrase, "consultative vote only." Since American Catholics are conditioned by a very legalistic culture, it is understandable that many Catholics would give "consultative" a narrow, legalistic interpretation."With the new Code," some complained, "we are back to the veto power. The pastor can consult us and then still do as he pleases." For them "to consult" meant "to ask for advice."

It was also not surprising in our legalistic culture that many Catholics tended to reduce the parish council to the precise words of the law. This tendency produced a possimism regarding the future of parish councils in this country. American Catholics are used to a democratic style of decision making. They find it difficult to accept the new Code's return to what they consider autocratic paternalism. They feel the new Code represents a step backward, a betrayal of both the spirit and the content of Vatican II.

A little reflection on postconciliar ecclesiology and a more historical interpretation of church law will show that this pessimism is not justified. On the contrary, "consultative," correctly understood, can yield an understanding of parish councils which is far removed from an arbitrary use of a veto or autocratic paternalism.

The first step toward this new understanding is to see "consultative" as an ecclesiastical category with its own history and ecclesial content. Of course, a good part of that content comes from Roman law and government, which the early Christians freely appropriated and incorporated into their own system. They were used to it and it worked.

But this unique history means that we cannot simply look to our modern civil or parliamentary forms of city, state, or federal government to discover the meaning of "consultative." Naturally, we can learn from these forms of government just as the early Christians did. We have no secret monopoly on the consultative process. But for now we need to remember that consultation in the church has for many centuries had its own path of growth and development.

If, for the moment, we concentrate on a rather narrow aspect of the ecclesiology of consultation, the canon law, we arrive at a much broader interpretation of the word consultation than the one often assumed by American Catholics. The new Code quite plainly "places more emphasis on the role of consultation in the life of the church," writes Fr. Michael Place. "In fact, it mentions five consultative bodies in each diocese. Two of these are obligatory: the presbyteral council (which includes the college of consultors) and the finance council. Three are optional, though recommended: the diocesan synod, the diocesan pastoral council and the episcopal synod.

"These consultative bodies," continues Fr. Place, "are not mere window dressings. The Code clearly specifies areas where the bishop must consult one or other of the consultative bodies and they must give their consent before the bishop can act. For example, both the college of consultors and the finance council must *consent* to any extraordinary act of administration of alienation of substantial patrimony (financial resources) of a diocese"[5] (Italics mine). In this instance the consent of consultative bodies has a deliberative force.

The increasing number of consultative bodies in the church since Vatican II indicates the growing importance of the consultative principle in the church. The synod of bishops held in Rome on a regular basis has become a part of church life. In addition, each diocese now has a number of consultative bodies. The most important of these is the diocesan synod which, according to the new Code, meets "when circumstances warrant it in the judgment of the diocesan bishop" (can. 461). Most dioceses now have a presbyteral council, a diocesan pastoral council, and a sisters council. Some dioceses have established additional consultative bodies to deal with special areas of the diocesan apostolate such, as communications, ecumenism, family life, liturgy, sacred art and architecture, parish life, and justice and peace.

Of course all these consultative bodies can become mere window dressing. That can happen, for instance, when a bishop or pastor simply does not call a meeting. But it can also happen by reducing the consultative principle to a narrow, legalistic interpretation, or by isolating it from its history and its ecclesial content. It can happen, finally, by not paying attention to the whole process of consultation, especially the obstacles to the consultative process. The rest of this chapter, therefore, will discuss: (1) The history of consultation in the church, (2) the ecclesial context, (3) some principles for interpretation of the new law, (4) the consultative process, and (5) some obstacles to consultation in the church.

History of Consultation

Already in the New Testament we see the beginnings of the consultative process. In Acts 6:1-4 we see the infant church responding to the problem of discrimination between the Hellenists and the Jews. First the Hellenists "murmured" to get the attention of "the Twelve." Then, responding, "the Twelve ....summoned the body of the disciples" and asked them to "pick out...seven men of good repute." The Hellenists then consulted with each other and presented seven from their group to "the Twelve" so they could be appointed to help with the daily distribution to the Hellenist widows.

The Council of Jerusalem (Acts 15) is a consultation among the elders, the apostles, the whole church, and the Holy Spirit: "Then it seemed good to the apostles and the elders, with the whole church..." (Acts 15:22). "For it has seemed good to the Holy Spirit and to us..." (Acts 15:28).

Paul, in that touching note to Philemon, writes: "But I did not want to do anything without your consent, that kindness might not be forced on you but might be freely bestowed" (Phil. 1:14). In the famous case of the incestuous man (1 Cor. 5:4), Paul once again asks the church of Corinth to assemble and expel the man from the community. No doubt the act of assembling included a process of consultation in reaching a decision.

In the early church the principle of consultation was especially evident in the election of bishops. The *Apostolic Tradition* of Hippolytus says simply: "Let the bishop be ordained after he has been chosen by all the people. When someone pleasing to all has been named, let the people assemble...All giving assent, the bishops shall impose hands on him..."[6] St. Cyprian, Bishop of Carthage, (258) felt the people had a divine right to be consulted in the selection of their bishops: "This very thing, too, we note, stems from divine authority—that a priest [actually, bishop] be chosen in the presence of all the people and under the eyes of all, and that he be approved as worthy and suitable by public judgment and testimony...."[7]

St. Leo is emphatic in requiring the consultation of the people before ordination: "Let a person not be ordained against the wish of the Christians and whom they have not explicitly asked for."[8]

After Constantine (337) the church came more and more under the influence of Roman law and government. Bishops became civil as well as ecclesiastical magistrates. It was natural, then, that these bishops should combine civil and church systems of government. They were ruling a Roman district, called diocese, in the name of the church and in the name of the emperor.

Since the fourth century before Christ the Roman consul under the unwritten constitution was vested with both *potestas* (power) and *imperium* (the right of commanding). With *imperium* the Roman consul was equal to a commander in chief in the military, with absolute power to issue and enforce orders.[9] Gradually in the Roman Republic there was a movement away from the "absoluteness" of the consul's *imperium*. The Roman Senate, a group of wise, old men, at first appointed by the consul, began to modify the *imperium* of the consul. It could pass a resolution called a *senatus consultum* (Senate's counsel). Later a process of deliberation was required before the consul could exercise his *imperium*. He could act against the Senate's advice "but only after he had sought that advice." In fact, consuls seldom went against the Senate's advice; wisdom, after all, is a most valued dimension of governance.

The people had in addition a type of veto over proposed

actions of the consuls. A consul would propose something. The people could agree or disagree. If they agreed, the consul was free to pursue his proposal or to drop it. If the people disagreed, the consul could not proceed.[10]
The old Code of Canon Law (no. 105) is a fairly close reflection of this Roman system. In the Code the superior (bishop) replaces the Roman consul. Fr. James Provost comments:

The bishop or superior has the ruling power. But to exercise it, there are times when, like the consul, he must give a group the opportunity to veto it. If they consent to his proposal, he is still the responsible agent and can decide whether to carry it through. If they object, their veto means he is not free to act. At other times the church superior, again, like the Roman consul, is free to do what he decides; but before acting, he must consult with a specified group. Failure to get their advice can lead to the act being invalid. Once he gets the advice, however, the bishop or superior is free to do what he decides and is not bound by the advice.[11]

One can hardly discuss the history of consultation in the church without a brief reference to conciliarist theories of the 13th and 14th centuries. In its simplest definition conciliarism is the doctrine asserting that a general council constitutes the supreme authority in the church. Conciliarism is a many-layered theory with a wide variety of theological nuances. Marsilius of Padua and William of Ockham developed the most extreme positions.

Marsilius taught that all power, ecclesiastical and civil, was vested primarily in the whole community and only secondarily in governors appointed by the community. In his system the pope, bishop, and priest are mere mouthpieces or spokespersons of the communities they lead. Conciliarism reached its high point during the Council of Constance (1415), which deposed two rival popes. Officially it came to an end during the faction-ridden Council of Basle (1431). Thirty years later it was condemned by Pope Pius II (1460) in his bull *Execrabilis*.[12]

But conciliarist ideas continued to spread and nurtured Gallicanism in France in the 19th century. No doubt Gallicanism was one of many factors that moved Pius IX to convoke Vatican I. After the definition of Papal Infallibility, with its famous "not from the consent of the church,"[13] it is simply not possible for Catholics to believe that dogmatic definitions get their validity or their "truthfulness" from the consent of the people. After the condemnations of the conciliarist theories, it is also clear that believers must hold that bishops get their power from God without any mediation on the part of the faithful. Although bishops are "servants of their brethren," they are more accurately described as trustees of the Lord and his word than as trustees of their congregations.[14]

Vatican II affirmed the holy people of God's participation in the priestly, prophetic, and kingly mission of Jesus Christ. It proclaimed that this people cannot err in matters of belief, thanks to a supernatural sense of faith. It went further and taught that this people is enriched by the Holy Spirit with charismatic gifts. From now on the whole consultative process needs to be considered in the light of this new Vatican II understanding of the people who are being consulted. For this reason it is now possible to take another look at the milder forms of Conciliarism as expounded by Nicholas of Cusa (d. 1464).

A cardinal, philosopher, and theologian of the church, Nicholas outlined his ideas on consent in his *De Concordantia Catholica*. Nicholas's theory of consent "is not based on the modern concept of natural rights. What is meant by consent is basically a theological concept of the existence of the Holy Spirit which creates harmonious agreement."[15] The nature of Christianity, Nicholas says, excludes all compulsion. "It is a beautiful reflection that all powers, spiritual, temporal, and physical, are latent potentially in the people, although, for the power to rule to be established, the form-giving radiance must come from above to put it into being, since all power is from above—and I speak of rightly ordered power."[16] Nicholas taught that the legislative power of the pope came from God, but that the authority of making laws depends not only on the pope, but also on common consent. "Rulership is from God through men and councils, by elective consent."[17] Nicholas was not interested in instituting a system of checks and balances, a system of controls. He hoped for "spontaneous agreement, a harmonious concord of ruler and ruled, head and members, working together in a spirit of free cooperation."[18] In that same spirit he proposed, with Cyprian of Carthage, that priests should be chosen with the consent of the laity.

In summary, we can say that Nicholas, like Paul, was interested in excluding compulsion from the Christian community. He affirmed the presence of the Holy Spirit in the people; he felt the process of seeking the people's consent was the way in which the Holy Spirit brought about a harmonious agreement in the church. These three elements provide an ecclesial context for considering the whole consultative process.

Even after the condemnation of Conciliarism, the church has continued the practice of consulting the faithful and, significantly, in doctrinal matters. Before he defined the dogma of the Immaculate Conception in 1854, Pius IX consulted all the bishops of the church as well as several theological committees. This consultation was all the more significant since Gregory XV in the 17th century had received numerous requests for a favorable definition, but had declined saying: "The Holy Spirit, although besought by the most constant prayers, has not yet opened to his church the secrets of this mystery."[19]

It is especially noteworthy that in 1950 Pope Pius XII, even after the definition of Papal Infallibility, placed considerable emphasis on the consultative process before defining the dogma of The Assumption of the Blessed Virgin Mary. On May 1, 1946, he sent an encyclical letter, *Deiparae Virginis*, to all the bishops of the world asking "what their clergy and *people* thought about the assumption and whether they themselves judged it 'wise and prudent' that the dogma should be defined"[20] (Italics mine).

Fr. William Hentrich S.J., in his compilation of the petitions for the definition of the Assumption, lists thousands of requests from the cardinals, archbishops, and bishops of the world. Then, quite significantly, he reports that more than eight million of the lay faithful were represented in the petitions.[21] Before solemnly defining the dogma of the Assumption

Pope Pius XII called a semi-public consistory on Oct. 30, 1950, to declare his intention of defining the Assumption. In his address to the cardinals, the pope referred to the responses to the question in his encyclical as a "nearly unanimous and certain wonderful harmony [*concentu*: lit. a singing together] of the sacred pastors and the Christian people."[22] He then asked the assembled cardinals to vote (*placet* or *non placet*) on the solemn definition of the Assumption. In the apostolic constitution, *Munificentissimus Deus*, in which the pope solemnly defines the dogma of the Assumption, he refers once again to the role of the faithful in the consultative process:

> In this pious striving (the studies and investigations), the faithful have been associated in a wonderful way with their own holy bishops, who have sent petitions of this kind, truly remarkable in number, to this see of Blessed Peter. Consequently, when we were elevated to the throne of the supreme pontificate, petitions of this sort had already been addressed by the thousands from every part of the world and from every class of people, from our beloved sons the Cardinals of the Sacred College, the archbishops and the bishops, from dioceses and from parishes.[23]

In the same apostolic constitution the pope reports that he asked that all these petitions should be gathered together and carefully evaluated. Evidence enough that, even after the definition of papal infallibility, Pius XII held the consultative process in high esteem.

The church is evidently very conscientious in following a consultative process in defining the doctrines of the faith. It would seem that that same process would have even more validity in disciplinary and administrative matters. These by their very nature relate more directly to the customs, culture, and educational level of the faithful.

In this short essay we can refer only briefly to the church's long and rich tradition of consulting the saints and the mystics.[24] The liturgical calendar holds up the lives of the saints for imitation by Christians. Their faith, their virtues, and, yes, their theology, are offered to the praying church for reflection and for guidance in the continuing process of spiritual and moral decision making.

As the church becomes more comfortable with its own mystical heritage, how could consultative bodies fail to consult the wisdom of St. John of the Cross and St. Theresa of Avila? Certainly, Latin American Catholics are gaining new insights into their own "dark night" by reflecting prayerfully on the dark night of John of the Cross.[25] Consultative bodies could well get into the habit of consulting the living saints too. If there is a Mother Theresa around, they could well seek her wisdom and experience. The practice of consulting the saints, both living and dead, could be a much needed corrective to the American tendency to consult only the lawyers, bankers, corporation executives, and management consultants.

As the Western church begins to rely more on consultative bodies, it might well pay more attention to the history of *oikonomia* as it has been applied in the Eastern churches. *Oikonomia* provides an ecclesial context for the application of the consultative principle. Literally, *oikonomia* means "household management"or "stewardship." In the New Testament it refers to the divine plan of salvation. Paul is fond of the word and the rich meaning it expresses. For Paul preaching the Word is *oikonomia*, a stewardship entrusted to him by God (1 Cor. 9:17). We should be regarded as "servants of Christ and stewards (*oikonomoi*) of the mysteries of God"(1 Cor. 4:1).

For Paul the divine plan for the management of salvation history has been entrusted to humankind. "More specifically, the 'management' or 'stewardship' belongs to those who fulfill the ministry of leading the church"[26] (Col. 1:24-25). In Titus 1:7 Paul says simply that the bishop is an *oikonomos*, a manager. In 1 Tim. 3:5 Paul writes about the bishop: "For if a man does not know how to manage his own household, how can he care for God's church?"

If the ministers in the church, like Paul, view the church more as a "household of the faith" (Gal. 6:10) it becomes easier to understand that the members of the household need to be consulted on a regular basis. While they live in the house, they are intimately affected by the decisions of the manager. Since all the members of the household are adults, not children, consultation becomes a condition for harmony in the house.

The Ecclesial Context for Consultation

With this historical background we can now provide a clearer description of the ecclesial context for consultation in the church. An awareness of this ecclesial context will lessen the danger of a legalistic reduction of the consultative process in our legalistic American culture. At the same time, it will keep us from looking to civil or secular models to find the meaning of "consultative only."

It hardly needs saying that the most important dimension of the church within which consultation takes place is faith. Before the law, there is faith. Before the dialogue begins, there is faith. Before, during, and after the meeting, there is faith. And faith constitutes the community of believers. Faith is a way of being church. It is the *way* Christians live and, therefore, the way they make their decisions. In its *Decree on the Missionary Activity of the Church* Vatican II writes: "The Bishop should be first and foremost a herald of the faith. . . ."[27] And in the same *Decree* we read: "The congregations of the faithful must every day become increasingly aware and alive as communities of faith. . . ."[28]

The decision-making process itself must first witness to the faith dimension of the community. The community finds its identity in its faith response to the Word when it shares one bread and one cup. That identity must remain intact when the community moves from the table of the Lord to the table of the meeting to make its decisions about its mission in the world. If the community, in moving to its decision-making meeting, begins to respond only to the law or to *Robert's Rules of Order*, it has betrayed its very identity. In fact, the decision-making process itself must nourish and enliven that faith. Whatever meaning the community gives to "consultative only," it can never be separated from the faith community's act of believing, its act of becoming. The community proclaims its identity to the world by sharing in the breaking of the bread and sharing in the making of its decisions."While they were worshiping the Lord and fasting, the Holy Spirit said, 'Set apart for me Barnabas and Saul for the work to which I have called them.' Then after fasting and praying they laid their hands on them and sent them off" (Acts 13:2-3).

Consultation in a community of believers is also carried out in the context of common discipleship. There are no degrees of disciples. From the pope to the poorest peasant all are together disciples of the same Lord. One does not lay hold of discipleship by entering upon a certain state of life. All the baptized have answered the call of the Lord. All are ready to lay down their lives for the Lord and for each other. This common discipleship constitutes one of the essential bonds of the church. The outward form of discipleship may vary from one disciple to another, but the form itself is secondary. The diversity of outward forms indicates the diversity of ministries the community is called to offer to the world.

When consultation takes place in the community of believers, one disciple is consulting another. And the disciple who consults will, at another time, become the one consulted. True consultation in the church will be a dialogic process in the community of disciples. It will respect the diversity of roles and functions, including those of hierarchic leadership. The consultative process strengthens, rather than diminishes, the bonds of common discipleship. It honors the fellowship's diversity of experience, of knowledge, of gifts, of competence. He or she who consults comes with reverence and respect before the faith experience of the disciple who is consulted. He or she may have part of God's own truth to offer for the upbuilding of the church.

Consultation also takes place in the context of Paul's image of the body. Vatican II, in its *Constitution on the Church*, highlighted Paul's ecclesiology of the body.[29] Just as we all belong to a common discipleship, so too we are all "baptized into one body"(1 Cor. 12:13). "As all the members of the human body, though they are many, form one body, so also are the faithful in Christ. Also in the building up of Christ's body there is a flourishing variety of members and functions."[30]

Faithfulness to Paul's body image shapes the consultative process; at the same time it interprets the words, "consultative only." For if consultation divides the church into "consultors" and "consultees," it divides the body. If consultation does not honor the usefulness of all the various parts of the body, then the church itself becomes a sign of a distorted, crippled body in which some of its parts do not function. To put it briefly, in consultation in the church, the foot is consulting the hand.

Consultation also takes place in the context of the common possession of the Spirit. *The Constitution on the Church* states unambiguously:

> He [Christ] continually distributes in his body, that is, the church, gifts of ministries through which, by his own power, we serve each other unto salvation...he has shared with us his Spirit who, existing as one and the same being in the head and in the members, vivifies, unifies, and moves the whole body."[31]

This common possession of the Spirit is revealed in the life of the church through the charismatic gifts given to all the baptized.

> Allotting his gifts "to everyone according as He will" (1 Cor. 12:11), he [the Spirit] distributes special graces among the faithful of every rank. By these gifts he makes them fit and ready to undertake the various tasks or offices advantageous for the renewal and upbuilding of the church. . . .[32]

To preserve order in the church it is important to see the various gifts in the context of the Pauline body image. A gift is never separated from the body; it is never separated from its upbuilding function; it is never given for its own advantage; and, of course, it is never separated from the Giver of all the gifts.

When we apply the doctrine of the common possession of the Spirit to the consultative process, we see one gift consulting another. Who possesses the gift being consulted doesn't make all that much difference. Since the gifts are given to "each according to the measure of faith" (Rom. 12:3), we can't confine the gifts to a caste system, to the ordained, to the educated, to the hierarchy, to the laity, etc. We cannot limit the consultative process to a gnostic elite, whatever its historical form, without at the same time denying the Vatican II teaching on the common possession of the Spirit.

Since Vatican II, consultation has to be carried out in the context of baptism as a common participation in the priestly, prophetic, and kingly mission of Christ.[33] This common participation in the one mission in virtue of baptism points to a basic equality among all the workers laboring in the same vineyard. "So neither he who plants nor he who waters is anything, but only God who gives the growth. He who plants and he who waters are equal..."(1 Cor. 3:8). Consultation takes place right there where the seed of the Gospel is being planted, and it takes place among "God's fellow workers." They share the mission, not by special mandate or by a bishop's "charge," but as a body of the faithful anointed by the Holy One. All the baptized witness to their common possession of the "royal priesthood" and the "common priesthood of the faithful" during their gatherings for liturgy; they also witness to it when they consult each other in the gatherings of their consultative bodies. While responsibilities are not equal, all are, nevertheless, responsible.

Consultation also takes place in the context of the church's common pilgrimage. For "the church, embracing sinners in her bosom, is at the same time holy and always in need of being purified, and incessantly pursues the path of penance and renewal."[34] If the church is responding to the Spirit's call and the changing signs of the times, it is constantly in process of going somewhere.

"Christ summons the church, as she goes her pilgrim way, to that continual reformation of which she always has need...."[35] Consultation takes place in the context of repentance and change of heart. All the baptized, whether ordained or not, are part of the imperfection of the church. Whether consulting or being consulted, all the baptized have as their primary duty to make an honest and careful appraisal of whatever needs to be renewed and achieved in the Catholic household itself.[36]

Consultation, then, takes place among repenting disciples

who together are making a careful appraisal of what needs to be renewed. Naturally such consultation requires a disposition to change that which needs to be reformed and renewed. The pilgrimage is a common search among sinners who now "see in a mirror dimly." While they may have found part of the truth, they have not found it all. Otherwise the pilgrimage would be over. The church is not divided between those who, like the Gnostics, have the truth and those who do not. Consultation takes place in a context where both the disciple who consults and the disciple who is consulted have an imperfect knowledge, an imperfect vision, an imperfect holiness.

The living church is constantly in conversation with its bishops, with its theologians, with its own tradition, with its mystics, with its saints, with its own people, and with the signs of the times. It is a conversation in which listening is more important than speaking. It is this listening attitude that leads to fruitful consultation in the church.

Vatican II was very much aware of the sign value of the church in dialogue. In *The Church in the Modern World* the bishops write:

> In virtue of its mission to enlighten the whole world with the message of the Gospel and gather together in one Spirit all men of every nation, race and culture, the church shows itself as a sign of the spirit of brotherhood which renders possible sincere dialogue and strengthens it.
>
> Such a mission requires us first of all to create in the church itself mutual esteem, reverence and harmony, and acknowledge all legitimate diversity; in this way all who constitute the one people of God will be able to engage in ever more fruitful dialogue, whether they are pastors or other members of the faithful.[37]

As the American church matures in a pluralistic culture and begins to share what truth it has discovered about war, peace, and the economy, it will need to see itself as a dialogic church. This "mark" of the church will be the ecclesial context for consulting through the consultative bodies at all levels in the church.

Consultation in the New Code of Canon Law

With a clearer understanding of the history of consultation and its ecclesial context, we come now to consultation in the new Code of Canon Law. One canon (536) deals specially with parish councils. The translation of the American Canon Law Society reads:

> After the diocesan bishop has listened to the presbyteral council and if he judges it opportune, a pastoral council is to be established in each parish; the pastor presides over it, and through it the Christian faithful along with those who share in the pastoral care of the parish in virtue of their office give their help in fostering pastoral activity.
>
> This pastoral council possesses a consultative vote only and is governed by norms determined by the diocesan bishop. [38]

Before we discuss the specifics of the law, we will do well to pause a moment to reflect on a few standard and well established rules for the interpretation of canon law. Church law is not civil law. Over the centuries the church has developed its own tradition for the interpretation of its own laws. Those who are accustomed to a rigid, Anglo-Saxon interpretation of civil laws, may feel the church interpretation is rather lax. However, the church is a community of mercy, of compassion, of saving grace. In the last analysis church interpretation must be inspired by the Gospel and the Holy Spirit. It must remain a form of ministry, modeled on the ministry of Christ, which "heals" the inherent deficiencies of the law. "Law is not self-implementing," writes Fr. James Coriden, "...nor is its application a purely mechanical, robot-like function. [39]

The first rule to remember in applying and interpreting the law is: Practice *epikeia*. Laws by their very nature are general. When applied to particular situations they are often deficient. "Epikeia," Fr. Coriden reminds us, "is a corrective for the inherent inadequacies of the law, and is really a sensible, wise, and prudent interpretation of the law, morally superior to its merely verbal application." [40]

A second rule that certainly has special application to canon

536 is: Consider your people. Here we need to be aware that conditions within the believing community shape the application of the law. We need to ask what is this particular community's cultural background? The educational level? The degree of sophistication? The experience in the consultative process? In participative management? Different communities can be obedient to the sense of the same law even though they apply it differently.

A third, very ancient rule is: Custom is the best interpreter of the law (Canon 27). "This rule means that the practice of the community, the way that the law is usually applied there, clarifies and confirms the meaning of the law, and that it is the best among all the indicators of the law's meaning."[41] An American custom of decision making can be a valid interpretation of the law. Canon 27 assumes the Spirit is present in the community and that the Spirit's direction can be discerned in the actions of the people. And sometimes that direction of the Spirit can mean non-observance of certain specifics of the law. To give but one example of non-observance, some American dioceses have never held a diocesan synod, even though the Code of 1917 required such synods to be held every ten years (canon 356).

In view of the ecclesial context explained earlier, it should come as no surprise that the fourth rule says: Law is subordinate and subservient to faith. It is an old axiom that it is not by the law that we are saved, but by faith. To borrow once again from Fr. Coriden's excellent article: "The interpreter must view the law in the light of faith, understand the law in a way that is consonant with and never in contradiction to the elements of faith, and strive to apply the law so that it is conducive to and supportive of this same faith."[42]

The final rule for the interpretation of canon 536 is simply: Vatican Council II governs the Code. So it is the ecclesiology of *The Constitution on the Church* and similar Vatican II documents that provide the context for interpreting and applying canon 536. Without repeating everything explained above, it is an ecclesiology of the people of God, of a communion of faith and love, endowed with the charisms of the Holy Spirit, in-

cluding the gift of discernment. The faith community receives
the law gratefully, with respect and reverence, but it does not
deny its own ecclesial identity in the process.

When consultative bodies begin to interpret and apply the
phrase "consultative only," they need to be aware of all these
rules for the interpretation of church law. At the same time
they would do well to seek some guidance from the canon lawyers themselves who have the ministry of interpreting the law
through the various commentaries. Discussing the meaning of
consultation in the new Code, Fr. Bertram Griffin writes:

> The fact that the presbyteral council and finance council
> are only consultative even though they are mandatory,
> should not discourage advocates of shared responsibility.
> Consultation in the revised Code is not a mere pro forma
> act. Canon 127 states that if consultation is required by
> law, the majority of the group to be consulted must be con-
> sulted for the validity of the administrative act, unless
> particular law provides otherwise. If consent is required
> by law, it must be obtained for validity. Moreover, the
> administrator (bishop or pastor) should not act against
> the advice of consultors, especially if they are concordant,
> unless he has a prevailing reason. Hence the Code clearly
> recommends consensus management as a decision making
> style and process in the church, allowing for discretion on
> the part of the bishop or pastor, but recommending that a
> consensus be achieved and that the administrator follow
> the consultation of appropriate bodies.[43]

One can safely assume the same "consensus management" applies also to the "consultative only" of parish pastoral councils
(canon 536). There is no indication in the Code that the consultative principle should suddenly have a different meaning
when it is used for parish pastoral councils. In fact Joseph A Ja-
nicki, commenting on this canon, tells us that the parish council
in the new Code is analogous to the Diocesan and Presbyteral
Councils:

> In this regard the parish council is analogous to structures
> such as the diocesan or deanery council, the presbyteral

council, and the college of consultors, which must be consulted in certain instances specified by law for an action to be valid. Similarly, the bishop could determine that in certain instances the parish council would have to be consulted...Diocesan norms could...indicate those instances in which the pastor must consult the council for the validity of an action.[44]

In effect, the individual diocese, through its published guidelines, can, at least in part, interpret the meaning of "consultative only" as it applies to parish councils. It can, like the Code itself, list the instances when the parish council must be consulted. In view of the history of consultation outlined above, a diocese could go further and indicate the cases when the pastors *must* have the *consent* of the council before acting. Such diocesan guidelines would do well to leave considerable room for pastoral judgment and discernment at the parish level. But diocesan guidelines that give real authority to the consultative process would certainly be justified in view of the history and ecclesiology of consultation and a truly pastoral interpretation of canon 536.

Since the promulgation of Vatican II's *Constitution on the Church* the parish has had its own ecclesial identity,[45] which must be respected and trusted with a meaningful and authoritative consultative process. Parishes, in consultation with the diocese, could well take responsibility for their own ecclesial identity by developing parish council guidelines indicating some areas where consultation seeks the consent, not the advice, of the parish council. In this way the council would become more aware of the ecclesial basis for the process of consensus decision making.

Of course, a large part of the meaning of consultation will depend on the parish community itself—its faith, its education, its decision-making process. No guidelines can ever spell out the final meaning of consultation.

Any attempt to do so will fall back into dead legalism. On the other hand, a parish that ignores the diocese's right to interpret part of the meaning could fall into Congregationalism.

This does not mean that both diocese and parish could not learn something from the Congregationalist system with its emphasis on an ecclesiology "from below." But it is not the Roman Catholic system.

When all is said and done, most of the meaning of consultation will come from the process, that mysterious combination of the human and divine dynamics that are always at work in the community of faith. So, to complete the picture on consultation in the church, we must reflect for a moment at least on the human and spiritual side of that process.

Discernment as a Method of Consultation

With the growth of numerous consultative bodies after Vatican II some dioceses have published a step-by-step method for carrying out the discernment process, especially as it applies to parish councils.[46] Because this chapter is primarily a theological reflection on consultation, it will not go into the details of the various methods of discernment. (Some information will be given in Chapter 10.) However, it can provide a theological context within which discernment can take place. Suffice it to say here that Christians would do well to look into the rich treasury of their own tradition before simply borrowing the consensus decision-making methods used by secular management boards.

Paul tells us that *discernment* is one of the gifts given to the baptized as "a manifestation of the Spirit for the common good" (1 Cor. 12:7:10). One can assume from Rm. 12:3 that this gift too is given "according to the measure of faith." Paul uses the word, *diacrisis*, which in its literal Greek means *appraisal, assessment, judgment* or *separation*. It also means the ability to *distinguish* between good and evil. For Paul the gift of discernment enables certain members of the community to sift, as it were, the wheat from the chaff in making an assessment of the mind of the church on matters pertaining to its spiritual welfare. Such gifts are given for the upbuilding of the church and it is through such gifts that the Holy Spirit leads the people of God.

For centuries religious communities have used discernment as a method for making community decisions. The constitution of one community says: "The manner in which monastic communities share in the mission of the church is dependent upon their tradition and their contemporary discernment."[47] In applying discernment to modern consultative bodies we would do well to consult the saints for their wisdom and guidance. In his *Spiritual Exercises*, St. Ignatius of Loyola (d.1556) gives 14 Rules for the Discernment of Spirits. He was "an astute operator and organizer—as his successor put it, 'a man of great good sense and prudence in matters of business.' "[48] He used his Rules for Discernment in a very practical way in resisting the pope and the emperor who wanted to make Francis Borgia a cardinal. In his letter to Borgia, Ignatius writes:

> It was as though I had been informed that the emperor had as a matter of fact nominated you and that the pope was willing to create you cardinal. At once I felt impelled to do all I could to prevent it. And yet, not being certain of God's will, as I saw many reasons for both sides, I gave orders in the community that all priests should say Mass and those not priests offer their prayers for three days for divine guidance, to God's greater glory.[49]

Of course, consultative bodies are not always composed of saints and they are not religious communities. But that does not mean they cannot learn the discernment process. It is part of our Christian heritage and it certainly can be used outside the boundaries of religious communities. It may in fact require a long educational process, spiritual direction, and growth in community prayer. But that could well be part of growing into the consultative process. That will not happen overnight. The guidelines of the Diocese of Columbus warn us:

> At a minimum, a communal discernment process would normally take at least a full evening to complete and could be carried on for a day or several days depending on the issues being dealt with. It should not be incorporated into an ordinary business meeting.[50]

It should not be assumed from the emphasis on prayer that discernment is a flight into supernaturalism. The Archdiocese of

Newark, describing one step in the discernment process, *gathering data*, asks for careful observation of all concrete circumstances of the situation, communication with experts on the subject, and dialogue among the community. "It is necessary," the Newark guidelines continue, "to examine all available data in order to achieve valid discernment. The presentation of new data requires new discernment."[51]

It should be clear from all the above that discernment is not a question of merely gathering the dominant feelings on a given issue; nor is it a new method for arriving at a majority vote. Christians who are conditioned by the parliamentary system of *Robert's Rules of Order* may be uncomfortable with discernment at first. Eventually, if they stick with it, they will discover it fits the Christian community much better.

It should also be clear from our brief reference to the process of discernment that the "success" or "authority" of consultation will depend very much on numerous intangibles that affect the dynamics of a specific consultative body. What is the trust level in the group? How much homework are the members willing and able to do on a given issue? Are there any hidden agendas at work? Is the group polarized and in need of reconciliation? What is the level of sophistication and education, especially in the application of the principles of group dynamics? Is there a strong, dominating personality whose voice carries the day? What is the group's competence regarding the issues being discussed? How long have the members worked with each other? Have they arrived at a common understanding regarding their own role and mission in their part of the church? All these questions already indicate that there can be some real obstacles to the consultative process.

Obstacles to the Consultative Process

When one is discussing obstacles to consultation, it is difficult to draw a clear and precise line between what is psychological and what is properly theological. Nevertheless, this discussion will be limited to a few of the theological obstacles that may now and then overlap a little with the whole psychological process.

After the Protestant Reformation theologians often viewed the church through dualistic constructs, such as visible and invisible, body and soul, or the *ecclesia docens* (teaching church) and *ecclesia discens* (learning church). Dividing the people of God into a teaching and learning church has had harmful effects on the unity of the church. Leonardo Boff writes: "There has been a great deal of violence and domination by some Christians over others owing to the acceptance of one church that speaks and teaches and another church that listens and obeys, all done in the name of a truth that only a select body of priests is presumed to possess."[52] In actual practice the clergy were defined as teachers and the laity as learners.

Vatican II, of course, did not retain the dualism of the teaching and learning church. In fact the ecclesiology of *The Constitution on the Church* eliminates the theological justification for that preconciliar distinction. It is now possible to refer to "The Teaching Authority of Believers."[53] The ecclesial themes developed in Chapter II of the Constitution, "The People of God," have gone a long way to bring about a greater unity. Nevertheless, the body of the church is still suffering from the residual trauma of that teaching-learning division.

If we reflect for a moment on the depth of this division, we will see why it can still be an obstacle to consultation in the church. Fr. Boff says: "The dichotomy of *Ecclesia docens* and *discens* is the result of a pathological view of the church's reality. The *Ecclesia docens* tended to be a separate sociological state. The creation of a body of experts dichotomized the community."[54] Since the clerical teachers, with their indelible character, were "essentially" different from the lay learners, this division tended to become an ontological separation. It meant that Pope Gregory XVI (1831-46) could write: "No one can deny that the church is an unequal society in which God destined some to be governors and others to be servants. The latter are the laity; the former, the clergy." And Pope Pius X could go even further: "Only the college of pastors [has] the right or authority to lead and govern. The masses have no right or authority except that of being governed, like an obedient flock that follows its Shepherd."[55] The division created a one-way street in which the hierarchy taught and the people listened.

Pius X's application of the shepherd/sheep image to church government, still common in our own time, is not helpful to the consultative process. If priests are shepherds and the laity are sheep, it will not be easy for the shepherds to get into the habit of consulting the "dumb" sheep. In John 10 the first and obvious meaning of the shepherd image is that Jesus "lays down his life for the sheep." All disciples, including the laity, are called to lay down their lives if they follow a Jesus who lays down his life for others. The shepherd/sheep image is primarily a Christological image.

The preconciliar division of the church into teachers and learners is still an obstacle to consultation in the church because some clerics still find it hard to see the laity as teachers. They have not yet internalized the truth that the whole church is the learning church. The whole church is the hearer of the Word. The whole church is the student of the one teacher, Jesus Christ. The whole church listens to the Spirit and learns from the Spirit. All the baptized are bound to believe that the same Spirit gives the gifts of "the utterance of wisdom," "the utterance of knowledge"(1 Cor. 12:8), and the gift of teaching (1 Cor. 12:28) according to the measure of faith. There is nothing in the Scriptures indicating that the Spirit distributes these gifts according to an earthly caste system. Many clergy and laity still need to grow into the habit of consulting these gifts whenever and wherever they find them.

A second obstacle to consultation in the church is also a leftover from preconciliar ecclesiology. In the 12th century the reformist Pope Gregory VII, with the help of Cardinal Humbert, proposed the idea that the church was a Christian society. Their proposal was primarily a response to Henry IV, the German King, who was in the habit of interfering in the internal affairs of the church, even to the point of appointing bishops and popes. Of course, kingship in those days was a clerical office.

But Pope Gregory VII went further and said the church, as a Christian society, is a *perfect* society. Now the pope did not mean that the church is a *morally* perfect society. He could hardly have meant that in view of the widespread simony and clerical concubinage existing in the church of his time. He meant that the church is complete, finished. It is a society whose goal is supreme in its own sphere and which possesses, theoretically at least, all the means needed to achieve that goal. It is *structurally* perfect. In its governance it doesn't need any help from the state, especially not from Henry IV.

Gregory's teaching became part of the Gregorian Reform and it was widely promoted in the church until Vatican II. So much so, that another Pope Gregory in 1832 could draw the following conclusions: "Therefore, it is obviously absurd and injurious to propose a certain 'restoration and regeneration' for her [the church] as though necessary for her safety and growth, as if she could be considered subject to defect or obscuration or other misfortune."[56] Pope Pius IX, in his 1864 *Syllabus* also condemned the error that "the church is not a true and perfect society." And in 1885 Pope Leo XIII wrote: "[The Church] is a society chartered as of divine right, perfect in its nature and in its title, to possess in itself and by itself through the will and loving kindness of its Founder, all needful provision for its maintenance and action."[57] By the turn of the 19th century theological manuals carried the thesis: "The church is a Perfect Society," with the theological note that this teaching is a matter of *divine faith.*[58]

After the Council of Trent (1545-63) the church became identified with the clergy who became the ruling class in their "perfect" society. Then the unspoken assumption was that the clergy possessed all the means needed to achieve the goals of their church. It is easy to see that the clergy would not be disposed to consult, or to ask for the advice they did not need. Even today clergy do not often feel the need to consult the sociologist, the psychologist, the historian, or the theologian. Many will not feel the need to consult so long as they feel they are the rulers in a perfect society. This lack of felt need on the part of the clergy will continue for awhile to be an obstacle to consultation in the church. Avery Dulles is certainly correct: "Even today, many middle-aged Catholics are acutely uncomfortable with any other paradigm of the church than the *societas perfecta*."[59] Vatican II tried to move away from that preconciliar triumphalism. However, some clergy still have not internalized its new teaching that "Christ summons the church, as she goes on her pilgrim way, to that continual reformation of which she always has need. . . ."[60]

The third obstacle to consultation in the church is the continuing struggle of all Christians to respond to the call to conversion or change of heart and mind. The word used in the New Testament *(metanoia)* (Mark 1:15; Matt. 3:2-11) calls for a change in the inner person, an interior change of belief and attitude. Jesus describes the process of conversion as becoming like a child (Matt. 18:3). As an attitude, *metanoia* is a disposition toward three kinds of conversion: moral, intellectual, and spiritual. This disposition is a seed of the kingdom growing in the community and world.

The consultation process will disclose new human and Christian possibilities. But it is not easy for those who consult to appropriate those new possibilities. An attitude of conversion means to remain open to as full a range of human-Christian experience as possible. It means that those who engage in the consultative process remain "radically undogmatic" or nongnostic.[61] William Thompson, quoting Hans-Georg Gadamer, explains: "The truth of experience always contains an orientation towards new experience. That is why a person who is called 'experienced' has become such not only through experiences, but is also open to new experiences."[62] Openness to former experiences equips a person to learn anew. *Metanoia* calls for an orientation to the past in terms of reflection and an orientation to the future in terms of possibilities. The consultative process, then, will work best in a context of prayer for conversion, for *metanoia*.

A fourth obstacle to the consultative process is a lack of understanding about the types of consultative bodies and their different roles and functions in the structures of the church. Diocesan and parish councils, except for specific cases mentioned in canon law, are not deliberative bodies like city councils or legislatures. They are not groups of peers coming together to make binding decisions. Nor should they be expected to implement policies. "An individual member of a consultative body may well want to get formally involved in policy implementation. If so, this should be on the basis of a separate relationship, not merely a continuation of serving on a policy making body."[63] Pastoral councils, both at the diocesan and at the parish level, are policy making, but not policy implementing. In most cases the policies they make will have to be implemented by professional, full or part-time staffs, who in turn, may work with small groups of volunteers. Fr. Provost's comments are very much to the point:

> People join a policy-making consultative body as a cross-section of the diocese, to reflect for example what the "average" Catholic lay person or priest thinks about the various issues. To expect such a person also to take on a more administrative function betrays the original psychological contract, asks more than the person is expected to do, and does not respect the question of personal or group competence.[64]

Those who become members of consultative bodies often do not realize how difficult it is to achieve an effective consultative process. Bishops and priests need to be aware of just putting in time with a consultative body. Attitudes of condescension or paternalism, of favoritism or prejudice can poison the whole process. At the same time they need to be sensitive to the possibility that "the people consulted can be inhibited by their subordinate role in the process, by personal or social factors, or even by a difference in culture."[65]

At the same time, those involved in a consultative process need to be aware of the various stages in the process: collecting data; clarifying criteria; identifying options; determining and agreeing on a recommendation. It is not unusual to see consultative bodies impatiently moving toward a recommendation when they are still supposed to be collecting information.

Of course, Catholics will learn by doing. Fortunately, the American bishops have been offering Catholics many opportunities to learn. They have experimented, rather successfully, with different forms of consultation. Before writing the two pastoral letters, one on the challenge of peace and one on the U.S. economy, the bishops organized a long and extensive consultation process. The Detroit Call to Action in 1976, in spite of some deficiencies, was a very useful experiment. Many dioceses organized consultations in preparation for the 1987 Synod on the Laity. No doubt as the American church gains more experience these consultations will become more and more fruitful for the upbuilding of the church.

Consultative bodies witness to a new way of being church. They are in a process of defining themselves and their mission in the postconciliar church. They will in time get through the growing pains of adolescence. But they will do it better if they reflect, now and then, on the history, the ecclesial context, the process and obstacles of consultation in the church.

NOTES

1. James A. Coriden, Thomas J. Green, Donald Heintschel, eds. *The Code of Canon Law:.A Text and Commentary* (New York: Paulist Press, 1985), p.xxiv.

2. *Ibid.* p. xxvi.

3. Vol. 42 # 2, 1982, p. 403.

4. *Decree on the Apostolate of Lay People*, Austin Flannery, ed. *Vatican II* (Northport, N.Y: Costello Publishing Co. 1975), p. 777.

5. "Twenty Questions on the Revised Code of Canon Law." *Chicago Studies*, Nov. 1986, p. 334.

6. "Apostolic Tradition." no. 394, *The Faith of the Early Fathers* (Collegeville, Minn.: The Liturgical Press. 1970), p. 166.

7. *The Faith of the Early Fathers*, Letter 67, p. 234.

8. Quoted by Herve Marie-Legrand in "Theology and the Election of Bishops in the Early Church." *Election and Consensus in the Church* (New York: Herder and Herder, 1972), p. 34.

9. Hans Julius Wolff, *Roman Law. An Historical Introduction* (Norman: University of Oklahoma Press, 1971), p.28.

10. James Provost, "Consultative Bodies," *The Jurist*, 40 #1, 1980.

11. *Ibid.*, p. 261.

12. L.M. Orsy."Conciliarism," *The New Catholic Encyclopedia* (New York:

McGraw Hill Book Co., 1967), Vol. 4. p. 112.

13. *The Teaching of the Catholic Church*, Josef Neuner and Heinrich Roos.-eds. (Staten Island, N.Y.: Alba House Press, 1966), p.229.

14. It may be helpful to distinguish between *consent* and *consultation*. To consent means to comply with or give approval to what is done or proposed by another. To consult means to ask the advice or opinion of another, to deliberate together. The consultative process often seeks the consent of those consulted. After Vatican I the truth of a dogmatic definition is not dependent on the consent or "approval" of the church. But that does not mean that *consent* is no longer part of consultation. No doubt, consultation will continue to have varying degrees of weight, depending on the process, the ecclesial context, the matter under consideration, etc. But consent remains *one* aspect of the wider and more complicated process of consultation in the church.

15. Morimichi Watanabe, *The Political Ideas of Nicholas of Cusa* (Geneve, Libraire Droz, 1963), p.48.

16. *De Concordantia Catholica*, Book II, XIX, p. 205.

17. *Ibid.*, Chap. xxxiv, p. 293.

18. Paul E. Sigmund. *Nicholas of Cusa and Medieval Thought* (Cambridge, Massachusetts: Harvard University Press, 1963), p.157.

19. E.D. O'Connor, "The Immaculate Conception," *The New Catholic Encyclopedia, op. cit.* Vol. 7, p. 381.

20. "Assumption in the Mind of the Universal Church," Editors, *The Catholic Mind*, Jan., 1951, p. 8.

21. *Ibid.* p. 4.

22. *Acta Apostolicae Sedis*, Vol. 42, No 15, Nov. 4, 1950, p. 775.

23. *National Catholic Almanac* (Paterson, New Jersey: St. Anthony Guild Press, 1951), p. 70.

24. See William Thompson's excellent book, *Fire and Light* (New York, Paulist Press, 1987).

25. Gustavo Gutierrez, *We Drink From Our Own Wells* (Maryknoll, N.Y.: Orbis Books, 1984), p. 129.

26. John Meyendorff, *Byzantine Theology* (New York: Fordham University Press), 1974, p. 88.

27. *The Documents of Vatican II*. Walter Abbot, ed. (New York: Herder and Herder, 1966), p. 608.

28. *Ibid.*, p. 608.

29. *Op. cit.* p. 20.

30. *Ibid.*, p. 20.

31. *Ibid.*, p. 21.

32. *Ibid.*, p. 30.

33. *Ibid.*, pp.26-27.

34. *Ibid.*, p. 24.

35. *Decree on Ecumenism, The Documents of Vatican II. op. cit.* p. 350.

36. *Ibid.*, p. 348.

37. *Vatican II*, A. Flannery, ed., *op. cit.* pp. 999-1000.

38. *The Code of Canon Law.* Latin English Edition (Washington, D.C.: Canon Law Society of America, 1983), pp. 206-07.

39. *Jurist.* "Rules for Interpretation." Vol. 42, 1982, p. 279.

40. *Ibid.*, p. 281.

41. *Ibid.*, p. 287.

42. *Ibid.*, p. 292.

43. *Code, Commuity, Ministry* "Diocesan Church Structures," (Washington, D.C.: Canon Law Society of America, 1982), pp. 56-57.

44. James A. Coriden, Thomas J. Green and Donald Heintschel. *The Code of Canon Law: A Text and Commentary* (New York: Paulist Press, 1985), p.433.

45. *Constitution on the Church.* Chap. 3, no. 26.

46. See *The Diocesan Guidelines* of Harrisburg, Penn. and Milwaukee, Wisc.

47. *Call to Life.* Sisters of St. Benedict, 1987, p. 39.

48. Paul Johnson *A History of Christianity* (New York: Atheneum, 1979), p. 361.

49. Quoted in *Life in Faith and Freedom* (St. Louis, Mo: The Institute of Jesuit Resources, 1979), pp. 204-205.

50. *Parish Council Guidelines*, (Columbus, Ohio: Diocese of Columbus) p. 36.

51. *Parish Council Guidelines*, (Newark, N.J. Archdiocese of Newark), p. 40.

52. *Church: Charism and Power* (New York: Crossroad, 1986), p.138.

53. See *Concilium* 180, *The Teaching Authority of Believers* (Edinburgh: T & T Clark Ltd., 1985).

54. *Church: Charism and Power. op. cit.* p. 141.

55. *Ibid.*, p. 142.

56. *Mirari Vos, The Papal Encyclicals 1740-1878.* Claudia Carlen, ed. (New York: McGrath Publishing Co. 1981), p. 237.

57. *Op. cit. Immortale Dei.*, p. 109.

58. J. M. Herve, *Manuale Theologiae Dogmaticae* Vol. 1. (Parisiis, 1957), p. 313.

59. *Models of the Church* (Garden City, New York: Doubleday and Co., 1974), p. 27.

60. *Decree on Ecuemism. op. cit.*, Chap. 2, no. 6.

61. William Thompson. *Fire and Light* (New York: Paulist Press, 1987), p. 56.

62. *Ibid.* p. 56.

63. James Provost. "Consultative Bodies" *Jurist*, Vol. 40, 1980, pp. 266-67.

64. *Ibid.*, p. 266.

65. *Ibid.*, p. 262.

Sharing

1. What is your first reaction to the council's canonical status as "consultative only?"
2. What, in your mind, is most significant in the history of consultation?
3. Do you feel your council should be consulted before the appointment of pastors? Of bishops?
4. How do you feel about the people's role in the interpretation of canon law?
5. Does your own parish constitution list any instances when the consent of the council must be sought?
6. How do you feel about discernment as a method of consultation?
7. Do you feel any of the obstacles to the consultative process listed in this chapter are still at work in your parish? Your diocese?
8. How could the consultative process in your own parish be improved?

CHAPTER 6

THE MINISTRY OF THE PASTOR

Tend the flock of God...not as domineering over those in your charge, but being examples of the flock" (1 Peter 5:2-3).

When parish pastoral councils first started, many pastors had an identity crisis. They didn't know how to relate to this new, shared decision-making body. They went in different directions, trying to figure out what their new role should be. They got all kinds of advice. Some sisters said: "We're all equal." And some laity concluded: "We're the corporation board. We run the parish. The pastor is our hired man."

In the confusion some pastors beat a hasty retreat: "This is the age of the laity. Let them run the parish." Or again: "I don't go to council meetings. That way the laity will feel more at ease. I can veto everything anyway." Others abdicated responsibility. They threw the ball to the laity and were disappointed that the laity didn't want to run with it. Some pastors, in a magnanimous gesture, gave up the veto power: "We've agreed to settle everything by majority vote. I told the council I wouldn't veto anything, no matter what." Not a few pastors, threatened by vocal and articulate laity, became arrogant and unyielding: "I'm the pastor here. I have full authority from the bishop."

The confusion of roles had its effect in shaping the pastoral councils. Since most pastors felt secure in the cultic and sacramental roles, they clung to "the spiritual" and gave finances and administration to the laity. As a result, many councils felt they were supposed to deal only with the nuts and bolts of maintenance. In more than one parish pastors identified their role with the veto power. They didn't see themselves as members of the council. They gave up their vote. As one pastor put it: "I didn't feel I should vote on the advice I gave myself."

As a result, some councils looked and acted like bodies organized against the pastor. Before Vatican II the church had been divided into clergy and laity. Now it was divided into decision makers (pastors) and advice givers (laity). In the early confusion at least four different models of parish councils emerged.

1) The *political* model. Power was the main concern. Council members tried to figure out how to get power from the pastor. And once they had it, they wanted to make sure they would keep it by putting it all in writing in a very detailed constitution. Members were very much concerned about representation. During the council meetings they felt they were representing their constituents. They insisted on a parliamentary system of voting.

2) The *business or maintenance* model. Here the main concerns revolved around money—spending it and, less frequently, raising it. Many lay persons felt they were so familiar with money and maintenance that they could relieve the pastor of this burden. He would then be free to devote all his time to the spiritual care of the parishioners. Most of the council's agenda was devoted to the care of the parish plant.

3) The *activity* model. Members were concerned about getting more people involved. There were more and more meetings, often with the same few people. There were numerous and lengthy reports of parish activities. Council members were so concerned about coordinating all these activities that they rarely had time for overall parish planning. Rarely did anyone ask how all this activity related to the goals and mission of the parish.

4) The *organization management* model. Here the emphasis was on the skills and techniques of management. Especially in the more affluent parishes, the assumption was that the modern management principles could be applied to the parish council. Members felt the parish was just like any other corporation and could be managed the same way. So there was a heavy em-

phasis on leadership skills, conflict resolution, and management by objectives.

Of course, the pastor had received no special training either in the seminary or in continuing education programs to help him with the development of parish pastoral councils. For many, understandably, the movement toward parish councils caused fear and anxiety. For this reason it may be helpful, even at this stage of development, to reflect on the ministry of the pastor as it relates to parish councils.

To get a clearer understanding of the pastor's role on the council, we have to look first at his role as pastor of the parish. The pastor who is appointed to a parish gets the ministry and job description from three different sources: (1) the pastor's office, (2) ordination, and (3) personal charisms.

The Pastor's Office

It may be helpful right from the start to distinguish the pastor's office as such from the particular priest who happens to occupy that office. Already in the New Testament, we see that a distinct office exists as something to which a person can aspire: "If anyone aspires to the office of bishop..." (1 Tim. 3:1).

Since the Spirit is in the church, it is at least possible that the development of the pastor's office is one of the fruits of the Spirit's activity, a gift (charism) to the church. One can hardly say, as a few Protestant theologians do, that the evolution of office is a corruption of the ideal, free-spirit church.

Of course, a particular pastor can exploit office for selfish purposes. He can use it as an authority crutch against the council. He can take refuge in it and so sidestep personal accountability. He can endow it with an aura of infallibility. He can make it appear so holy and sacred that any questions about it will seem irreverent or sacrilegious. He can act as if it were a "thing" awarded to him as his personal possession. He can use it as power, rather than service. In short, he can forget that office is in the service of the church, not of the pastor. The pastor's office, like the president's office, can be abused.

On the other hand, office as such can be a positive good in

the church. It can, to some extent, deliver the parish and the council from the pastor's personal whims. It can deliver the people from the cult of personality condemned in 1 Cor. 3:4-9. It can arrest the privatizing tendencies in religion. It can serve as a more or less objective standard for holding the pastor accountable. Finally, it can provide some continuity with tradition.

The pastor's office is, of course, not an absolute. It is the product of a long historical development. And, like the church itself, it is always in need of renewal and reform. Two developments in this reform are worth mentioning: the associate pastor's role, and the more recent experiment with team ministry. With the growing shortage of priests, associate pastors are becoming a rarity, and more and more lay men and women are serving as pastoral associates; some are also being appointed to the pastor's office as administrators. These developments will usher in a new phase of renewal and reform. More about that later.

Someone will always remain responsible for the duties and responsibilities attached to the pastor's office. It is possible to distinguish four factors that shape the pastor's office: (1) the shepherd image, (2) the presiding chair, (3) canon law, and (4) Vatican II.

1) The Shepherd Image. In Ephesians 4:11 we read: "And his gifts were that some should be apostles, some prophets, some evangelists, some pastors. . . ." In the New Testament period "pastor" evokes the image of the shepherd leading his sheep to green pastures. In our urban, industrialized society the shepherd/sheep image can hardly be applied literally to the pastor and "the faithful." Sheep are dumb, passive, and easily led. Today's Catholics, on the other hand, are often as well educated as the pastor, and they aren't easily led.

The first point of the shepherd image is that, like Jesus, "the good shepherd lays down his life for the sheep" (John 10:11). The pastor, therefore, is called to lay down his life for his people. Second, as the shepherd knows his sheep by name (John 10:3), so the pastor is called to know his people by name. Third, the shepherd goes out looking for the lost sheep (Matt. 18:12). In so doing, he proclaims God's mercy for the sinner. So the pastor, in virtue of his office, is called to search for and accept those who have gone astray. Fourth, the shepherd leads the sheep to green pastures. He cares for them. He protects them from the teeth of wild animals. So too, the pastor, in virtue of his office, is called to have pastoral care for his people, to be concerned about their physical and spiritual welfare.

Of course, the council members are joined in a partnership with their pastor or pastoral team. In virtue of their baptism they share in these four responsibilities of the pastor's office. The shepherd image is a Christ image. This means that all who are baptized in Christ are called to be his witnesses in laying down their lives for others, in showing mercy to the sinner, in caring, like a shepherd, for the physical and spiritual needs of the Lord's flock. The shepherd image is not the property of clerics or officeholders in the church. At the present time in the Catholic church, however, the pastor bears the blessed burden of ultimate responsibility at the parish level. Council members, therefore, cannot take over ultimate pastoral responsibility without taking over the pastor's office itself.

2) The Presiding Chair. In 1969, St. John's University, Collegeville, Minnesota, established the chair of Jewish Studies. It was endowed by a Minneapolis foundation. The occupant of that chair may change through the years, but the chair with its teaching responsibilities will remain.

After Vatican II many pastors, responding to the liturgical reform, renovated the sanctuary. They carried the statues into the church basement. They dismantled the communion railings and stored the wood in the janitor's workshop. When the storm was over, three pieces of furniture remained: the altar, the pulpit, and the presiding chair.

Instead of "saying Mass" the pastor now "presides at the liturgy." While the word preside seems new to us, it actually conveys an old idea. St. Justin (c. 150), describing the liturgy of his time, refers to the presiding priest as the president: "Then is brought to the president of the brethren bread and a cup of water and wine. . . .When the president has given thanks and all the people have assented. . . ."[1]

"Preside" comes from the Latin *praesedere*, meaning "to sit before, or in front of." It can also mean "to have the care or management of." The Greek word expressing the same idea is *prohistemi*, "to be at the head of." This word is used in 1 Tim. 5:17: "Let the elders who rule well be considered worthy of double honor...."

As early as the second century, the bishop *presided* over the liturgy from the presiding chair. As a liturgical symbol the chair acquired a twofold meaning:

In the first place, sitting was associated with teaching. This is so in the gospels, particularly as applied to Jesus, but also to the rabbis. In the second place, sitting was associated with government. These two lines of thought converged upon the bishop's chair. For the bishop sat in his chair to teach true doctrine. And the bishop sat in his chair to preside over the corporate life of the believing community.[2]

The presiding chair came to have highly symbolic meaning in the installation of new ministries:

...before there were any other rites for the inauguration of ministries in the Christian congregation, one primitive rite obtained everywhere, namely the leading of the new minister to take his place in the seat appropriate to his office. For when, at the end of the second century, the notion of continuous succession from the apostles came to expression, it did not do so in the form of a consecrated from consecrators, but altogether as a continuity in the occupation of a certain chair.[3]

The chair of Jewish Studies at St. John's University remains even after the occupant dies or moves. So too, the presiding chair in the sanctuary remains even after the pastor dies or moves. The chair remains as a sign of the pastor's office. It will hand on its list of responsibilities to the new pastor when he arrives.

Of course, the pastor's chair doesn't exist by itself. It gets its meaning, its list of responsibilities, in continuity with the teaching and governing mission of the larger church. For this reason, the presiding chair is best understood as a replica of the bishop's chair in the cathedral, which in Greek (cathedra) means "a chair." The pastor who occupies the presiding chair is therefore a delegate of the bishop's presiding chair in the cathedral. His duty to represent the diocesan church continues even if the bishop's chair is vacant. That is part of his responsibility as occupant of the pastor's office.

The presiding chair with its current list of responsibilities is not an absolute. It is not of divine law. It's not necessary, for instance, that he who presides over the liturgical celebrations also preside over the administration of the parish. It is quite possible that in the future an ordained minister will preside over the eucharist and a non-ordained minister will preside over administration. Since presiding and administering are two distinct ministries, they could, in Paul's view of the church, easily be separated. The presiding chair may be a helpful symbol, but it should not become a justification for one ministry to absorb all others. In canon 230 the new Code of Canon Law allows "lay persons...to exercise the ministry of the word, to preside over liturgical prayers, to confer baptism, and to distribute Holy Communion. . . ."

3) The New Code of Canon Law. A rather long section in the new Code of Canon Law is devoted to the duties of pastors. Even though these laws for pastors are rather long, it may be helpful to include them here. Many lay councilors do not have ready access to the Code. Yet, if they are going to relate to the pastor in shared ministry, they need to know what their pastor's *official* ministry is all about. So here are three of the main laws outlining the pastor's official duties:

Canon 528 #1. The pastor is obliged to see to it that the word of God in its entirety is announced to those living in the parish; for this reason he is to see to it that the lay Christian faithful are instructed in the truths of the faith, especially through the homily which is to be given on Sundays and holy days of obligation and through the formation which he is to give; he is to foster works by which the spirit of the gospel, including issues involving social justice, is promoted; he is to take special care for

the Catholic education of children and young adults; he is
to make every effort with the aid of the Christian faithful, to bring the gospel message also to those who have
ceased practicing their religion or who do not profess the
true faith.

#2.The pastor is to see to it that the Most Holy Euchar-
ist is the center of the parish assembly of the faithful; he
is to work to see to it that the Christian faithful are nou-
rished through a devout celebration of the sacraments and
especially that they frequently approach the sacrament
of the Most Holy Eucharist and the sacrament of penance;
he is likewise to endeavor that they are brought to the
practice of family prayer as well as to a knowing and active participation in the sacred liturgy, which the pastor
must supervise in his parish under the authority of the diocesan bishop, being vigilant lest any abuses creep in.

Canon 529 #1. In order to fulfill his office in earnest the
pastor should strive to come to know the faithful who
have been entrusted to his care; therefore he is to visit
families, sharing the cares, worries, and especially the
griefs of the faithful, stengthening them in the Lord, and
correcting them prudently if they are wanting in certain
areas; with a generous love he is to help the sick, particularly those close to death, refreshing them solicitously
with the sacraments and commending their souls to God;
he is to make a special effort to seek out the poor, the afflicted, the lonely, those exiled from their own land, and
similarly those weighed down with special difficulties;
he is also to labor diligently so that spouses and parents
are supported in fulfilling their proper duties, and he is to
foster growth in the Christian life within the family.

#2. The pastor is to acknowledge and promote the proper
role which the lay members of the Christian faithful have
in the Church's mission by fostering their associations for
religious purposes; he is to cooperate with his own bishop
and with the presbyterate of the diocese in working hard so
that the faithful be concerned for parochial communion and

that they realize that they are members both of the diocese and of the universal Church and participate in and support efforts to promote such communion.

Canon 530. The following functions are especially entrusted to the pastor:

1) the administration of baptism;

2) the administration of the sacrament of confirmation to those who are in danger of death, according to the norm of can. 883,3;

3) the administration of Viaticum and the anointing of the sick with due regard for the prescription of can. 1003, nos. 2 & 3, as well as the imparting of the apostolic blessing;

4) the assistance at marriages and the imparting of the nuptial blessing;

5) the performance of funerals;

6) the blessing of the baptismal font during the Easter season, the leading of processions outside the church and the imparting of solemn blessings outside the church;

7) the more solemn celebration of the Eucharist on Sundays and holy days of obligation.[4]

Canon 528 #1 presents the pastor as teacher and sanctifier; the second outlines his role of governance; the third simply lists his main functions as a parish priest. Mostly the ministry of the pastor is an extension of the teaching, sanctifying, and governing functions of the bishop. Canon 529 #2 highlights the Vatican II idea of *communion*. The pastor is supposed to promote the participation of laypersons in the life of the diocese and parish, no doubt through the parish and diocesan pastoral councils.

4) Vatican II. Some other duties coming with the chair of the pastor's office can be drawn from Vatican II's *Decree on the Ministry and Life of Priests*:

1) to serve as the chief proclaimer of the Word and presider over the eucharistic celebration

2) to be the public reconciler of the members of the community

3) to serve as the public witness of the diocesan church to the local community and vice versa

4) to be the chief minister of unity in the community

5) to be the public leader of community prayer

6) to be a leader of the general spiritual formation and growth of the community

7) to nurture, support, and unify the various charisms within the community

8) to witness to the faith of the community

9) to witness to the church's universal call to holiness

10) to oversee the teaching mission of the church in his parish.

In actual practice, the pastor often delegates some of the above responsibilities and shares them with associate pastors, team members, or deacons. It may be an eye-opener for new councilors to see what the pastor's "boss" (canon law, Vatican II) expects him to do.

Ordination

In North America, the pastor is usually an ordained priest. Ordination is a time when the people of God accept the priest as their leader. They affirm that he is fit and suitable, and then they support him by their applause. It is also a time when the bishop imposes hands and gives the priest "his marching orders." And—let's face it—in the Roman Catholic system those orders aren't subject to review by the parish council.

In the rite of ordination, we see that the priest is ordained to "preach the gospel, sustain the people of God, and celebrate sacred rites especially the Lord's sacrifice." In his instruction, the ordaining bishop lists some of the priest's duties:

In baptizing men you will bring them into the people of God; in the sacrament of penance you will forgive sins in the name of Christ and the church; with holy oil you will relieve and console the sick. You will celebrate the liturgy, offer thanks and praise to God through every hour of the day, praying for the people of God and the world as well. As you do this, always keep in mind that you are a man chosen from among men and appointed to act for men in their relations with God. Do your part in the work of Christ the Priest with the unfailing gladness of genuine charity, and look after the concerns of Christ, not your own.

Ordination means that the priest is accountable to the diocesan church, to its bishop, and to its diocesan offices, for example, education, liturgy, tribunal. The priest ministers within a context of defined relationships with the diocesan church. If he steps too far out of line, he'll hear it from the chancery office.

This relationship is very much in process and may change, but, at the present time, the pastor often relates to the council partly from his pastoral office and partly from his ordination. Fr. Orville Griese has summarized the state of the pastor's relationship to the council in three basic pre-suppositions:

1) There can be but one head of the parish; the pastor shoulders that blessed burden.

2) The pastor does not work for or under the parish councils; the parish council does not work for or under the pastor.

3) Both pastor and parish council are to work with one another for "Thy kingdom come" on the parish level and beyond.[5]

The Pastor's Personal Charisms

As one clerical wag puts it, pastors are a lot like people. They come in various shapes and sizes. Each has his own history, experience, and personality. Each has a different level of competence or incompetence. Each is "gifted" with different talents and charisms. Each is flawed by the mystery of evil still at work in his life and world.

Some don't care about administration; others love it. Some actually like meetings; others hate them. Some are good catechists for children; others are a disaster. Some have a great need to do everything themselves; others delegate freely. Some are rigid and legalistic; others are more relaxed. Some are easily threatened by articulate laity; others are glad the lay people are finally speaking out. Some are shy and reserved; others are the life of the party. Some seem holy and prayerful; others seem worldly. Some are good preachers but poor builders; others are good builders but poor preachers. And so it goes.

Pastors, in other words, do not come from the seminary in set molds, like cars from an assembly line. Since Vatican II it should be plain to everyone that pastors, like the rest of humans, cannot be lumped into any kind of stereotype. Whatever the pastor's strengths and weaknesses, his personal skills and his personality become part of his ministry in the council and in the parish. One would hope that the council would be an accepting and supportive community that would maximize his strengths and shore up his weaknesses. He is, after all, a responsive human being who is susceptible to change. He isn't immune to the human and divine dynamism of a faith community. Shared prayer and shared pizza can do wonders for the most Neanderthal pastor.

Unless the pastor is very new, he'll probably know more about running the parish than the average councilor. He has received as least four years of graduate training in theology. Over the years, he has picked up a lot of practical know-how about "pastoring." After all, he's full-time. He lives at the control center of the parish. His nose can quickly detect the more bizarre religious behavior. He also knows where the roof leaks and where the extra altar linens are.

To summarize: The pastor, as pastor of the parish, gets his role from the pastor's office, from ordination, and from his personal skills. It remains now to discuss how the pastor relates to the parish council.

The pastor relates to the council: (1) as a partner with the council in the discernment/consensus process; (2) as ratifier of council deliberations; and (3) as a member of the council with his own unique ministry of pastoral leadership.

Early Council History

When parish councils first started, they spent all kinds of time discussing their competence and authority. Were they merely advisory to the pastor? Or were they decision-making groups? Unfortunately, the whole discussion was narrowly focused in either/or terms. The question came out of a legal, preconciliar mentality. Then, too, there was an atmosphere of mistrust. Both priest and laity were anxious to get it all down in writing, in a constitution. After all, "the council might get out of hand."

Such attitudes were understandable. Pastors knew enough

church history to have some fears about a recurrence of the lay trusteeism of the 1840s. And they were conditioned to see authority (jurisdiction) coming from above. They were the bishop's helpers. They were accountable to him alone.

Most pastors, therefore, answered the simplistic, either/or question in favor of themselves. The council would be advisory only. And many laypersons were quite willing to accept a merely advisory status. After all, whether it was in the confessional or in the pulpit, many laity were conditioned to accept final answers from their pastors. Then, too, many laity felt advising the pastor was better than nothing. It was quite a promotion from the "pay, pray, and obey" status of yesteryear.

If the council was merely advisory, then everything hung on the pastor's veto power. The council had to come up with the pastor's answer. Otherwise, he would say "No." The possibility, if not the threat, of veto hung as a spectre over all council discussion. It was not exactly conducive to mutual trust or to shared ministry.

Fortunately, most councils have moved beyond the legalism of their early days. Pastors and laity have begun to trust one another. They also have acquired a deeper appreciation of what it means to be partners in a Christian community. They are more ready to understand their relationships in terms of a sharing faith community.

The Pastor as Partner in Discernment/Consensus

As we discussed in the last chapter, consultation in the church is a dialogic process that respects the diversity of roles and functions, including that of the pastor-leader. The method many councils are using for this dialogic process is prayerful discernment and consensus. The goal of the process is to seek that consent in which the Holy Spirit brings about a harmonious agreement in the community, and to eliminate compulsion. This process is very different from voting for or against a matter and waiting to see what stand the pastor will take.

In the discernment/consensus process, the council and pastor are partners in making decisions for the common good of the parish; they witness to the basic equality of Christian partnership.

This partnership is rooted in the Spirit's activity in the church, that is, the whole people of God. The Spirit is one and will not be divided up. The Spirit is not present as only advice-giver in one part of the church and as decision-maker in another. This Christian partnership is also based on the fact that all the faithful, in virtue of baptism, share in the priestly, prophetic, and kingly mission of Christ. Such participation is part of Christian life as such and cannot be reduced to giving advice.

It is also worth noting in this connection that in our country the laity are conditioned by democracy and participative deci-sion making. Many have considerable experience in the shared decision making of corporation boards and modern management systems. Their time is too valuable to waste in meetings that do not result in real decisions. A council that is not primarily deci-sion making (consultative in the fullest sense) is a denial of al-most everything we said in Chapters 2, 3, and 5. Such a council can hardly contribute to the growth of adult Christian responsi-bility, and is reduced to a dependent, rather than interdepen-dent, relationship. By structuring such a relationship a council may do more harm than good.

We must always keep in mind that the church is mystery. And so is the Christian community. The process of council deci-sion making is too complex to be reduced to strictly legal catego-ries—many gray areas will remain. Suffice it to say these gray areas need to be discussed and resolved in an atmosphere of trust, prayer, study, and discernment. As councils grow and develop, they will see themselves more and more as faith communities and will come to trust the discernment process.

The Pastor as Ratifier

Before we discuss the pastor's role in ratification, we need to examine the principle of ratification by the diocese. The prin-ciple of ratification flows, in a sense, from the very nature of the church. In the first place, the gospel proclaimed by the priest in the parish is not subject to vote. The gospel does not evolve out of the opinions or consent of the parishioners. The preached gospel is the Lord's word, not humanity's. It includes the truth of the apostolic tradition, the truth of the historical Jesus. Thus the main message of salvation comes from the Easter community of the New Testament. It has a historical transcendence. It is the Good News which the herald brings, from outside, into the parish community. It is an announcement, a proclamation. Neither its truth nor its power depend on a consensus or vote of the parish council. It forms the basis for the council's discernment in parish life.

Second, the church as a community of salvation historically antecedes the faithful and constitutes them, that is, it brings them into existence as believers. The baptismal font with its power exists before the baptized faithful. The church precedes the faithful in Christ in three essential points: (1) By the revelation of the mystery of the Trinity and of the Kingdom of God, Jesus established the messianic people in respect to their faith. (2) By his priestly acts, he instituted the sacramental life by which the faithful enter into a true communion with Jesus and with one another. (3) By calling his disciples and by sending them forth, he gave the messianic community an apostolic ministry. So before any vote is taken, the church possesses the treasure of faith, the treasure of the sacramental life, and the treasure of the apostolic ministry. These are the Lord's gifts that bring a new community into existence. They come from the Lord directly.

The diocese's right to ratify also flows from two other theological principles: (1) the need for the parish to retain its doctrinal communion with the diocesan church; and (2) the need for the parish to witness to the truth that it is a smaller, dependent community within the larger, more independent diocesan church. A few words about each principle may be helpful.

1) The parish and its council need to build up a living communion with the diocesan church. As the head is one with the body, so the parish is one with the diocese. The parish witnesses to its union with the diocese by professing the same faith, by following the same Lord, by obeying the same gospel, by celebrating the same baptism, by breaking the same bread and

sharing the same cup. When the pastor ratifies the council's consultation, the whole council is sharing in a sign of unity which, like breaking bread, witnesses to the diocese's communion with the parish. It would be helpful, of course, if the diocese listed the areas in which the council does not have competence. The Archdiocese of Milwaukee's Norms for Parish Councils state in this connection:

> So that the spirit of shared responsibility of the Second Vatican Council be lived out, the parish council, after prayerful study and dialogue, formulates policies concerning parish and pastoral matters. The pastor's presence and active participation in the dialogue is a necessary element in the process of formulating a policy. The council's policy decisions are to be consistent with faith and morals, civil and church law and archdiocesan policy. The council in this way reflects the working union of the parish with both the Archdiocese and the Universal Church.[6]

2) The second principle for ratification is the truth that, in the Roman Catholic tradition, the parish is a smaller, dependent cell in the larger body—the diocesan church. The Catholic parish is not a Congregationalist church. It is neither autonomous nor independent.

The diocese is not merely the bishop or the chancery office. Nor is it merely an organizational linkage of small, independent congregations called parishes. The diocese is church in its own right. It is a portion of the people of God constituting "a particular church in which the one, holy, Catholic, and apostolic church of Christ is truly present and operative." It can ordain all the ministers it needs. It can celebrate all the sacraments.

The parish, on the other hand, is dependent on, and relative to, the diocese, just as the hand is dependent on, and relative to, the body. All council decisions, therefore, need to remain open to the body of the diocesan church. Ratifying a council decision is one way of expressing that openness to the diocese.

Remaining open to the diocese in a positive way isn't easy for many parishes. Often the diocese is seen as the "enemy," and the parish as "where the action is." Because the diocese is usually too large, both numerically and geographically, it is seen more as an impersonal, administrative bureaucracy than as a warm, loving, Christian community. As a result, parishes often become parochial, like isolated cells in the body of the diocesan church. Such parochialism is, of course, detrimental both to the parish and to the diocesan church. The parish must remain in doctrinal communion with the diocesan church, which retains the right of ratification over some council decisions.

In current practice, the pastor, as delegate of the diocesan church, is the ratifier of the council's decisions. Ideally, this should happen within the discernment/consensus process; as Sr. Mary Benet McKinney says in her book, *Sharing Wisdom:* "the pastor discerns the discernment."[7]

In the normal course of events, withholding ratification will be rare. This is especially true if the council uses the discernment/consensus model. If a pastor or lay administrator feels he or she cannot ratify a council decision, he or she needs to explain why to the full council. After hearing the reasons, and after further discussion, the council can, by a new discernment/consensus process, appeal to the appropriate diocesan office or committee to resolve the dispute. This process of appeal is further explained in Chapter 13.

One should not assume, however, that ratification is the pastor's responsibility alone. All members share in the parish's responsibility to maintain communion with the diocesan church. For this reason, the whole council should be sensitive to what can, and what cannot, be ratified. Then it will never, for example, recommend that beer and pizza replace wine and bread in the liturgy.

Further, one should not assume that the power to ratify goes with ordination. With the growing shortage of priests, bishops have begun to appoint religious women as administrators of parishes; some lay pastors may also be appointed. Such persons then represent the diocesan church and may serve as ratifiers of the council decisions.

It hardly needs saying that the pastor cannot give up the power of ratification without giving up the pastoral office itself. He may not abdicate his responsibility in a false move toward equality. The council is not meant to bring about a grand leveling of all the members. It is meant to support all the diverse gifts and ministries, including the unique ministry of the pastor.

If all council members see themselves as having a unique ministry, it is a waste of time and energy to argue about who has the most authority or whose voice carries the most weight. The amount of authority will depend on each person's gift and on the issue being discussed. On an educational issue, the gift of the teacher may have the most authority. On a family issue, the gift of the mother of a family may have the most authority. On a farm issue, the gift of the farm worker may have the most authority, etc.

In the future, the unique ministry of the pastor, in the model just described, will probably be in tension with the concept of shared ministry as outlined in Chapter 3. There are no simple formulas for resolving that tension. In actual practice, pastors and council members may have to deal with that tension on a day-to-day basis.

Tension is, of course, a sign of life and growth. Both pastor and council members need to accept this tension with a positive attitude, praying and hoping that the Spirit will use it to give birth to new forms of ministry both for the pastor and for council members.

The Pastor's Ministry of Leadership

As new ministries converge in the council, the pastor needs to adjust his pastoral role. (In many cases this is already happening when co-pastors or pastoral associates are appointed to the parish.) The pastor needs to evaluate his own ministry and its relationship to these new ministries. The parish council is an excellent, experimental laboratory for reflecting on the new directions in the pastor's own ministry.

Today's pastor can be grateful that the Spirit's gifts are superabundant. Ministries are blossoming. A new Pentecost is indeed occurring. The Spirit continues "to equip the saints for the work of the ministry for building up the body of Christ"(Eph. 4:12). The pastor no longer needs to do everything in the parish.

Now the business manager can balance those books; the new pastoral associate can take that wake service over at the funeral home; there are now many volunteers in the parish to develop and carry out new ministries.

On the other hand, even though he no longer does everything himself, the pastor needs to place high priority on the ministry of presence. He will not learn to relate to other ministries unless he is present to them. Besides, by absence the pastor conveys the subtle message that his priestly ministry is really more important than the other ministries. He gives the impression that he is entitled to pull rank. The lay ministers on the council may have equally compelling reasons for being absent.

Today's pastor needs to minister in the context of accountability. Secrecy, hidden funds, arbitrary and unilateral decisions are out of place. The pastor is a model of trust and openness. He takes the council in his confidence. He constantly reports back to it. Whether closing the school or launching an adult education program, the pastor participates fully in the council's discernment process. Sometimes this open, consensus style brings the pastor into tension with diocesan procedures. But that may be a fine opportunity for the parish to give an example to the diocesan church about accountability and shared ministry.

The pastor also needs to see himself in a positive and supportive relationship to the council's ministries. This means he creates an atmosphere in which lay ministers feel free to risk, to test, their ministries. He is always available to help councilors reflect on "mistakes" and turn them into learning experiences. He affirms and encourages them.

He would do well, in this connection, to practice the principle of subsidiarity, modeling a decision-reaching process whereby issues are dealt with and policies are established at the most appropriate level, rather than spilling over into the meeting of the council. In this way, the committee's ministries would grow toward maturity, because they would be encouraged to exercise real responsibility.

He has to be aware, too, that councils, like growing children, "will go through phases of contrariness in order to acquire their own personalities."[8] They may indeed take a stand against him at times just to assert their own individuality and their own new found competence. They are going through a period of growth, and the pastor has to be patient and not take the council's opposition personally. (He may be going through some changes too as he grows toward a new style of governance.) He has to realize that it takes time to train leaders. (And to be trained in the process.) But that's his job—training leaders who can assume responsibilities without being dependent on him. When he has completed his task, the Lord will call him elsewhere, as he called St. Paul, to begin the same task all over again.

The pastor needs to challenge the councilors to adopt a broader vision of the church and its mission in the world. Lay councilors tend to concentrate on the school, the athletic program, the parish plant, etc. So the pastor has the responsibility of delivering the council from its parochialism and opening it to the diocese, to the church and to the world.

To do that effectively the pastor needs a broad vision himself. The mark of a good leader is to have a vision and be committed to it. Martin Luther King, Jr., had a vision of racial justice in America. Dorothy Day had a vision of enabling the poor. St. Paul had a vision of proclaiming the Gospel to the whole world. Once the pastor is committed to a vision, he will, by his contagious excitement and energy, communicate it to his people.

Then, too, in this age of shared ministry, the pastor needs to be vulnerable, to be ministered to. He needs to be seen as a man who is human enough to own his real needs and failings and to be accepting of the ministry of others. He can't walk on water. He needs to receive as well as give. That's what shared ministry is all about.

The pastor is called to build an atmosphere of faith and prayer. And that means more than saying a prayer before and after the meeting. In times of conflict the pastor can interject: "Could we all pray about this matter for a few minutes?" Or: "Let's see what the gospel has to say about this."

It's easy for the council to get lost in financial and administrative details. The pastor, by guiding the preparation of the agenda and by appropriate questions during the meeting, can lead the councilors to reflect on the issues in the light of faith. Christian ministry, after all, flows out of faith and prayer.

It is in the context of faith and prayer that the pastor serves as a minister of healing and reconciliation. During the beverage break and before and after meetings, the pastor listens to the councilors' hurts and gripes. He makes room for different opinions in a pluralistic church. When discussion generates more heat than light, he leads the way in reconciling the dispute. The ministry of reconciliation is not limited to the words of sacramental absolution.

As new ministries emerge, the pastor needs to be on guard that he doesn't spread his sacramental ministry, as a wide umbrella, over all the other ministries. Historically, the ordained ministry tends to overwhelm and absorb all the other ministries. Rather than being the master of the ministries, he is merely one among many of the Spirit's enablers of ministries. He should not assume that his liturgical ministry is so sacred that he is exempt from the questioning and challenging process that goes on during the meetings. He has to remember that he is not one over many but one among many. The pastor's ministry, like all ministry, is always in need of feedback and evaluation. He needs to build a climate that makes it easy for councilors to offer that feedback.

The pastor also needs to hold up high ideals for the councilors. Since all ministry is for the public good and in the name of church, he can require that councilors be adequately prepared and that they meet certain standards of performance. The bus driver and airline pilot have to pass examinations. They need to have certain qualifications. They must have good physical and mental health. They need to know the rules of the road or of the sky. Only then are they allowed to "minister" transportation to the people.

All public ministry, whether ordained or not, requires faith, skill, knowledge, and competence. Good will isn't enough. Lay readers, deacons, pastors, councilors, and ministers of the eucharist need to be evaluated. They need to meet certain standards of performance. The needs of the common good (the people of God) have priority over the needs and desires of the individual minister. If a lector doesn't pass the test, doesn't read well, then that person should not be allowed to minister the word of God. The people of God's right to hear the word of God has priority over the person's desire to serve as lector. In the same way, if ministering councilors promote division, if they are incompetent, or if they refuse to study the issues in the light of the gospel and the mission of the church, then they should not be allowed to minister as councilors.

Now all this emphasis on skill and competence doesn't mean that the council is supposed to be an exclusive group of skilled and educated elite;the council must always be open to the hidden gifts of the Spirit given to the poorest and humblest parishioner. But it does mean that even the humblest gift may have to be formed and developed according to some standards that grow out of the discernment of the larger community. (Chapter 9 contains a list of qualifications for ministering on the council.)

The pastor has a difficult leadership role because he shares in a special way in the prophetic mission of Christ. Sometimes the pastor must offer the service of "brotherly against." This means that, on some issues, he may have to take a stand in opposition to the community he leads.[9] He has to challenge it to obey the Gospel even if it means giving up his pastoral office or his life. He has to confront the conscience of his council on racial and sexual discrimination, on its insensitivity to poverty, world hunger, and justice and peace issues. The pastor is not a man who merely responds, in political fashion, to the likes and dislikes of his parishioners. He serves their real needs precisely by remaining faithful to the often unpopular and painful demands of the Gospel and of the church.

In today's church, the pastor may need to improve his leadership skills and learn from group dynamics and from current management theory, much of which promotes styles of leadership that are enabling rather than authoritarian, and which encourage participative decision making. He will need to be a learner, informed and willing to change as needed.

In his 1986 lenten message to his priests, Bishop Francis Quinn (then of Sacramento) lists the 10 pastoral rules observed by an effective pastor in a southern California diocese:

1) I must develop listening skills. 2) I must trust my people. 3) I must be ready to endure the messiness of shared decision making. 4) I must give volunteers and staff people in the parish permission to fail. 5) I must demand that lay leaders serve limited terms. 6) I believe in my own prophetic gifts. 7) Not all good ideas come out of the diocesan offices. 8) There are no problems, just opportunities. 9) Less control over the parish requires more maturity on my part. And, 10) I must not stop growing.[10]

Today, more than ever, pastors and all ordained ministers may need to internalize the truth that the ministry of enablement is one of their primary ministries. This form of ministry is described rather well by James Fenhagen. It's a ministry that gives top priority to the following four values:

1) It is more important for the ordained ministers in a congregation to enable others to identify and carry out their ministries than to do it themselves.

2) Recruiting persons for ministry is only half the task. Without consistent and ongoing support—the hard follow through—enablement will not take place.

3) Interdependence is preferable to dependence.

4) The greatest gift a pastor has to give to another is not the right answer but the authenticity of his or her own search.[11]

Now finally, here are some brief practical applications for the pastor and the council:

1) The pastor should not identify his ministry with ratifying or not-ratifying the council's consultation. He should not narrow his ministry to one function.

2) If the council develops a conflict and becomes split into two factions, the pastor has to be careful he doesn't become identified with a single faction in the parish. If he does, he'll lose his power to reconcile the two factions. He has to keep enough distance so that neither side can claim him in order to

prove the rightness of its position against the other. He has to remain free enough and objective enough to minister healing and reconciliation to both sides.

3) In virtue of his unifying ministry, it is the pastor's special responsibility to build up positive feelings between the diocesan church and the council. He is not doing much to foster unity, for instance, when he introduces a diocesan program by saying: "Now I don't like this anymore than you do, but the diocese says we have to do it (stewardship, liturgical changes), so we better do it." Speaking and acting as if there is a conflict between the diocesan church and the parish doesn't build up the church, either diocesan or parish. Then, too, if the diocesan church loses its credibility because of negative image making, it will not be able to offer a mediating ministry when the council needs outside help to reconcile a dispute.

4) The pastor needs to be on guard lest he foster competitive spirit between "his" council and those of neighboring parishes. He may be doing just that when he says: "We've got the best council in town," or "We're way ahead of all the other councils in the diocese." Such remarks are often not based on actual knowledge of the neighboring councils, and they foster the notion that "his" council has nothing to learn from the neighboring councils. They build a spirit of competition rather than cooperation.

Now that we have a clearer understanding of the unique ministry of the pastor, we can move on to discuss the mission of the parish and its council.

Notes

1. *Documents of the Christian Church*, Henry Bettenson, ed. (New York: Oxford University Press, 1943), pp. 93-94.

2. W. Telfer, *The Office of Bishop* (London: Darton, Longman & Todd, 1962), p. 202.

3. *Ibid.*, p. 204.

4. *Code of Canon Law* (Washington, D.C., Canon Law Society of America, 1983), pp. 201-03.

5. "Pastor-Parish Council Collaboration," *The Priest* 33 (Feb. 1977), p. 20.

6. *Living the Spirit, a Parish Council Manual*, Archdiocese of Milwaukee, 1987.

7. *Sharing Wisdom,* S. Mary Benet McKinney, O.S.B. (Tabor, 1986), p. 61.

8. Walbert Buhlmann, *The Coming of the Third Church.* (New York: Orbis Books, 1977), p. 273.

9. E. Schillebeeckx, "The Catholic Understanding of Office," *Theological Studies* 30 (December, 1969), p. 572.

10. *Origins,* "Golden Age of the Priesthood," Vol. 15, 1986, p. 645.

11. *Mutual Ministry* (New York: The Seabury Press, 1977), p. 105.

Sharing

1. In what ways does the council process affect the ministry of the pastor?
2. How do you feel about the pastor's official job description?
3. How do pastoral teams and pastoral associates shape the ministry of the pastor?
4. Do you feel the parish structure encourages and supports the pastor's personal charisms?
5. How would you explain the principle of ratification in your own words?
6. How does the principle of accountability affect the ministry of the pastor?
7. How can the ministry of enablement be improved?
8. How do you feel a pastor could best exercise a prophetic leadership?

CHAPTER 7

THE MISSION OF THE PARISH AND ITS PASTORAL COUNCIL

In the first 20 years of their existence councils often concentrated on budgets, maintenance, and running the plant. They tended to devote most of their time to the crisis of the moment, and little time to long-range, pastoral planning regarding the mission of the parish. No doubt, in many instances, this is still true. Because the lay council members have been inclined to view the visible, practical issues of parish life—finances and structures—as their proper concern, the broader aspects of parish mission and ministry, particularly the future of parish life, have rarely appeared on council agendas.

To determine its mission and goals, the council needs to ask two very basic questions: What is a Christian community called to be? What is it called to do? Once these two questions have been answered, the council will be ready for a third—that is, what system of committees, commissions, and teams should be set up to carry out the mission of the parish? This chapter will discuss the first two questions. The next chapter will take up the third.

It is good to be clear that the greatest challenge to the Christian comes in his or her daily life in society, and not primarily through any church activity. In a sense, it is the major task of the council to enable the people of God to present their Christian witness in the world where it is most needed. The parish council is only one of many ways in which the Christian shares in the mission of Christ, and is usually a temporary commitment. Whatever the form of involvement, the Christian constantly needs to ask: What does the Lord call me to be? What does the Lord call me to do?

What Is a Christian Community Called to Be?

The first item on the agenda of every council meeting should be: How do we become a true Christian community? A person has to *be* in good mental, physical, and spiritual health before the person *does* anything. So too, the council should try to become a healthy Christian community before it moves into action. "So every sound tree bears good fruit, but the bad tree bears evil fruit" (Matt 7:17).

To be an authentic Christian community the council needs to become a true partnership. To remain a member of this partnership requires an equal willingness to give and an equal willingness to receive. A true partnership doesn't exist if all the helping is going one way, in the direction of the pastor. It has to be a communion of services. This partnership of services is always reaching outward. It exists not only for itself, but for the world. Like Christ, it is always laying down its life for the world.

1) This Christian community, and therefore the council, is called to be a partnership in faith. The council is not merely a team working together, like football coaches or a management board. It becomes a true partnership because the members are "bonded together" by a deep personal faith in Jesus/Lord. They do everything in his name. They believe together before they work together. The risen Lord, who unifies and reconciles, makes the partnership.

Because of their faith in the risen Lord, the members of the partnership become capable of a living, trusting, working relationship with one another. The partnership, therefore, doesn't come about because all the members are protesting against the Protestants or against the neighboring parish or against the chancery office, etc.; or because they all submit themselves to the same law or constitution; or even because they all like and admire their pastor. Paul vigorously rejects a partnership based on a personality (1 Cor. 3:5-6). The partnership of a council can be based on no other foundation than faith in Jesus Christ (1 Cor. 3: 11).

2) The council, before it does anything, is called to holiness. Vatican II's *Constitution on the Church* teaches:

The church...is held, as a matter of faith to be unfailingly holy....Therefore, all in the church, whether they belong to the hierarchy or are cared for by it, are called to holiness.... All Christians in any state or walk of life are called to the fullness of Christian life and to the perfection of love, and by this holiness a more human manner of life is fostered also in earthly society.[1]

For Paul the church is a communion of "those sanctified in Christ Jesus, called to be saints..." (1 Cor. 1:2). As lectors the "saints" minister the holy word of God; as "saints" they minister the holy sacrament of baptism in emergencies; as ministers of the eucharist, they serve the holy body and blood of the Lord to the people. By their holiness of life, "the saints" are signs or "sacraments" ministering holiness to the whole parish. So it is the business of the council to help its members to grow in holiness. If it misses that, it has missed it all.

It hardly needs saying that a council must be a praying community. The comments of Bishop Frank Rodimer (Paterson, N.J.) are pertinent:

The first thing a council must do is pray. The parish council is not a board of directors, not a blue ribbon panel, not a house of representatives.... Council members are a group of people trying with the grace of God to discern the voice of the Holy Spirit, trying to be one with Christ, trying to acknowledge his presence in their midst.[2]

At every meeting, therefore, the councilors need to devote some time to shared prayer. The council, if it hopes to stay on the right track, needs to be in dialogue with God, searching for God's will as it seeks to make decisions for parish life. (Chapter 12 will more fully discuss growth in holiness and the spirituality of the parish council.)

The council also needs a conversion to a sense of community, to an understanding of the parish as a community.... The understanding of the church—and of the parish—as a community is not dominant or primary in most people's minds. The parish, as an institution, is—that's why most parish councils consider their main area of activities to be finances, properties, and schedules.[3]

3) The parish council, as council, is a communion of disciples. All the baptized are called to be disciples of the Lord. This is the basic Christian vocation. No one lays hold of discipleship merely by entering a certain state of life, such as by becoming a sister, a brother, or a priest. Discipleship is never a question of religious garb, of titles, of grades, of status, of privilege or even of the celibate state. There are no degrees of discipleship. (A priest is not more of a disciple than Sister Margaret merely because he's a priest.) All are still in the process of becoming more perfect disciples. St. Ignatius of Antioch (c. 107), looking forward to his martyrdom, writes to the Romans: "Then shall I be truly a disciple of Jesus Christ, when the world shall not so much as see my body."

4) The council is a community endowed with the common possession of the Spirit. "I will pour out my Spirit on all flesh" (Acts 2: 17). Paul writes: "Now there are a variety of gifts, but the same Spirit...to each is given the manifestation of the Spirit for the common good" (1 Cor. 12:7). In 1 Cor. 12, Paul gives a list of these gifts. Of course, Paul never intended to give a closed list of all gifts for all time. Because of the Spirit's continuing activity in the church, each parish is the fertile soil for the flowering of new and diverse ministries. They are formed partly by the faith of the community and partly by the concrete response to the local needs of the parish and the civic community. The council is called to foster, nurture, and develop the gifts given "to each," both in the council and in the parish.

5) If the parish council is truly carrying out the mission of Christ, it will be a community that ministers healing. In Matt. 4:24 we read: "So his fame spread throughout all Syria and they brought him all the sick, those afflicted with various diseases and pains, demoniacs, epileptics and paralytics, and he healed them." The society in which we live is geared at a hectic pace to production and consumption. It is focused more on things than on people. For this reason, many people suffer de-

spair, mental illness, neurosis, estrangement, and loneliness. The pressure of a competitive, success-oriented society drives many to sex, drugs, alcohol, and suicide. In every parish and civic community, many people also suffer physical pain and sickness. They may be in clinics, hospitals, convalescent homes, or in their own homes.

The parish council, as the model of a ministering community is called to minister the healing power of Jesus/Lord—to promote life in all its richness. It is called to be a healing, humanizing community, offering warmth, acceptance, and compassion to those who have fallen by the wayside in a cold, mechanical, "number" society.

For example, one parish adopted a prostitute. It offered her a warm, accepting community in which she could start a new life. Three times she attempted suicide. Each time the members of the community took turns sitting by her bedside, offering care, compassion, and understanding. They became the healing environment enabling her to build a new life. All council members, therefore, are called to support a ministry to the sick, especially the poor. They can do this by visiting the sick personally. But they can also set up a committee on health care. Such a committee would be concerned, both on the state and the national level, about legislation promoting health care.

In summary, then, a council is called to be a community of disciples who, in faith and prayer, respond to the Spirit, strive for holiness and minister healing to those who are sick or hurting in the church and in the world. In this way, it serves as a model for what the whole parish is called to be.

What Is the Christian Community Called to Do?

In determining the number and kinds of council committees, it is often assumed that the council must serve the needs of the parish and the community. When the council's committees are formed, they are often a response to the "need" crisis of the moment, for example, finances. Or, they are a response to the *felt* needs of those who lobby for a particular point of view, such as supporting the parish school. Thus, the committee system sometimes reflects more what is than what ought to be. At other times, it is nothing more than a reorganization of parish societies with a heavy focus on institutional needs, such as the members' concern for education for their children, or for comfortable physical facilities.

If the council is going to get on the right track, it needs an order of priority in assessing needs. Of course, the needs relating us to God come first. Thus, we need to praise God. So the council first needs to devote itself to prayer and worship. The gospel needs to be proclaimed in word and deed. So the council needs to proclaim the gospel through some kind of evangelization. The church, and therefore the parish, needs to be catholic. Therefore, the council needs a *world* vision. The church needs to be missionary. Therefore, the council needs a missionary thrust, etc.

All these needs come before the *felt* needs of the parishioners or the needs of the various special interest groups in the parish. For this reason, the mission of the parish and of the council must respond to: (1) God's "needs," (2) the church's needs, and (3) the people's needs. Of course, the council doesn't set up a special committee to respond to every need. The council as a whole can respond to some needs. And one committee can very well respond to a whole series of different needs. More about this in the next chapter.

The main point is that a committee system ought to reflect the truth first, that God's "needs" are primary, and second, that the council is concerned not only about where the parish is, but especially where it ought *to go.* Thus the committee system may challenge and discomfit many plant-oriented Catholics. For instance, in spite of numerous social encyclicals and bishops' pastoral letters, many Catholics can't figure out why a council should have a committee on justice and peace or social concerns. In this area, many parishioners have a need to be challenged by a specific committee even though they don't know it, and do not *feel* they need it. In view of this priority of needs, the mission of the parish and its council can be described under the following ten headings:

1) *To proclaim the gospel: to be missionary.* The Christian community is missionary by its very nature. "It is clear, there-

fore, that missionary activity flows immediately from the very nature of the church."[4] The parish, and the council, must constantly reflect the nature of the church as missionary.

The first business of the council, therefore, is to herald the *kerygma*, to announce the Good News of salvation to those who have not heard it. Its first mission is to the non-baptized in its own territory and in the world. This missionary responsibility is not discharged by throwing a few bucks in the collection basket on Mission Sunday. Moreover, this mission "is mutual, not one-directional. Christian peoples and local churches will share the Gospel with one another in various ways, form each according to its special gifts and abilities, to each according to its needs."[5] Sharing the gospel could mean developing a relationship with a parish in the inner city or in another country; it could mean involving the entire parish in an evangelization process that would begin simply with an effort to become more welcoming and eventually include establishing an RCIA (adult catechumenate) team in the parish.

2) *To establish the baptized believers in the faith.* There is a constant need to deepen, to intensify the faith of those who are already baptized. The parish usually responds to this need through Sunday homilies, family and adult education programs, Catholic schools, and, more recently, the development of small, faith-sharing groups in the parish, for the mutual support and enrichment of lay persons in their life situations. The parish is also called to reach out to those who have been alienated from the church in the past.

3) *To offer the liturgy of prayer, praise, and thanksgiving to God.* The Christian community by definition is a "thanking" and praying people. The council is called to respond to the community's need to sing God's praises. The council might respond to this need by offering the liturgy together (perhaps in the home of the chairperson), by sharing prayer during meetings and weekend retreats, and by giving high priority to a committee on worship and spiritual life.

4) *To build up the Christian community.* The mystery of evil is at work until the Lord comes again. It reveals itself in the ef-

fects of original and personal sin. For this reason, sin, selfishness, and factionalism tend to divide the Christian community. Building up the community means being concerned about unity, reconciliation, and ecumenism. The hurts, wounds, factions, and divisions, both within the Christian and the secular communities, need to be healed. As many grains of wheat become one bread, so the Christian community is always in the process of becoming one. The council, as model for the whole parish, is called to witness to the Lord's call to unity by building bonds of dialogue and prayer with members of other faiths and with the civic and secular communities.

The council is also called to discern the Spirit's gifts to build up the community. In 1 Cor. 12: 10, we see that discernment is one of the many gifts the Spirit gives to each believer for the common good. We can assume that the Spirit is *superabundant in allotting these gifts*. They are given not only for the individual, but especially for the church. The gifts, therefore, become a variety of ministries. Every parish has them; they need to be discerned. This is one of the most challenging tasks of the council.

5) *To offer diakonia or service.* The Christian community offers threefold service—to the Gospel, to the Lord, and to the world. The council, like Christ, is always in an attitude of self-giving. A council turning inward, geared primarily to preserving itself and its institutions (even its own school), is betraying its call from the Lord to lay down its life for the world. The council is called to feed the hungry, to give drink to the thirsty, to clothe the naked, to accept the sinner, and to visit those in prison. The council goes especially where the city, state, and government workers do not go.

6) *To read the signs of the times in a particular time and place.* Vatican II teaches:

At all times the church carries the responsibility of reading the signs of the times and of interpreting them in the light of the gospel, if it is to carry on its task.... We must be aware of and understand the aspirations, the yearnings, and the often dramatic features of the world in which we live.[6] Our age is characterized by power, wealth, violence, poverty, urbanization, interdependence, disintegration of the family, high technology, electronic communications, the alienation of youth, racial and sexual discrimination, the explosion of knowledge, and the challenge of the "new" morality. These signs of the times change constantly. The council is living in a rapidly changing culture and society and, as a result, is always called to conversion and action. The U.S. bishops write,

> We should not be surprised if we find Catholic social teaching to be demanding. We are always in need of conversion, of a change of heart. We are richly blessed, and as St. Paul assures us, we are destined for glory. Yet it is also true that we are sinners, that we are not always wise or loving or just, that for all our amazing possibilities, we are incompletely born, wary of life, and hemmed in by fears and empty routines. We are unable to entrust ourselves fully to the living God, and so we seek substitute forms of security: in material things, in power, in indifference, in popularity, in pleasure. The Scriptures warn us that these things can become forms of idolatry. We know that, at times, in order to remain truly a community of Jesus' disciples, we will have to say "no" to certain aspects in our culture, to certain trends and ways of acting that are opposed to a life of faith, love and justice.[7]

To respond to the changing signs of the times, the council might institute an ad-hoc committee on youth and the family, Hispanic ministry, or women in leadership. Or it may choose as a priority the formation of neighborhood renewal communities within the parish. No outsider can program the council's response in advance.

7) *To be a sign of the inbreaking of the kingdom of God in a particular time and place.* In a world where there is discrimination, the council is called to witness to the kingdom of God where there is neither Greek nor Gentile, neither slave nor free, neither male nor female. In a world of hate, revenge, and balance of terror, the council is called to be a sign of love. In a world of mistrust and triple locked doors, the council is called to be a

sign of trust. In a world of harsh and unequal justice, the council is called to be a sign of God's forgiveness and healing mercy. In a world of creeping despair and pessimism, the council is called to be a sign of a new heaven and a new earth where there is honesty and freedom, "truth and life, holiness and grace, justice, love and peace" (Preface of Christ the King). The council's service to the inbreaking of the kingdom can't be reduced to a specific committee or program. All committees, all forms of Christian discipleship, are so many different responses to the power of the kingdom breaking into the present world, for the kingdom comes on God's terms, not humanity's. Visible here and there to the person of faith, it, nevertheless, remains mystery.

8) *To exercise Christian stewardship over the material goods of the parish community.* Already in New Testament times, Christians were involved in financial and material affairs. Paul writes: "...I am going to Jerusalem with aid for the saints. For Macedonia and Achaia have been pleased to make some contribution for the poor among the saints at Jerusalem" (Rom. 15:26). "...And they sold their possessions and goods and distributed them to all, as any had need" (Acts 2:45). In 1 Cor. 12:28 Paul lists "administrators" among the gifts given to the body of Christ. One Scripture scholar thinks Paul himself was a full-time tentmaker and part-time preacher of the Gospel.

In his resurrection, Jesus has redeemed and sanctified the world in its material form. All of creation, including money, is holy again. The council is called to witness to the truth that Christ has eliminated the distinction between the sacred and the profane. Just as bread, wine, water, and oil are holy enough to "minister" the liturgy, so too money, buildings, and properties are holy enough to "minister" the mission of the church. Those who administer the finances and properties of the community are engaged in a holy ministry. In 2 Cor. 9:12 Paul calls the collection itself a diakonia, a ministry.

Now that we have a clearer picture of what the Christian community is supposed to be and what it is supposed to do, it will be easier to figure out what kinds of committees the council might set up. That will be the task of the next chapter.

Notes

1. *Dogmatic Constitution on the Church,* in *Vatican Council II,* pp. 396-97.
2. *Origins,* Vol 6, p. 728.
3. *Ibid.*
4. *Decree on Missions,* in *Vatican Council II,* p. 820.
5. *To the Ends of the Earth,* U.S. Bishops' Pastoral on World Mission.
6. *Church in the Modern World,* in *Vatican Council II,* p. 905.
7. *Economic Justice for All,* U.S. Bishops' Pastoral on the Economy, 23.

Sharing

1. What is the greatest challenge for the Christian? How can the council enable this?
2. In what way is the parish council a true partnership for mission?
3. Discuss the council's responsibility to be stewards of the material goods of the community? Why is this a "holy ministry"?

CHAPTER 8

A SYSTEM OF COMMITTEES

Committees are the working arms of the council. Despite all the jokes about them, without the committee system, the council would find its job overwhelming. Effective committees serve the parish community in important ways, but especially by broadening the representation and participation of parishioners in parish mission. Committee members bring to this service their skills and gifts as well as their Christian faith and a sense of working for the benefit of the parish and the church as a whole. Committees are the "backbone" of council activity. The saying goes that if we didn't have them, we'd have to invent them.

Relationship to the Parish Pastoral Council

The committees' relationship to the council is the key to their effectiveness; the relationship should be one of interdependence, collaboration, and trust. After consultation with its committees, the council develops policies and establishes goals and priorities that deal with parish-wide concerns. Implementation then becomes the responsibility of the committees and staff. A sense of trust between the council and its committees is extremely important—the function of each group is vital to parish life. The committees relate to the council and through the council to one another, as arms and feet relate to the body, and through the body to one another. It is the council's responsibility to give the committees good direction, encouragement, and affirmation.

The council retains a good grip on its own identity and remains sharply focused on its main tasks—to pray, reflect, study, learn, listen, plan, develop skills, establish broad policies, build a community of faith, and think creatively about the parish mission. The toughest job of the council is to dream dreams and lay out broad vision. (It may actually be easier to serve on a committee, where tasks are neatly defined.)

The council must also learn to delegate authority and responsibility for implementing portions of the parish mission to its committees; the council can then hold them accountable. When understood and practiced, the principle of subsidiarity (which simply means sharing the decision making with appropriate groups) prevents the council from becoming bogged down in details and from duplicating committee tasks. Committees do not make policy on their own; they recommend and carry out the council's policies.

Building a good relationship between council and committees requires effort, planning, and good communication. More and more, councils are initiating ways to make this happen. One example is a once-a-year planning session that brings together council and committee members for common prayer and review of the current mission statement, followed by individual committee goal-setting sessions.

Setting Up a Committee System

It may be helpful, initially, to clarify the terms describing the committee system. Some councils use "commission" to designate their four or five standing committees. They use "committee" to designate those committees serving under the commissions. They use "subcommittee" for those committees serving under the commission's committees. They use "ad hoc committee" to designate any committee set up on a temporary basis for a specific task or purpose. Often both ad hoc committees and subcommittees can be responsible either to the full council or to one of its standing committees or commissions. Other councils use "committee" to designate their four or five standing committees. They use "subcommittee" for any committee responsible to a standing committee. They use ad hoc committee as defined above. Subcommittees are responsible either to the full council or to a standing committee.

In this chapter and in the rest of this book, unless otherwise noted, "committee" will indicate a standing committee of
the council. "Subcommittee" will indicate any committee responsible to a standing committee or to the full council. An ad
hoc committee will be any committee set up on a temporary basis
to accomplish a specific task or purpose. It can be responsible either to the full council or to a standing committee. The number
and kinds of committees varies from diocese to diocese and from
council to council. With too few, the council may miss an important aspect of the mission of the church; with too many, the mission of the council becomes too scattered, and there is danger of
overlapping tasks. Councils probably work best when they have
four to six committees. (In very small parishes, there may even
be fewer, with some committee functions combined.) If more committees are needed, it might be best to set them up as subcommittees, or as teams devoted to one particular ministerial task.

Parish needs, organization patterns, and ways of living out
the church's mission vary a great deal from parish to parish.
At an early stage in its development, a council will have to decide which committees and subcommittees it will set up to carry
out the mission of the church in the parish; the committees and
their responsibilities will be the fruit of a discernment process
by each parish community. Each council's committee system,
however, should be a real response to the call of the Lord, the
demands of the gospel, and the mission of the church, as well as
the unique needs of the parish community.

If the council is going to carry out the mission of the church,
it will need at least the following committees: (1) spiritual life
and worship, (2) Christian formation/education, (3) social ministry, (4) administrative services (finance), and (5) parish and
community life. These will make up the core committee system.
In partnership with the full council, they will oversee and coordinate other subcommittees that could have more specific responsibilities. Some dioceses require separate "finance councils," based on the stipulations in the revised Code of Canon
Law. (More about finance councils later in this chapter.) In other areas of the country, councils may not have standing commit-

tees (all committees are ad hoc) or the committees are accountable to the staff or pastor.

When setting up its committee system, the council also looks to the diocesan church, and its priorities and pastoral plan. The committees of the diocesan pastoral council could serve as models for parish council committees. Diocesan offices and departments can provide resources for committee work and council committees should be in communication with them.

Before we discuss the various ministries of the individual committees in the core committee system, we can name some general principles about committee organization.

Committee Organization

Effective council committees do not just happen; they are organized well by councils and staffs who are aware of their importance. These elements should be considered: purpose, scope, structure, operation, and spiritual growth.

Purpose: Why does the committee exist? What will be its contribution to the mission of the parish? The council needs to give clear direction to each committee and help those serving on the committee to relate their tasks to parish mission. (If the council has developed a parish mission statement, this is the vehicle through which a committee can key in on its mission and ministry.)

Scope: The committee needs a clear understanding of its limitations and relationships. What are the requirements of civil law, church law, or archdiocesan policy that affect the committee's ministry? How does it relate to (or overlap with) other committees, the council or parish organizations?

How does it relate to parish staff?

Structure: What members will the committee have? What will its particular responsibilities be, and how will it carry them out? What subcommittees/teams may be necessary? How will its chairperson be chosen — by the committee or by the council? (If committee chairpersons are discerned by a committee, a liaison to that committee from council membership is necessary in order to link the committee with the council.)

Operation: Committees need to meet regularly and follow a well-planned agenda (since committee members often tend to be talented and task-oriented, it is sometimes difficult to keep them to an agenda.) A brief, monthly report to the council, outlining the committee's activities, is important in order to keep the council well informed. The committee sets yearly goals for its ministry, relating them to the council's goals, with appropriate timelines. When a proposal is presented to the council on an issue or concern, several alternatives, not just one recommendation, should be part of the proposal, enabling the council to choose the alternative most suitable for the community. Just as the council works by consensus, the committees also seek to come to consensus in their deliberations. Committee members all have something to offer and should be encouraged to think for themselves, present insights and possibilities rather than problems, and be enthusiastic about the work of the committee. Committee members need a clear idea of what resources— physical, financial, people's gifts—are available for the committee's ministry, thus avoiding unrealistic planning. Parish staff members who work with committees must exercise an enabling relationship, rather than a controlling one, and function as a resource for committee ministry. Sometimes, a resource person from outside the parish can be called upon to help the members in their planning.

Committees ultimately serve the parish community. Regular communication with the parish forms the basis for committee planning—a needs survey or informal needs assessment is crucial to the committees' planning. Most especially, committee personnel need to be listeners, attuned to how people in the parish are dealing with their life situations in family or workplace, how they are changing and revealing new needs. In this way, committees truly develop into "servant communities."

Spiritual Growth: Committees, like councils, can also be caught in the activity trap—church activity is not Christian just because it is church activity. Spiritual formation growth for committee members, therefore, is as important as it is for council members. It is an integral part of the activity of any committee or other group representing a Christian community. The members of any committee, just as parish councilors themselves, need a clear grasp of the importance of their role in making Jesus present within the community. Committee meetings ought to include time to pray, to reflect on Scripture, to study resource material relating to the committee's ministry, and just to dream dreams—time for the reflective spirit. Opportunities to share faith and to socialize occasionally, or to participate in a retreat, help the committee members grow into a small faith community, enriching not only the committee but the whole council process.

The role of the committee chairperson is a most important one. He or she works to create an atmosphere of trust, openness, and respect for all members' ideas and abilities, while leading committee members in planning for committee mission and ministry. The chairperson does not pursue personal objectives or instruct, but skillfully helps the committee to seek out needs, and to plan and identify resources in the parish and the broader community that will help meet needs. (Parishes are wise if they provide committee chairpersons with training in specific skills and education in the committees' ministerial responsibilities.)

Evaluation: It is the council's responsibility to ensure that committees annually evaluate their service to the parish mission. (See Appendix for a possible committee evaluation form.)

In general, there are some basic functions common to all committees. The following were published as part of the Archdiocese of Milwaukee guidelines for parish councils, *Living the Spirit*[1]:

1) To identify the needs of the parish in an aspect of the parish mission;

2) To communicate these needs to the Council, discerning with them which needs can realistically be addressed and where intercommittee collaboration might be effective;

3) To formulate long-range goals and objectives after prioritizing needs;

4) To develop means to implement the goals;

5) To submit the proposed means (programs) to the

Council for approval and support;

6) To communicate with the pastoral team about the implementation;

7) To maintain communication with the parish concerning programs, encouraging active support and involvement;

8) To maintain communication with the respective archdiocesan offices for guidelines and resources;

9) To provide ongoing formation of committee members in areas of concern through workshops, study, spiritual formation, etc.;

10) To participate in planning a reasonable budget; and

11) To periodically evaluate existing programs and activities.

Now that we understand these general principles about the council/committee structure, we are ready to discuss the various ministries of the council's standing committees. (See chart on following page.)

The Spiritual Life and Worship Committee

Liturgy is the "summit toward which the activity of the church is directed. At the same time, it is the foundation from which her power flows. It is in the Liturgy that we celebrate who we are and what we believe as a Christian community."[2]

This committee is concerned with the worship and prayer life of the parish community. Since Vatican II, we have come to realize more clearly that liturgy is not the property of the clergy but the central activity of the church, the gathered assembly of Christians. For this reason, it is altogether fitting that members of the parish community share, not only in the actual celebrations but also in their preparation. We have also come to realize that the parish should be nurturing the spirituality of people in their daily lives. The Diocese of Nashville describes the work of this committee well: "The overall purpose of the spiritual life and worship committee is to plan and provide for the spiritual development of each member of the parish through liturgical celebrations, significant experiences, and spiritual growth programs."[3] This committee might also pro-

THE PARISH COMMUNITY

Proclaims the Word	Prays and Celebrates the Liturgy	Serves the People of God	Builds Community

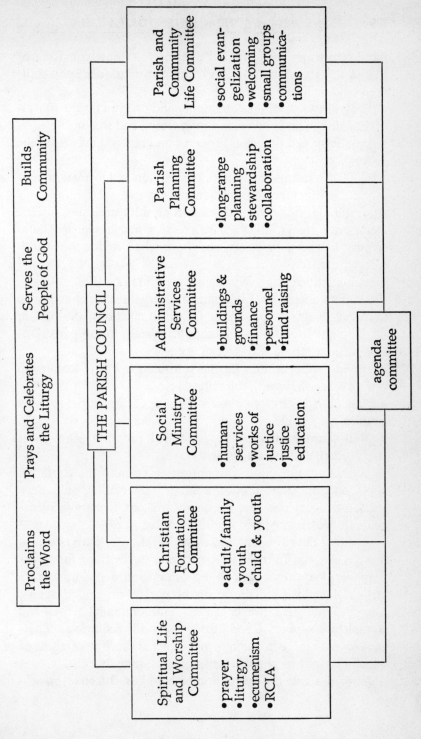

THE PARISH COUNCIL

Spiritual Life and Worship Committee
- prayer
- liturgy
- ecumenism
- RCIA

Christian Formation Committee
- adult/family
- youth
- child & youth

Social Ministry Committee
- human services
- works of justice
- justice education

Administrative Services Committee
- buildings & grounds
- finance
- personnel
- fund raising

Parish Planning Committee
- long-range planning
- stewardship
- collaboration

Parish and Community Life Committee
- social evangelization
- welcoming
- small groups
- communications

agenda committee

mote ecumenical activity and oversee the implementation of the adult catechumate (RCIA). The committee's responsibilities could be listed as follows:

• study the needs of the community and prepare for the liturgical celebration on Sundays and major feasts and seasons
• provide special prayer experiences and renewal events for the parish
• establish a means of continuing education and formation in liturgical matters for all parishioners
• coordinate and provide formation for all liturgical ministers: lectors, ministers of the eucharist, ushers, music ministers, altar servers, sacristans, greeters, and those who provide the liturgical environment
• evaluate liturgical celebrations, including homilies
• evaluate all present programs and organizational activities involved in the deepening of the spiritual life of the parish; develop a spiritual plan and support system for all parishioners, including those with special needs
• provide opportunities for the spiritual growth of leadership groups—parish council, committees, etc.
• plan parish retreats or retreats for special groups, such as couples, singles, etc.
• plan ecumenical activities that will promote ecumenical cooperation, understanding, and prayer
• coordinate with other committees, especially the Christian Formation and Education committee, in developing guidelines for sacramental rites: baptism, eucharist, confirmation, reconciliation, matrimony, and anointing of the sick.

Spiritual development and the celebration of faith is a continuous process. To make these experiences enriching for all parishioners requires a lot of time, effort, and dedication; it requires the close collaboration of parish priests, deacons, liturgical ministers, prayer leaders, environmental artists, and committee members. Good liturgy especially requires skill, talents, knowledge, competence, and monetary resources, some of which may not be possible without a full-time liturgist.

A word about the evaluation of homilies. Effective preaching is desired by almost everyone who participates in Sunday liturgy, as many surveys indicate. Since preaching is the prerogative of the clergy, including deacons, some of whom may not possess the gift of giving good homilies, this is a sensitive issue. The spiritual life and worship committee has the responsibility for setting up criteria for the evaluation of homilies in an honest, supportive way. Priests who have had the experience of dialogue about the Sunday readings with lay people within the context of a small group session have recommended such dialogue as being very helpful in homily preparation. In future years, it may be possible for lay persons who have the gift of preaching to be able to share it with the parish.

A subcommittee of the spiritual life and worship committee on ecumenism would handle all ecumenical activities in the parish in cooperation with the efforts of the other committees:
• promote the spirit of ecumenism in the parish
• invite and guide dialogue with our neighbors not in the Catholic communion (study groups, etc.) and educate people about ecumenical practices
• plan ecumenical programs, social events (i.e., Seder supper) and prayer experiences, especially during the Week of Prayer for Christian Unity
• cooperate with neighborhood churches in local activities and efforts.

In a smaller parish, an ecumenical liaison could be appointed who would work with already existing committees and organizations to promote ecumenism in the parish.

The Christian Formation and Education Committee

One of the most challenging tasks of the parish council is to define and plan for the educational mission of the parish. The bishops' pastoral message, "To Teach as Jesus Did" clearly teaches that the whole Catholic community has the responsibility for the educational mission of the church:

Under the leadership of the Ordinary (bishop) and his priests, planning and implementing the educational mission of the church must involve the entire Catholic community. Representative structures and processes should be the normative means by which the community, particularly Catholic parents, addresses fundamental questions about educational needs, objectives, programs and resources. Such structures and processes, already operating in many dioceses and parishes in the U.S., should become universal.[4]

The Diocese of Harrisburg describes the educational mission of the parish as follows: "to provide all its members with religious learning opportunities aimed at fostering a personal faith and expressing that faith through service."[5] In some parishes, there has been some confusion about whether the council or the school board is the official and final "representative structure" for overseeing the educational mission for the entire Catholic community. Often there has been tension between the council and the school board because in many parishes school boards came first. These boards were not disposed to "step down" in favor of the emerging parish councils that defined themselves as the top policymaking body for all parish programs and activities. In many cases, this tension has been resolved by making the school board part of the Christian formation and education committee under the parish council, yet able to freely administer that portion of the parish pastoral plan that deals with the school.

The Christian formation/education committee can be divided into three subcommittees: adult education, religious education for children not in Catholic school, and school board. Or, where school boards do not exist, the latter two could be combined into a subcommittee called "child and school ministry." Staff members who work in the parish in educational ministries serve as ex-officio members.

The greatest challenge facing this committee is the education of the adult parishioners, especially the young adults in the parish. Again from the bishops' pastoral:

Catechetics for children and young people should find completion in a catechetical program for adults. The content of such a program will include contemporary sociolog-

ical and cultural developments considered in the light of faith, current questions concerning religious and moral issues, the relationship of the "temporal" and "ecclesial" spheres of life, and the "rational foundations" of religious belief. Adult religious education should strive not only to impart instruction to adults but to enable them better to assume responsibility for the building of community and for Christian service in the world.[6]
The committee must always be mindful of this challenge and never "let adult education get pushed aside by the many demands for children's education."[7] Jesus himself hugged the children and taught the parents!

The responsibilities listed below can be distributed to the various subcommittees according to local needs and situations:
• develop a long-range plan for the lifelong religious formation/education of all parishioners, including young adults and families
• monitor and evaluate all school and educational programs
• provide for the selection, training, spiritual development, and evaluation of all catechists and coordinators in the religious education program
• assist with recruiting of catechists and teachers
• identify and train adult education group discussion leaders
• supervise parish library/bookracks
• maintain a relationship with neighboring public school system
• develop ecumenical education programs
• oversee an apostolate to students in colleges who may be within parish boundaries
• work with the spiritual life and worship committee in education for the sacraments
• study available resources on how adults learn.

If there is no family life committee, the Christian formation and education committee may wish to also provide family development programs and activities, support groups for the divorced and the widowed, or marriage encounters, and engage the parish in pro-life efforts.

Since the family is regarded as "the domestic church," it

makes sense to imbue all parish activities with a *family perspective*.

The Social Ministry Committee

(This committee may also be called human concerns or Christian service committee.) A committee responding on the parish level to the church's long tradition of teaching on human dignity and justice would seem, after all this time, to be virtually mandatory. Vatican II's *Constitution on the Church in the Modern World*, the numerous papal encyclicals and pastoral letters, especially the recent U.S. bishops' pastorals on peace and the economy, both inspire and challenge Catholics to be leaven in the world. This committee strives to "involve the parish in projects for world hunger, housing, racial discrimination, migrant workers, women's rights, prison reform, respect life issues, or legislation on social justice."[8]

These issues may involve people next door, or halfway around the world; they may involve immediate aid, or long-term efforts to empower others. They may not be popular issues, so members of this committee will need to stand together to seek support from the parish council.

A listing of responsibilities could be:
• identify resources to meet the human needs of all people in the parish community (compile a directory of human services available in the community)
• promote empowerment efforts such as the Campaign for Human Development
• study issues that impact on the community of which the parish is a part, and recommend action (example: participation in a food pantry)
•study world-wide and environmental issues and recommend action (example: become a "convenant parish" in Bread for the World)
•provide for the visitation of the sick, lonely, and shut-ins
•with the Christian formation and education committee, educate the parish on justice issues—hold forums and study group sessions

•work cooperatively with community organizations for the betterment of neighborhoods.

Most importantly, the social ministry committee works to involve everyone in the parish in social ministry and action, and to help connect people's gifts with needs in the parish.

A subcommittee focused on missions is a good idea.

Since the people of God live in communities, especially in dioceses and parishes...it belongs to such communities to bear witness to Christ before the nations. The grace of renewal cannot grow in communities unless each of them expands the range of its charity to the ends of the earth and has the same concern for those who are far away as it has for its own members.[9]

Some of its responsibilities could be:
• promote the work of the Propagation of the Faith
• adopt a mission parish in another country or a poor parish in the inner city
• sponsor a lay missionary to another country (arranged through the diocesan Propagation of the Faith office)
• prepare special publicity and worship experiences for Mission Sunday
• promote educational programs on the missions in the school and religious education programs
• sponsor a parish event for the benefit of the missions.

The Administrative Services Committee

This committee offers the service of administration to the council and to the parish community. As mentioned earlier, administering is one of the ministries given to the church by the Spirit for the common good (1 Cor. 12:28). Like the rest of the committees, the administrative services committee is accountable to the full council. And it has no more authority than the other committees. While it prepares the budget, it does not approve it. Only the full council can do that. Nor does the administrative services committee determine parish priorities. That too is reserved to the full council. This committee's main service is to support all the other committees to see that they have the money, personnel, and facilities they need.

The administrative services committee is concerned with parish resources, parish budget, parish support, and the effective use and maintenance of parish facilities. It is often divided into two subcommittees: finance, and properties and maintenance (Occasionally, there is a third, fund-raising or development).

The following responsibilities can be listed for each subcommittee:

1) Finance:

• In cooperation with the other committees, to prepare and present an annual budget for both operating and capital expenditures based upon the goals and objectives determined by the entire parish council. This approved budget is published and made available to all parishioners

• To periodically review income and expenditures to determine if the parish is operating within the approved budget

• To provide parishioners with periodic (quarterly, semiannual, or annual) reports on the financial position of the parish

• To approve financial statements for submission to the chancery

• To assist parish council committees and subcommittees in preparing and submitting annual budgets

• To study parish revenue and make recommendations to the parish council for maintaining or increasing revenues to meet parish objectives and priorities

• To educate parishioners to the need for good sponsorship of time, talent, and treasure in church support

• To coordinate any fund-raising programs, including the annual diocesan appeal

• To coordinate parish business and financial activities with the diocesan office of finance/administration

• To establish a program of job classification and salary administration for all employees of the parish

• To review and approve all banking arrangements, capital expenditures, and long-term contracts.

2) Maintenance:

• To periodically inspect all parish properties and review and recommend additions or repairs according to the priorities esta-

blished by the committee; to plan for future requirements
• To prepare an inventory of all parish equipment, furnishings, and facilities along with a schedule of replacement or servicing
• To prepare guidelines concerning use of parish facilities, lighting, security, heat, and janitorial needs
• To procure qualified engineers or professionals for maintenance and custodial personnel
• To develop teams of parishioners, skilled and unskilled, who will donate time and talents for parish maintenance tasks
• To promote economical preventive maintenance practices concerning parish grounds and facilities
• To study parish needs for heat, lighting, and air conditioning with the aim of conserving energy
• To check whether rental and leasing of parish buildings complies with the laws of the state and the diocese
• To analyze the feasibility of financial investments, purchase of land, new building projects, and the sale or rental of land and buildings
• To study the insurance needs of the parish and make recommendations to the parish council, with special reference to diocesan insurance policies
• To inspect the facilities annually for fire, safety, and security hazards
• To recommend to the parish council necessary maintenance, personnel, and services for the parish properties.

As mentioned earlier, the finance committee has to be careful it doesn't become the dominant committee on the council. Ordinarily, finance matters should not get more time on the council agenda than other parish concerns. (The annual approval of the parish budget is, of course, an exception.)

Canon 537 in the revised Code requires a finance council in each parish, subject to special norms established by the diocesan bishop, and composed of members of the parish selected according to those norms. The task of the finance council is to assist the pastor in administration of the property and finances of the parish.

In some dioceses, the finance council is separate from the parish council, with a tenuous connection, causing some anxiety about separating the mission of the parish from the means to carry it out. In other dioceses, the finance council/committee remains as a committee of the parish council. A national parish council conference held in 1986 surfaced these "pros" and "cons" about the finance council vs. finance committee:

> These were seen as advantages of separate structures: freeing the parish council to be more pastoral; focusing on skilled people. Disadvantages were given as: making the parish council more abstract; dividing the parish mission; playing one group against the other; difficulty in developing consensus.[10]

Retaining the finance council as a committee of the parish council was seen as having these advantages: holistic structure; clear lines of accountability; and consistency in ministry. One disadvantage was described as: "the tail wagging the dog."

Several factors that may help parish councils make the transition to a satisfactory arrangement, which will retain effectiveness while fulfilling the canon law mandate, are:

1) Appoint liaisons between finance council/committee and parish council;

2) Implement an annual budget procedure to bring expertise together;

3) Develop a good pastoral plan;

4) Make certain the finance council/committee receives good spiritual and theological formation;

5) Clarify the roles of each group, to one another and to the pastor;

6) Identify the responsibility of the finance council/committee with relation to: plant, budget, funding, personnel. Whichever system is used, it is obvious that there must be good communication and cooperation between the two groups. Where parishes have formed separate finance councils, it would be wise to provide a liaison between the finance council and the parish pastoral council other than the pastor (who is already at risk for burnout), and to also provide at least two opportunities a year for the two groups to meet for common visioning and plan-

ning, preventing them from moving in different directions.

Increasingly, as paid staff in the parish grows, personnel committees are being formed to develop personnel policies to recommend to the parish council. This group may be a separate standing committee of the council, a sub-committee of the administrative services committee, or a personnel committee that reports to the parish staff. The basic functions of a personnel committee are to develop a sound method of personnel administration on the local level, to monitor its implementation, and to participate in personnel planning. Personnel administration in the parish should be grounded in justice and a sense of giftedness and vocational call.

Some of its responsibilities might be to assess personnel needs, develop and review job descriptions annually, consider employee needs as well as the needs of volunteers, assist with evaluation procedures, recommend wage scale of salaries and benefits, and maintain equal employment opportunities.

It is important to stress that the actual hiring, supervising or evaluating of employees, or terminating their employment, is the role of the parish administrator—in most cases the pastor. Much frustration could be avoided if this point is well understood.

The Parish and Community Life Committee

Each parish is a unique and diverse blend of people, gifts, needs, interests, and points of view. It is also a gathering of believers. In a society that is very mobile and extremely individualistic, belonging to a parish community is important and valuable for many people. People need a sense of community in their lives; they want to feel welcome and to be a part of parish life.

This committee is concerned with building community in the parish and with fostering a sense of belonging. It encompasses all efforts that strengthen the Christian community in love. One of its important roles is to help the parish to assume its responsibility for evangelization.

Evangelization does *not* mean proselytizing (an image of an aggressive Jehovah's Witness comes to the mind of many Catholics). What it does mean is living the gospel in word and deed. Jesus himself told us to do that: "Go into the world and preach the gospel to the whole creation" (Mk. 16:15). No doubt Pope Paul VI will be remembered in history for the many times he urgently called the whole Catholic world to evangelize:

Those who have received the Good News and who have been gathered by it into the community of salvation can and must communicate and spread it....Evangelizing is in fact the grace and vocation proper to the church, her deepest identity.... Thus it is the whole church that receives the mission to evangelize and the work of each individual is important to the whole.[11]

This committee educates the parish in understanding this concept of evangelization: sharing the good news with all people within the context of their lived experiences. As a foundation for their work, committee members study Pope Paul's document *(Evangelii Nuntiandi)*, which reminds us that any outreach to the alienated and unchurched has to be joined simultaneously to an evangelization effort with active Catholics as well. Evangelization begins with each one of us! The committee, sensitive to the Gospel, will try constantly to discover the prime moments for evangelization: the death of a family member, a wedding, an illness, holidays such as Thanksgiving or Christmas. It is up to the committee to discern when and where the gospel speaks to the pain and the joy, the tears and laughter, of the human pilgrimage, and to develop ways to invite the whole parish to respond.

Few parishes today (especially the larger ones) have a well developed welcoming procedure for newcomers to the parish. This committee could oversee an effort to make the parish a more welcoming community, especially at liturgy on Sundays, which may be the only point of contact with the church for many Catholics. Teams could also be trained for home visitation to invite people into parish life and discern needs.

The Christian community needs the many different gifts of people to carry out the mission of Jesus. Another responsibility of this committee might be to devise ways to help parishioners discern their gifts and offer them to the parish and community in service. A stewardship of time and talent process could begin with a parish census. This information would then be referred to the appropriate committees for follow-up.

A listing of the responsibilities of the parish and community life committee might look like this:
• to enable the parish to become an evangelizing community
• to be concerned with building community among all parish members
• to develop welcoming and home visiting programs to reach out to newcomers, the alienated and inactive, and the unchurched, and to train evangelizers with approaches to such groups
• to sponsor social activities for parish fellowship
• to develop a stewardship program to help parishioners discern gifts of time, talent, and treasure
• to conduct periodic census and parish surveys, with appropriate follow-up
• to publish parish communications
• to cooperate with the spiritual life and worship committee in conducting the adult catechumenate
• to form small groups of parishioners to reflect on the gospel and relate it to their lives
• to supervise the council's orientation/nomination/election process.

The Pastoral Planning Committee
While the council bears the major responsibility for developing a parish pastoral plan, a planning committee would be helpful to assist the council with the tasks in each step of the planning process. Its responsibilities might include:
• to keep abreast, with careful and continuous research, of the long-range needs of the parish community and the factors affecting the faith growth of its members
• to develop and keep current a "parish profile"
• to give input to the council at each step of the process
• to help the other committees to plan

- to plan and conduct the annual parish meeting
- to assess the present and future use of all parish facilities.

Whatever planning process is chosen should be preceded by a renewal experience so that a vision for the future of the parish is shared. The process should be prayerful, flexible, and allow considerable input from the parish.

Other committees or subcommittees may be formed as the needs of the parish community dictate. Cooperation among all the committees serving the council eliminates overlap and encourages interdependence.

Once the committee system is in place, parishioners will have a clearer idea about how their particular skills and talents fit into council ministry.

That is one of the purposes of election: to fit the skills and charisms of parishioners to the various parts of the council's task in carrying out the parish mission. It is time therefore to move on and see how the council will select its members to do the job.

Notes

1. *Living the Spirit: A Parish Council Manual*, Archdiocese of Milwaukee, 1987.

2. *Constitution on the Sacred Liturgy*. Vatican II.

3. *Called to Serve with Vision*. Parish Council Guidelines, Diocese of Nashville.

4. *To Teach as Jesus Did.* A Pastoral Message on Catholic Education, USCC, 1972.

5. *Called to Serve*. Parish Council Guidelines, Diocese of Harrisburg.

6. *To Teach as Jesus Did.* p. 13.

7. *Called to Serve.*

8. *Ibid.*

9. *Decree on the Church's Missionary Activity.* Vatican II

10. PADICON (Parish and Diocesan Council Network) newsletter.

11. U.S. Catholic Conference, *On Evangelization in the Modern World*, pp. 12-13.

Sharing

1. Discuss the relationship between the parish council and its committees. What is working and what needs to be improved?

2. Is there a need to revise the committee structure or add a committee in order to carry out the parish mission? How will we make sure our committees are well formed spiritually as well as organizationally?

3. How can we make certain the finance committee/council is in communication with the parish council, so that the resources of the parish serve the pastoral plan envisioned by the council?

CHAPTER 9

SELECTION OF MEMBERS

Once a year most parish councils elect new members. Sometimes they appoint a special election committee to serve on an ad hoc basis. Other times one of the standing committees, such as communications, is given this added responsibility. Whatever system is adopted, elections of new members is a serious and important event for the whole parish. The word *election* has a heavy political connotation. It brings with it visions of kissing babies, campaign speeches, and partisan debate between opposing candidates. While *election* may be a good word to describe an important aspect of democracy in action, it is hardly the best word to describe that Spirit-inspired process whereby a Christian community discerns who is gifted with the ministry of leadership for the parish council.

In the Christian community, it might be better to talk about *selection*. When a Christian community chooses its leaders, it is indeed involved in a process of spiritual discernment. This discernment takes place, first of all, in a context of prayer for light and guidance from the Spirit. It also takes place in a context of certain spiritual criteria. In the first selection process, in Acts 6:3, the apostles lay down the following criteria: "...pick out from among your own number seven men of *good repute full of the Spirit and of wisdom...*" (Italics mine). "To be of good repute" means that the community respects them for their public Christian witness in their daily lives. Since ministry in the church is by its very nature a public function, the public needs to have a high regard for the minister even *before* he or she is selected.

The phrase "full of the Spirit and of wisdom," clearly recalls Nm. 27:18: "Yahweh answered Moses, 'Take Joshua, son of Nun, a man in whom the spirit dwells...give him a share in your authority, so that the whole community of the sons of Israel may obey him.' "

The first requirement, then, is that those selected for the council be people of deep faith who are responsive to the wisdom of the Spirit. They will be people who are more concerned about God's will than their own. That detachment from willfulness is the quality that needs to be discerned in a spirit of prayer and reflection. In Acts 13:2 the Spirit selects Barnabas and Saul while the church of Antioch is "worshiping the Lord and fasting." Because service on the council is a true public ministry, the ministers need to meet certain criteria for ministering in and to the church. It's not enough that they are articulate spokespersons for a particular faction in the parish. Nor is it enough that they represent a particular point of view, such as liberal/conservative, for or against the pastor, etc. Nor yet is it enough that they are persons of good will who are willing to run for election. The process of selection and discernment may mean that the election committee *selects* some who are in fact *not* willing to run.

God called some persons to be prophets even when they were unwilling. Jeremiah protested to God: "Ah, Lord Yahweh, look, I do not know how to speak: I am a child!" (Jer. 1:6). And Isaiah objected: "I am a man of unclean lips" (Is 6:5). And Jonah was so unwilling to serve that he "decided to run away from Yahweh" (Jon. 1:3). But God chose them all anyway. St. Augustine (430) didn't want to be bishop. But after he got the approval of the people and the neighboring bishops, he gave his consent. St. Ambrose (397) didn't want to be bishop either. But the people of Milan shouted: "Let Ambrose be our bishop." Ambrose, feeling afraid and unworthy, fled the city by night. But eventually he agreed to serve as bishop. In view of the history of both prophets and saints, it is at least possible that those who are *unwilling to run* may actually be the best candidates for the council. Of course, such candidates, through prayer and dialogue, would have to arrive at a point where they can accept their call to serve before actually running for election. A councilor who *remains unwilling* and then sits on the council because "Father asked me" will probably do more harm than good.

The pastor, as a member of the election committee, should not hesitate to actively recruit candidates for the council. After all, if God is going to call an unwilling parishioner to minister on the council, he may very well do so through the pastor's gift of discernment. If the pastor is practicing the pastoral principles explained in Chapter 6, he will know who will and who will not make a good candidate for the council. Of course such candidates would still be submitted to a process of discernment by the election committee.

The process of discernment asks if the prospective candidate is a person of faith and prayer. Is he or she in step with the changing church? Concerned about all the people? More concerned about the demands of the gospel and the needs of the church than about a particular pressure group? The discernment that selects candidates for the council operates on two levels: first, in the elections committee that *screens* and *discerns* the prospective candidates; second, in the discerning vote by the people.

1) *Preparation of the People*

   a) Plan a timetable of three months.

   b) Use pulpit, bulletin, special inserts, and visual aids.

   c) Explain the role and purpose of the council in the parish.

   d) Publish and distribute copies of the council's constitution.

   e) Distribute copies of election procedures (from the constitution).

   f) Hold public, parish forums, preferably in parishioners' homes on a regional basis. These meetings will find out how the people feel about the council and how it is dealing with parish problems.

   g) Distribute a summary report on the council's past activities.

   h) Stagger elections on a two or three-year rotation basis so that not more than one-half or one-third of the council is elected each year.

2) *Nominating Procedure.* Before discussing the actual process of nominations and elections, it may be helpful to discuss the relationship between the *representative* and the *functional* principles. People are concerned about the representative principle when they say: "We need a black nominee to represent the blacks, a youth to represent the youth, a senior citizen to represent the senior citizens." People are concerned about the functional principle when they say they need a teacher to serve on the education committee, an accountant to serve on the finance committee, a liturgist to serve on the liturgy committee. Conditioned as they are by democracy, councils often place too much emphasis on the representative principle, to the detriment of the functional principle. A good mix of age, sex, and color may seem very democratic and very representative. But it doesn't mean the council has enough skill, talent, knowledge, and expertise to effectively carry out the *functions* of the parish. If the parish has a mission in education, the council needs members, of whatever sex, age, or color, who have skill and knowledge in the area of education. If the parish has a mission to promote Christian family life, it needs members who have knowledge and experience in Christian family life.

In determining who will offer the *best* ministry on the council, the primary question is: can the members of the council do the job the council is called to do? Age, sex, and color do not, by themselves, contribute to the council's skill, knowledge, or competence in carrying out the mission of the church. It is worthy of note that Paul in his three lists of gifts and ministries that build up the body of Christ (1 Cor. 12, Eph. 4, Rm. 12), lists only functions: healers, helpers, teachers, administrators, etc. Nowhere does he mention age, sex, or color. The assumption is that all the ministries listed are given by the Spirit according to the *measure of faith*, not according to age, sex, or color. Paul's church gets built up by upbuilding *functions.* It doesn't get built up merely because representatives from various castes, classes, factions, or pressure groups have come together.

Adequate representation, however, is still important in putting together a council. But representation in a Christian community is based not on any historical form of democracy, but on the Pauline principle that the manifestation of the spirit "is given to each" (1 Cor. 12:7). For this reason the council cannot discriminate against any groups in the parish. And, therefore, adequate representation of age, sex, and color remains important, not to be democratic, but to witness to the biblical truth that the Spirit is given to all the baptized. In selecting members for the council, however, the functional principle is primary; representation, while still important, is secondary. Often the two principles can be combined in the same person. For example, a black councilor can be an accountant, an Indian can be an educator, etc.

The election committee itself should have broad representation. It should be composed of members who are thoroughly familiar with the workings of the council and with the people of the parish. On the other hand, it shouldn't be an inner circle or parish clique that invites candidates from its own narrow circle of friends. It's especially important that the pastor be a member of the election committee. He may have information of a confidential nature that may eliminate a particular candidate. If he's on the nominating committee, his input will be available at an early stage. It will save the committee the embarrassment of eliminating a candidate after he or she has agreed to run.

The election committee, therefore, has two functions—*to screen* and *to select*. Both are functions of discernment. In exercising its screening function, the election committee will do well to agree in advance on a list of qualifications. Since service on the council is a parish ministry, the committee can indeed insist on certain basic qualifications.

Such a list of qualifications will also help the election committee to be more objective. It will keep the committee from playing favorites or being arbitrary in making its selections. The list of qualifications should, of course, be kept to a minimum. It should also allow for a very flexible interpretation. The council should definitely not become the exclusive preserve of an educated elite, of company executives, of financial experts. That would soon become gnosticism. Salvation is not in

knowledge. The following list of qualifications may be some
help to the election committee's discernment process:

a) Age 18 or over

b) Active, registered member of the parish

c) Believing, praying Christian

d) Adequate knowledge about the parish and its tasks; skill,
gift or talent to offer

e) Desire to serve the church and to grow spiritually

f) Desire to unify and reconcile the whole parish and the
community

g) Willingness to participate in ongoing leadership formation, including an initial orientation process

h) Willingness to devote considerable time and effort to meetings and committee work; ability to relate to other members as
a team

i) Acceptance of the teachings of Vatican II

j) Good reputation and moral character.

The second function of the nominating committee is to select
prospective candidates. The committee should consider the following steps:

a) Select some nominees from existing council committees to
ensure continuity. Ask council committees themselves to recommend names.

b) Select some nominees who have specific skills, i.e., accountants, educators, liturgists, musicians, etc.

c) Invite all parishioners, preferably in groups, to submit
nominees in accordance with published elections procedures.

d) Encourage parishioners to nominate themselves.

e) Ask the pastor to review the list of nominees at an early
date. He may have information about a nominee's reputation
or moral character that will eliminate this nominee before
the name gets on the final list.

f) Obtain nominees' consent in writing.

g) Insist on nominees' commitment to attend an orientation
session, as preparation for service on the council. They might
even be asked to sign a *commitment to service,* if elected.

h) Be sensitive to the need for adequate representation

from all geographical areas and from different groups, such as women, youth, senior citizens, etc.

i) Avoid cliques both on the council and on the nominating committee.

J) Invite the diocesan director of the parish council office, if there is one, to meet with the candidates to share insights regarding diocesan structures and services.

k) Invite nominees to express their concerns and their reasons for offering their service to the council.

Some councils ask candidates to run for council as chairs of specific committees. Then they print their ballots accordingly. Other councils ask candidates simply to run for the council, and, when elections are over, the executive committee or the full council, after dialoguing with the new councilors about their special gifts, talents, and interests, appoints them to serve on a specific committee. Still others ask committees to elect their own representative to the council (not the committee chairperson, however). Care must be taken to ensure that these committee-elected representatives have the entire parish mission as their concern and not just a particular committee's mission. If this latter method is used, an equal number of at-large members should also be elected.

All of the above seem to work. The main point to remember is that each new councilor should end up on the committee that will provide maximum opportunity for exercising his or her unique ministry. All at-large councilors should be encouraged to serve on a specific committee; otherwise, they will soon lose interest in the council.

3) *Getting to Know the Candidates.* In large parishes especially, it is important that people get to know the candidates. Since the people's vote will be a form of discernment, the parishioners need to know who is gifted with the most useful ministry to build up the parish community. It won't do to vote merely out of friendship or because the candidate has a familiar ethnic name. To help the parishioners to get to know the candidates the elections committee could consider the following:

a) Print special bulletin insert with resumes of all candidates. Resumes should be limited to 75 words or less and include name, address, and phone number, areas of concern and interest, past activities in parish and community, recent picture, brief statement regarding the service the candidate expects to contribute to the parish as a council member.

b) Conduct meet-your-candidate sessions. These may be held before or after all the Masses, in parish hall or in neighborhood meetings.

4) *Selection.* At election time, the election committee could consider the following:

a) Celebrate special liturgy on the discernment of gifts and the call to service in the church.

b) Provide plenty of opportunity to vote.

c) With proper explanation, invite parishioners to vote before or after Sunday liturgy: "On one occasion, while they were engaged in the liturgy of the Lord and were fasting, the Holy Spirit spoke to them: 'Set apart Barnabas and Saul for me to do the work for which I have called them' " (Acts 13:2).

d) Print clear, simple ballots, listing candidates by committee, with different colors for different geographical areas.

e) Mail ballots to all registered parishioners. That way they will have more time to think about their selections.

f) Do not allow any nominees to count ballots.

After elections it may be necessary for the pastor, *after consulting the full council,* to appoint one or two members to the council. This can happen when the council is lacking in sufficient representation (for example, not enough women) or in expertise (no one who understands stewardship). In any case, *at least half* the council should be elected by the parishioners.

5) *Installation Ceremony.* Because service on the council is a parish ministry, it is fitting that there be a parish installation ceremony. It is common practice to have a ceremony to install lectors, religious education teachers, and ministers of the eucharist. In the same way, some brief installation ceremony for

newly elected council *ministers* is entirely appropriate. In preparing for the installation ceremony, the election committee could consider the following:

a) Discuss the reasons for an installation ceremony with the new members.

b) Invite their input in planning the ceremony.

c) Plan installation ceremony with the Sunday liturgy.

d) The ceremony itself could include the following elements:

   i) thanks and *certificate of appreciation* to all outgoing members.

   ii) thanks to all those who ran for election

   iii) announcement of the winning candidates

   iv) installation ceremony

v) conferral of certificate for ministry on new members

vi) reception with refreshments in the parish hall.

Discernment of Leadership:
An Alternative to Election

Over the years, the way of electing parish leadership described above has presented some concerns: a declining number of people participating as electors and candidates (in some cases, not enough to fill the open positions); the need for an orientation process that involves more parishioners; the need to give people a chance to express their concerns and share their vision of the parish; the need for a better understanding of the concept of shared responsibility; and the need to affirm and support all those gifted for leadership in the community. Parishes across the country have recently been developing a way of choosing leadership through a prayerful discernment process that is sensitive to these concerns and which provides an alternative to the "popular" election process: discernment by the nominees themselves. This process calls upon the Spirit to be present, is open to the broadest possible input from the community, provides an opportunity for prayer and reflection at each step of the process, and includes strong formation and orientation for council candidates.

Although each parish entering prayerful discernment to

choose leadership must develop its own unique process, the following are necessary steps:

1) *Formation of the Total Parish.* The whole parish is encouraged to pray intensively and prepare for the calling forth of leadership. On a special Sunday (the feast of the Baptism of the Lord is ideal), the entire parish is invited to submit names of persons they feel would be good council leaders for the Christian community (spiritual as well as pastoral leadership qualities are emphasized). Parish organizations and committees can also be encouraged to pray, reflect, and submit nominations. Usually, when the parish is well prepared, a good number of nominees is identified. In the discernment process, what happens to the parish community, not just to the leadership, is of utmost importance. This step is *crucial* to the process since there is no general election later and this is the parish's opportunity to call forth its leadership.

2) *Orientation of Nominees.* All nominees are contacted by the election committee to determine their willingness to serve. They are invited to participate in a mandatory orientation session that carefully outlines a councilor's role, responsibilities, and relationships. Some nominees will decline the nomination after both step #1 and this step, which is to be expected. All are asked to carry through their participation as "electors," if not candidates. A knowledgeable, prayerful staff member could be available to help nominees decide prayerfully whether they have a call to serve. The parish continues to pray for those who have accepted nomination and for the success of the process.

3) *The Actual Discernment Process.* Unlike the "popular" election, the new councilors are chosen by the group of nominees and "electors"; current members of the council may also be included. A skilled facilitator is very important to the discernment process. When the nominees and electors gather and are welcomed and introduced, they are seated in a circle and the process proceeds as follows:

Prayer: affirmation for our heritage; affirmation of present efforts of the community; preparation for reflection and faith sharing; call for an openness to the Spirit.

Scripture Reading and Reflection

Sharing of the needs of the community and the responsibilities of leadership. (The facilitator could read the mission statement of the parish.)

Declaration of Candidacy: Each candidate is invited to present a brief oral statement of her or his concern and what each feels she or he can contribute to the council leadership.

Dialogue (preferably in small groups) and *Faith Sharing.* (People may wish to move around freely as they dialogue.) (Omitting this sharing imperils the entire process.)

Prayer to the Spirit for the Gifts needed to lead.

Balloting: a written ballot is taken and __ persons are chosen and announced. Group sings an Amen! Alleluia!

Break

Second Balloting: After prayerful reflection for a few moments, a second written ballot is taken and the ____ persons chosen on this ballot become the parish councilors. Their names are announced, there is a round of applause, and a joyful song is sung.

(Note: The *number of candidates decides the number of ballots*—small parish may need only one or two ballots; a larger one, several; usually, just two persons are discerned on one ballot.)

Affirmation and Closure: The process ends with celebration. All the candidates are thanked for offering their service to the church, and those who were not discerned are encouraged to become active on committees. The evening concludes with a prayer of thanksgiving and song.

The keys to the discernment process are prayerful dependence on the Holy Spirit, informal sharing, and a spirit of collaboration (as opposed to a more competitive election procedure), as well as a recognition of each person's unique gifts.

Several benefits are apparent. The participants find the process affirming, unifying, and supportive. There are no winners or losers; those chosen to lead are supported by all. The total parish is called to prayer and to a deeper faith life. The process also surfaces new and more prayerful pastoral leadership—people are discerned through this process who may not have been able to win a "popular" election.

Much of the foregoing part of this chapter outlines the selection of at-large members of the council. A word should also be said about ex-officio members. The pastor, of course, is the most important ex-officio member. Parish trustees may also be regarded as ex-officio members. The associate (pastor(s), a permanent deacon or religious attached to the parish, other staff members such as a liturgist or school principal may be given seats on the council as well. In some parishes that have two or more associate pastors, only one may serve on the council; in others, all associate pastors are considered members.

Once councilors have been selected (elected or discerned), it will probably be time to go to the first meeting. Naturally they will hope the meetings will be a successful and satisfying experience. But successful meetings don't just happen. They have to be planned. The next chapter, therefore, will offer some pointers on how to plan efficient and satisfying meetings.

Sharing
1. How do you feel about the distinction between "election" and "selection"?
2. How would you feel about nominating yourself?
3. How do you feel about screening and discerning prospective candidates?
4. What are the pros and cons of election? Of discernment?
5. What are some of the advantages of an installation ceremony?
6. How would you plan to get the whole parish involved in the selection/discernment process?
7. How does your current selection system compare with the one suggested in this chapter?

CHAPTER 10

EFFICIENT AND SATISFYING MEETINGS

In North America, people like speed and efficiency. That's why fast food places are so popular. That's also why we pay attention to efficiency engineers and management experts. We like to "get things done." Efficiency is usually defined in terms of production. It means "the capacity to produce desired results with a minimum expenditure of energy, time, money, or materials." As most people know, parish pastoral councils are rarely models of efficiency. They don't often get things done with a minimum expenditure of time and energy.

Parish councils can hardly be blamed if efficiency is not their top priority. After all, Jesus wasn't all that big on efficiency. He chose poor fishermen as his first disciples. He invited conflict by choosing a tax collector (Matthew) who was working for Rome and a zealot (Simon) who was working against Rome. Besides that, he left them all to fend for themselves without bylaws, group dynamics, or mission statements.

Like the first disciples, councils have a different priority. They have to take time to pray, to discern the Spirit, to figure out what is God's will here and now. They have to take time to be human and more time to be Christian. And that may not get them a high rating on the efficiency scale. On the other hand, we are called to be good stewards of God's gifts (1 Cor. 4:1-12). We all have a vocation to get on with the work of the Lord.

Time itself is a gift from God. We are accountable to God for its use in service to our sisters and brothers. This chapter will offer some pointers on how to plan and run effective council meetings.

When council meetings are over, the members sometimes reconvene at the nearest bar. There they express their real feelings about the meeting just concluded: "What a drag!" "I thought Carol would never shut up." "I had the feeling Father wasn't telling the whole truth about our parish finances." "What a waste of time." "The pits!" Councilors often feel something went wrong but they don't know what will make it go right. They want to get something out of a meeting, but don't know what they have to put into one.

Meetings can indeed be boring. "A long-winded exchange of mutual ignorance!" "The penance we do for our sins!" On the other hand, they can be exciting, stimulating, productive. Everything—well, almost everything—depends on planning and preparation. While there is no sure-fire formula for success, meetings will be much more satisfying if both planners and participants pay special attention to the following: (1) motivation, (2) preparation, (3) process and dynamics, and (4) leadership skills. Let's take them in order.

Motivation

1) Every council meeting should be an experience of faith. The council meeting is a communion of those who are sharing and growing in their faith in the Lord. They have gathered as disciples in their own "upper room" to make decisions in dialogue with, and in prayerful obedience to, their Lord. They have come to hear the call of the Lord—a call that will become concrete through prayer, dialogue, and discussion.

2) Every meeting should be an experience in spiritual growth and development. Contrary to the slogans of religious Pelagianism and secular pragmatism, the Lord wants his disciples' love more than he wants their work. The meeting will advance the kingdom of God only insofar as the Lord's disciples become more effective servants. It is the Lord's holiness, working through the baptized members of his body, that will renew the

parish. It's not so much neatly designed programs as effective Christian witness that will change the face of the earth. Every agenda needs to foster and nurture this growth in holiness; otherwise, the council meeting will be just another board meeting. (See Chapter 12, Open to Me the Gates of Holiness.)

3) Council meetings should be a community building experience. They should be warm, pleasant, friendly. Members should know one another on a first name basis. An occasional party with wine and cheese or beer and pizza will help bring about a meeting of persons. Prayer for sick members, their wives, husbands, and children, get-well cards, visits to the hospital, celebrating the birth of a new baby or a job advancement—all of these will go a long way in building a loving, human, Christian community. Motivation can never be taken for granted. It needs to be nurtured and recharged constantly. True commitment is always a process of recommitment. For this reason, every council meeting has to pray special attention to the faith, the spiritual life, and the community spirit of its members.

Preparation

With due deference to the miraculous intervention of the Holy Spirit, meetings will succeed if they are well planned; they will fail if they are poorly planned. In general, planning a good meeting requires (1) a careful preparation of an agenda and choice of a facilitator, (2) preparation of the physical arrangements and, of course, (3) preparation by the committees and the individual councilors. Let's consider briefly these four kinds of preparations.

1) *The Agenda*. The first step in getting ready for a meeting is the preparation of the agenda. Usually an agenda or executive committee, composed of the pastor and two or three officers of the council, prepares the agenda. Sometimes councils use the last few minutes of each meeting to prepare the agenda for the next meeting. It should never be prepared by one person alone, whether that be the pastor or the chairperson; otherwise councilors will easily suspect the meeting is being manipulated through the agenda. To control the agenda is to control the meeting. It's true

that committees can also control the agenda and therefore manipulate the meeting, but it's less likely. To make sure that the agenda preparation remains an open process, the chairperson could announce, now and then, that all members, indeed all parishioners, are welcome to suggest items for the agenda.

In preparing the agenda, the committee goes through a sifting process. It has to make sure, *first*, that only policy matters are placed on the agenda. There is a rather important distinction between policy and administration. A policy is a broad course of action that allows for a certain amount of personal interpretation. Thus a parish council could accept a policy to hire minority-owned businesses, whenever possible.

This policy sets a context within which each individual decision can be made regarding the specific instance at hand. Policies cannot, and should not be written to cover every conceivable situation. Policies should be written to cover only those situations calling for major decisions. Minor decisions must be left to the discretion of the individual person responsible for that particular program.[1]

Administration, on the other hand, is concerned with technique and procedure. Often it requires the skill, training, and competence of full-time staff, such as the pastor, the director of religious education, the minister of music, and maintenance personnel. It's up to them, not the council, to determine when a Mary Jones is ready for confirmation, when the parish hall needs to be painted, etc. Although it's not always easy to distinguish between policy and administration, the council needs to be aware of its proper role in the overall parish structure. It has neither the time nor, in most cases, the competence to oversee the details of administration. When it gets into administration, it is overstepping the boundaries of its authority. (The best way to lose a good janitor is to let the chairperson of the administration committee hover over his shoulder.)

The Code of Canon Law, for instance, establishes the principle that the pastor is responsible for hiring and firing the parish personnel. It is his responsibility, therefore, and not the council's, to oversee and supervise their work. That's part of his job as full-time administrator of the parish.

Second, getting back to preparation for the meeting, the agenda committee, in consultation with the full council, has to decide what should be discussed by the council and what by the individual committees. Thus, if the church roof leaks, it may be an agenda item for the administration committee, but not for the full council. If the school tuition needs to be raised, it may be an agenda item for the Christian formation committee, but not for the full council. If a prepared agenda contains picayune details, like a new carpet for the rectory, everybody will feel compelled to deliver themselves of an opinion regarding the kind and color of carpet to be purchased. Precious time, which could be devoted to serious policy matters or to planning, will be wasted. Council meetings aren't committee meetings. They should not discuss matters best handled either by one of the standing committees or by the full-time staff.

Third, the agenda should include fact sheets or an "agenda notebook" on the more complicated issues. This notebook contains background information on the items on the agenda. Fact sheets should be prepared by the appropriate council committee or by the agenda committee. Thus a proposal for hiring a director of religious education, could include a brief history of the religious education program, the number of students enrolled, the number of teachers, type of training programs, the diocesan guidelines for the religious education programs, etc. Such fact sheets encourage members to prepare for the meetings and save important time during the meetings. Discussion will then begin with common knowledge of the pertinent facts.

Fourth, the agenda, along with the minutes of the last meeting should be in the hands of the council at least 10 days before the meeting, an important responsibility of the council secretary. Significant agenda items should also be published in the parish bulletin two weeks before the meeting, the better to engage the interest, reactions, and expertise of the whole parish. Such parish and council interaction will also increase parishioner interest in the next council elections.

The meeting agenda might follow this general format for a

2-1\2 hour session:

1) *Formation Session* (30 minutes)

Prayer, scriptural reflection, faith sharing, and study. (Council members take turns leading this part of the meeting; the study portion could be dialogue on a passage from one of the bishops' pastorals, a current article on some aspect of parish life, etc.)

2) *Purpose of Meeting* (10 minutes)

Brief statement on the purpose and objectives of the meeting by the chairperson; (agreement on agenda and approval of minutes of last meeting are included here; the names of those present should be listed in the minutes by the secretary.)

3) *Ongoing Parish Life* (60 minutes)

a) Decision-making issues for discernment of the council—adapting a new policy, approving a budget, committee proposal, etc. (A discernment/consensus process may be used.)

b) Issues for dialogue (not decision making), sharing, reaction, proposing, etc.

c) Reports from staff committees on current issues in ministry. (These should be brief; committee reports are succinct, in written form, and sent ahead with the agenda. It's wise not to have verbal committee reports and to allow only clarification questions by councilors, if needed.)

4) *Voice of the Parish* (10 minutes)

Comments from visitors (be sure this part of the meeting is well regulated.)

5) *Planning and Visioning* (40 minutes)

Long-range planning, visioning, and "dreaming" together. This part of the meeting could include reviewing and adjusting annual and long-range goals; in-depth consideration of the ministries of one of the committees, or consideration of the broader issues in the community, such as hunger or homelessness.

The time limits listed are approximate and may be adjusted according to needs. If a major issue is to be considered by the council, more time must be allowed. Reflective prayer may be interspersed throughout the meeting as needed in order for councilors to remain centered in the Lord, an important consideration when a discernment/consensus process is used.

The "purpose of the meeting" portion helps councilors to focus on the purpose of the meeting and to "buy into" the agenda items. Councilors can be invited to prioritize the items on the agenda, and to agree on what time the meeting is going to end. The "planning and visioning" part of the meeting is the one most often skipped because councils are unaccustomed to a planning process and often are not future-oriented. When committees prepare proposals for the council, alternative recommendations should always be included for the council's consideration.

The following checklist might be helpful to the agenda committee. Did we:

a) Determine the purpose and objectives of the meeting?

b) Decide when the meeting will begin and end?

c) Plan who will facilitate the meeting and arrange for other necessary personnel? Decide who is responsible for the formation session?

d) Prepare an environment conducive to sharing prayer and dialogue?

e) Make sure the council has all necessary materials and information to make their work effective?

f) Evaluate and plan for follow-up action?

1) *Physical Arrangements.* When the agenda or executive committee has completed the preparation of the agenda, it may be time to check out the physical arrangements for the meeting. The physical setting ought to be such that it fosters and sustains a feeling of community. The room (and the chairs) need to be comfortable for adults, creating a climate for a conference meeting. If at all possible, classrooms and church halls are to be avoided. Libraries and rectories are better choices.

To promote better eye contact, councilors are seated in an oblong, circular, or horseshoe style (never rectangular). Only voting members are in the circle. Beverages may be available before and during the meetings. Naturally, the meeting room is to be well ventilated for the health and comfort of all. The meeting room would also contain all the materials necessary for the meeting: paper, pencils, lectern, blackboard, chalk, newsprint, overhead projector, etc. It's a good idea to make a checklist and go over it for every meeting. Other groups may have used the room and removed some of the equipment.

3) *Committee and Parishioner Input.* If the meeting is going to be a success, all council committees will have to do their homework. They are the working arms of the council; they gather the facts and do the necessary research. Then they discuss the issues in the light of the council's stated priorities. If the committees don't do their work adequately or if they fail to meet, the council meetings may be a waste of time. Of course, the individual councilors have to do their homework too. They prepare for the meeting by studying, consulting, and reflecting. At the minimum, they read the fact sheets that come with the agenda. At the maximum, they read pertinent articles in books and journals and study the resource materials available from the diocesan offices.

Members also need to consult with other parishioners, especially with those who have some experience in the matters to be discussed. They could even go a step further and make some phone calls to get the feelings and opinions of the parishioners who have seen the agenda in the parish bulletin. Finally, the councilors spend time in reflection. They put together what they have read and what they have heard, and then reflect prayerfully on what demands the gospel is making of them and of the parish in regard to the topics on the agenda.

The Process and Dynamics

Some attention must also be paid to the process and dynamics of the meeting; how the councilors relate to one another and how they actually go about getting through the business of the meeting. In spite of the best advance preparations, a meeting can still fall on its face. The style, method, or atmosphere of the meeting can generate negative, hostile, or passive-aggressive feelings. In other words, the meeting can go sour because the process and dynamics aren't right.

While the human and divine chemistry of any council meeting is to some extent unpredictable, there are, nevertheless, certain processes that can be helpful in creating a healthy, wholesome, satisfying climate for conducting the meeting. Let's talk about five of those processes: (1) consensus decision making, (2) discernment, (3) problem solving, (4) conflict resolution, and (5) evaluation.

Consensus Decision Making

Most councils are familiar with the parliamentary form of decision-making. In this system a simple majority rules. If a motion gets 51% of the votes, it passes. A few motions, such as unseating a member, require a two-thirds majority. The parliamentary system of voting is derived from the English Parliament. General Henry Robert incorporated that system into his famous *Robert's Rules of Order*, in use since 1915. This system is useful in keeping some kind of order in meetings of large assemblies. However, when used in council decision making, it can divide the council into winners and losers. Even if it doesn't polarize the council it often means the losers are not disposed to support the "other side's" decision. At best, they feel it isn't really their decision. At worst, they feel angry and frustrated. In either case, they won't jump with ecstatic enthusiasm when it's time to commit their time and energy. Many councils feel that the win-lose syndrome, which is often a by-product of the parliamentary system, is inappropriate for a Christian community and that there is nothing distinctively Christian about *Robert's Rules*.

Traditional rules of order are based upon debate as the single process by which decisions may be made. Debate begins with a proposal, a main motion, that someone offers the group. With a second to support it, if the assembly is large, the proposal can then be debated.

Because debate requires participants to identify with the pro or the con of an issue, people's egos become attached to the victory or defeat of the proposal. When the vote is taken, one side wins and the other side loses. In such debates, wisdom is lost, the purposes of the organization are lost, the cohesiveness and camaraderie of the participants are lost, the interests of the membership are ill-served, and the organization loses the participation of those members who cannot see much joy in battle.[2]

In recent years, more and more councils have adopted the consensus form of decision making. It is a process in which a workable decision is reached through dialogue, compromise, and modification of the contribution of all council members. Many councils feel this community way of making decisions has a number of advantages; it puts more emphasis on maintaining the unity of the Christian community in the council; it gives a higher priority to persons and the growth of the council as a community of persons: it is less rigid, formal, and competitive; it is another way of saying, contrary to tendencies in our modern society, that people are more important than efficiency and productivity. It provides a better forum for exercising the gift of discernment and for the emergence of the prophetic voice. In 1 Cor. 12:10, it is clear that the gifts of discernment and prophecy are given to every baptized Christian. Decision-making systems need to be in the service of the Spirit's gifts.

Consensus decision making can be described in two phases: the first deals with consensus on broad goals and objectives; the second deals with the group process regarding specific issues discussed during a particular meeting. Councils generally work toward a consensus on the broad goals and objectives during a weekend planning session. (See Chapter 11.)

The second phase of consensus decision making concerns how specific issues are discussed during a council meeting. In the consensus system there is a communal dialogue, but no vote. Consensus is achieved when everyone can live with the decision. In actual fact, no one has achieved exactly what he or she wanted. But everyone has offered input that has been taken seriously.

In most cases the proposal under discussion has changed because of this input. Thus more people can identify with and support the final decision.

The facilitator seeks consensus by listening to the dialogue and by watching for signs of agreement. Each person is allowed to state his or her position once during the initial dialogue period and is asked to refrain from any remarks that depart from the issue. The facilitator may have to ask specific questions like: "Joe, do you feel you can go along with this decision?" The facilitator may also encourage members to present alternatives that could result in consensus (the group is continually working through possible alternatives to reach its decisions). Again, the facilitator "tests" for consensus. If consensus seems to be reached, it is very important that the facilitator confirm this by stating: "We have a consensus decision that. . . ." When the facilitator moves toward stating consensus, no further dialogue is allowed.

If, in spite of dialoguing for some time, the council cannot reach consensus, the facilitator is careful to try to define the exact area of disagreement, asking for all the reasons on the negative and all the reasons on the affirmative side. Finally, he or she asks: "Do we have all the facts?" At this point the council may be willing to table the issue to allow more time to gather additional data or to study the issues at greater length. This is especially true when a straw vote indicates the council is really divided on the issue. Generally, additional facts and more time will move the council toward a compromise solution.[3] In such cases, it may be helpful to refer the matter back to an appropriate committee.

Generally, consensus should be used for major decisions affecting parish life; at times, a simple majority vote may serve as well. The consensus system will not be effective when councils are not genuine faith communities, are polarized around strong personalities, or are being manipulated by pressure groups. In such cases, the council would do well to honestly admit these obstacles and then set aside some meeting time to build up the council as a faith community and to reflect on its internal dynamics. If the council is not at least trying to become a faith community, long discussions about decision-making techniques will be a waste of time.

The words "decision making" carry with them a real danger of a misplaced emphasis. In actual practice councils spend most of their meeting time, not in decision *making*, but in decision *reaching.* They learn, discuss and share information. They may need four or five meetings of this kind of sharing before they reach the point of decision making. The whole *process* of decision reaching is, of course, more important than the *moment* of decision making.

The Discernment Process

Since Vatican II, we've added many new words to our Catholic vocabulary. Discernment is one of them. It is closely related to the consensus decision making just described. Its use is indeed becoming more common in the meetings of parish councils across the country.

Right off, let's explain what discernment is not. First, it is not a Catholic form of democracy. It's not merely a question of getting a majority vote on a difficult issue. It's not a new process for diagnosing the dominant feelings about a question being discussed. It's not a system designed to manipulate the consent of the council. Like so many of the "new" words, discernment comes right out of the New Testament. In 1 Cor. 12, Paul is talking about the spiritual gifts given by the Spirit to each believing Christian. First, he mentions the gifts of healing, of working miracles, and of prophecy; then, in verse 10, he mentions the gift of discerning of spirits.

The word "discernment" *(diacrisis)* in its literal Greek can also mean *appraisal, assessment, judgment, separation,* or finally, *distinguishing,* especially between good and evil. The word, in its Old Testament sense of judgment, is used in the context of the process that reveals the will of Yahweh. In Paul's writings the use of the word is not separated from his firm belief in the omniscient God who is the judge and who sees humanity through and through. Nor, of course, is it separated from faith in the Spirit. Discernment needs to be understood in the context of the other spiritual gifts. These are all distinguished by their conformity to the Christian faith. Even though they are diverse in their operation and manifestation, all the gifts come from one divine source. They are all directed to the aim of building up the well being of the church, the peo-

ple of God. In fact, the value of the individual gifts is measured by their usefulness in building up the church. Such gifts are
not always to be considered extraordinary, for Paul includes in
his lists teaching, serving, helping, exhorting, administering,
and giving aid.

In Paul, the gift of discernment is one enabling certain members of the community to sift, as it were, the wheat from the
chaff in any assessment of the mind of the church on matters
pertaining to its spiritual welfare. Against the background of
the unbridled religious enthusiasm of Corinth, Paul is saying
that God wants his creatures to use the faculties he has given
them. The use of common sense and intelligence should be
ranked among such faculties. Paul is saying, further, that the
gift of discernment may not be as striking as the gifts of oratory,
prophecy, or speaking in tongues. But it is important, nevertheless. In the midst of all kinds of ecstatic outbursts, it is no small
gift to the church when members can disentangle their thoughts
from their emotions and prejudices and *think straight*.

In its biblical meaning, therefore, the act of discernment is a
participation in the process that reveals God's will on earth.
It's a process in which God is the active agent, and Christians,
who are humbly and prayerfully disposed, become the blessed
receivers of some of the wisdom and knowledge of God.

In her book, *Sharing Wisdom*, Mary Benet McKinney presents
a "wisdom model" for church group decision making:

Before the process is even begun, the group must agree to
accept a majority decision if necessary, and to accept it as
the will of the Spirit. This is not the same as agreeing to
go with the majority and to support the decision. The
shared wisdom model asks group members, in advance of
the decision, to agree to see and to embrace the decision of
the majority as the discerned decision, the will of the
Spirit, the voice of the Lord being heard by this group at
this time over this issue. Only this position will bring the
peace and contentment that is the indicator of the gift of
the Spirit.[4]

The wisdom model presupposes a mature spiritual life on the

part of each member of the council. The council (and the parish) is called to deep prayer, scripture reflection, and active and attentive listening to the truth of the Lord so that authentic discernment can happen. Human feelings, attitudes, and concerns must be sorted out. Trust in God and one another must replace insecurity; receptiveness to divine insight must overshadow personal opinion. Discernment "is not a unanimity of opinions and ideas but a shared felt sense that this is God's word to this community at this point in its history."[5]

There are several important prerequisites for communal discernment:

1) Communion—a sharing in "a common vocation from the Holy Spirit"; a common faith in Jesus, a conviction that the Lord has called the parish together to be church

2) "Common agreement on the basic expression of this communion in words here and now," the "core vision" that makes the parish a community

3) "Common commitment to carrying out the decisions reached through communal discernment"; this common commitment is entered into before discernment.[6]

The following steps are basic to the discernment process:[7]

• Preparation; prayer and reflection for discernment of the Spirit and for wisdom

• Clear formulation of the question to be discerned

• Data gathering

• Alternating periods of prayer and sharing of insights on the pros and cons of the issue: each member's comment or clarification should help move the group toward a decision

• Withdrawal to seek a sense of the Lord's will (personal discernment)

• Sharing of personal discernments

• Confirmation

• a sense of peace and satisfaction.

These steps may be adjusted somewhat to accommodate diverse circumstances of decision making. It is crucial that enough time be allowed for the process. There is a periodic testing for consensus throughout the process.

An important criterion for recognizing the results of a true discernment process is a feeling of peace. "But the Spirit produces love, joy, peace, patience, kindness, goodness, faithfulness, humility, and self control" (Gal. 5:22-23).

When a consensus seems to have emerged from the process, and members feel an inner calm and peace, that peace is identified as the gift of the Holy Spirit assuring that the decision is indeed God's will. The facilitator of the process seeks to determine whether members are truly at peace with the results. If so, then the conclusion should be duly recorded in the council records as resulting from a discernment process of the council.

If a consensus does not occur and does not seem possible, then the decision will have to be arrived at in another way or postponed until later.

Another criterion might well be: Will the results be for the upbuilding of the church? Will the council's resolution be for the common good? "Let all things be done for upbuilding ..." (1 Cor. 14:26). And, finally, is the resolution truly the fruit of faith, prayer, and listening to the Word of the Lord?

It's not facetious to say that at times it may be necessary to have a process of discernment to find out if genuine discernment of the Spirit has occurred. After all, the conclusions of communal discernment may very well be repugnant to human nature and desire. They may challenge us to respond, even though we are unwilling, to the tough demands of the Gospel. The peace of discernment is a truly spiritual peace that comes from a knowledge that the council is answering the call to self sacrifice and is sharing in the difficult, prophetic mission of Christ.

Problem Solving

Councils often have to wrestle with some tough problems. Sometimes it's an internal problem growing out of the human chemistry of the council. Other times it's a parish concern, such as closing the school. At still other times, the problem may be that no one can figure out what the problem is. In any case, councils need to develop some skill in dealing with problems. Again, it's impossible to come up with a sure-fire system to solve all council problems. On the other hand, many experts in group dynamics have developed some common sense principles to help small groups deal with problems. Many of these principles can be used by parish councils.

The following pointers for problem solving have been adapted from *T.E.T. (Teacher Effectiveness Training)*. They can be used by the chairperson or a special outside facilitator who has a special ministry for group dynamics and problem-solving. They are arranged in five steps:

Step One: setting the stage

1) Make sure the time is acceptable to the council.

2) Have a pencil and paper or chalk and chalkboard.

3) Explain that the solution must be acceptable to both (or all) parties in the council.

4) Use active listening in all phases, e.g., when coming up with the proper time to discuss the problem.

5) Do not require the members to justify their ideas.

6) Begin with an "I" message. Councilors must *own* their feelings. ("I feel angry.")

7) Don't let anyone introduce a *new* problem during the problem-solving process.

Step Two: defining the problem (getting to the real needs)

1) State your need in a good "I" message.

2) Use active listening whenever feeling is expressed.

3) Don't buy "promises" that things will get better. "I'll try not to do that anymore."

4) Stand your ground that problem-solving has to be done.

5) Don't start off with *your* solution to the problem.

6) Don't start generating solutions until everyone agrees with the statement of the problem and some kind of understanding of everyone's needs. Check them out — "As I understand the problem, it is ...."

Step Three: generating solutions

1) Try to get the councilors to offer their possible solutions first.

2) Do not judge or evaluate any solutions—even the "far out" ones.

3) Write down all the solutions offered.

4) Feel free to contribute your solutions. If they are judged immediately, say: "We'll settle that later. Right now we only want all possible solutions."

5) Offer feedback, i.e., lead the discussion.

6) Restate the problem when things bog down.

7) Don't settle for only a few solutions. Try to get as many as possible. Don't push for *your* solution.

Step Four: evaluating solutions and making decisions

1) Get in there and think with the others on the solutions.

2) Use a lot of active listening, i.e., give the speaker frequent and continuous feedback so she will know you have received the message accurately.

3) Find points of agreement on the easier issues and then move on the more difficult ones.

4) Be honest in expressing your own feelings.

5) Push for a decision. Test solutions out on them: "What do you think of...?"

6) Write down the decision and read it back to them and get an O.K. from the group.

7) Don't try for a "perfect" solution. Settle for the acceptable one—the one that seems to meet everyone's needs.

8) Let them know that either party to the disagreement can modify the solution and re-problem-solve the situation at any time.

9) Be willing to settle for "Let's try it for a while" basis.

10) Do not vote.

11) If necessary, take a straw vote only.

Step Five: implementing the solution

1) Make sure the decision includes: *who* is to do *what* by *when*. Don't allow any vagueness.

2) *Never* take the role of reminder or enforcer—leave that responsibility to the council.

3) Do not build in punishment. Say only: "We'll have to work on this again if this solution doesn't work. "

4) Make sure that everyone understands and is satisfied.[8]

Conflict Resolution

After the meeting, council members often express the feelings they are afraid to express during the meeting. Such debriefing may take place at the corner bar or at the home of a member where they feel they are with friends *they can trust.* Such sessions often surface the conflicts and mistrust repressed during the actual meetings. Conflicts should, of course, be expected among free-thinking Christians. In the New Testament we see that the first Christian community experienced conflict. There is that famous case in Gal. 2:11 when Paul "opposed Cephas to his face" on the matter of circumcision. And Luke reports other conflicts in the early church: "This led to a disagreement and after Paul and Barnabas had had a long argument with these men it was arranged that Paul and Barnabas and others of the church should go up to Jerusalem and discuss the problem with the apostles and elders" (Acts 15:2). "Barnabas suggested taking John Mark, but Paul was not in favor of taking along the very man who had deserted them in Pamphylia and had refused to share in their work. After a violent quarrel they parted company and Barnabas sailed off with Mark to Cyprus" (Acts 15:38-39).

In A.D. 155, St. Polycarp, the bishop of Smyrna, had a disagreement with Pope Anicetus about the right date for celebrating Easter. Eusebius, an early church historian, describes the conflict:

And when the blessed Polycarp was at Rome in the time of Anicetus, and they disagreed a little about certain other things, they immediately made peace with one another, not caring to quarrel over this matter. For neither could Anicetus persuade Polycarp ... nor Polycarp Anicetus.... But though matters were in this shape, they communed together, and Anicetus conceded the administration of the Eucharist in the Church to Polycarp, manifestly as a mark of respect. And they parted from each other in peace.[9]

It's not un-Christian, therefore, to experience conflict. Denial of conflict or refusal to deal with it, however, can indeed become un-Christian. Besides generating mistrust, bitterness, and anger, such behavior shows a lack of faith in the Lord's reconciling power, which is always at work where two or three are gathered in his name (Matt. 18:20). There can be at least five different responses to conflict:

1) We can just refuse to see it. "It's the neighbor's house that's dirty, not ours."

2) Even if we see it, we can refuse to see it as a *problem*. "After all, it's our dirt — and that makes it o.k."

3) We can see it, but refuse to take any personal responsibility. "It's *our* dirt, but not *mine*. After all, if those stupid people came around to my point of view, there wouldn't be any conflict."

4) We can see it, but decide (by doing nothing) not to deal with it, either because we don't have the nerve or because we're afraid. After all, we might get dirty in the process. We aren't ready. Our faith community is too fragile. We'll come apart at the seams. When conflict does raise its head, we take refuge in humor. (Crack a joke.) Or change the subject. We feel more comfortable in clinging to the false assumption that all is just fine. "Let's give each other the handshake of peace and sing a song."

5) We can see it and honestly and courageously deal with it. We can overcome our fear and then trust in the Spirit and in one another. We can learn to disagree without becoming disagreeable. Together, we can take one giant step toward a more mature and more Christian council.

It's impossible, of course, to lay down a lot of rules for dealing with conflict in the council. There are too many unknown and intangible factors. For instance, what is the trust level in the council? How comfortable are the members with one another? Do they often pray together? Do they share their spiritual life with one another at deep levels? Every council is a unique and mysterious chemistry of the human and the divine. The dynamics of the council, especially that of conflict, cannot be guided in advance by neat rules from a printed page. Nevertheless, some *general* guidelines may still be helpful. It's up to individual councils to use, adapt, or reject them as they see fit.

John Burns recommends the following principles for dealing with conflict:

1) The parties involved must realize and indicate to themselves and to each other that a conflict is taking place between them.

2) Each party must be brought to objectively see the nature, character, and implications of his or her position.

3) Each party must be brought to objectively see the nature, character, and implications of the other party's position.

4) There must be a common language or set of meanings employed.

5) Resolution must be defined by both parties as advantageous or at least acceptable.

6) The parties must interact in a mutually communicative way in which each can pick out clues that the other offers for resolving the conflict.

7) The duration and intensity of the conflict must be considered by the negotiator of a conflict if one is present.

The following points also should be considered when attempting the resolution of intergroup conflicts:

8) Awareness of what each group considers to be defeat and victory. On the personal level as well, there should be a consideration of what each party will accept in the resolution and still believe a sense of self-respect has been maintained.

9) There should be an understanding of the role and character of leadership within each group.

10) As much of a cultural understanding as possible should be encouraged between the parties. Differences in ways of viewing things or doing things by two different cultures can reinforce basic conflict situations.[10]

Naturally, no one should assume that all conflicts can be resolved. As mentioned earlier, tensions and conflict are part of the normal life in a Christian community. Conflicts can, however, be used to clarify diverse points of view. They can also deliver persons from a dogmatic absolutism in their positions.

In the last analysis, councils need to learn to live with some conflict out of respect for the freedom and dignity of their fellow Christians.

Evaluation

As a way of monitoring their own process and dynamics, councils ought to evaluate their meetings at least twice a year. This can be done by inviting an outside observer from a neighboring council to critique a typical meeting. Norman Lambert explains the role of this outside observer:

> The observer should sit outside the group, not taking part in the discussion but rather noting those things that seemed to affect the way that the group worked together at reaching (or not reaching) consensus. When the group reflects on this exercise, members can ask the observer for a complete report or simply for his or her input regarding a specific issue that they might raise.
>
> The observer's role is to help the group understand its own processes of decision making. She should be careful, therefore, to report only what he/she actually heard and saw, and not to interpret the behavior of any group member. Nor should she "punish" members who may have dominated the group or excluded certain other individuals from the discussion. Her role is to facilitate the group's learning about itself; the members must decide what to do with the information she provides.[11]

Another way of evaluation a meeting is simply to distribute a survey sheet to all the councilors after a typical meeting. Members should answer the following three questions: (1) What did you like best about this meeting? (2) What did you like least? (3) What suggestions do you have for improving future meetings?

The unsigned surveys can be collected and then redistributed for reaction and discussion by the council. This system of self-evaluation encourages all members, not just the chairperson, to assume responsibility for both the process and the progress of the council meetings. As a final point, it may seem to be a small matter in the overall process and dynamics, but meetings will go faster and smoother if visitors do not sit in the same circle or at the same table with the voting members. A council meeting, after all, is not a town hall meeting. Nor is it a grand free-for-all. It's a meeting of duly elected or discerned members who have come together to conduct the official business of the parish. The form of the meeting should respect the vote of the parishioners. They did not, in fact, vote for the visitors. If the council gives equal voice to visitors and to voting members, it is ignoring the will of the parishioners as expressed through the election. As time goes on, many parishioners will not bother to vote in an election that to them seems to have lost its meaning.

Leadership Skills

All council members are, of course, called to be leaders. Each councilor, however, will lead through his/her own unique gifts and skills. Each will develop a personal leadership style. While the different styles may not necessarily be right or wrong, some styles will be more effective than others. All styles can, to some extent, be improved and adapted to changing situations. But to do this, one must be aware of one's own leadership style. It may be helpful, therefore, to reflect on the leadership role of the chairperson of the council and then finally, on the possible leadership styles of the council members.

The Role of the Chairperson The chairperson has a key role in creating a pleasant and positive atmosphere for council meetings. He or she fosters a climate of trust and openness, and shows genuine respect for the members' ideas and abilities. The chairperson is the yeast that enables the councilors to grow to their full potential as ministers in the church. To do this job well she or he should at least be striving for the following qualities:

Spirituality: the chairperson's relationship with Christ and appreciation of gospel values is the keystone to effectiveness in directing the activities of the parish council.

Fairness: A healthy detachment from vested interest instills trust and confidence.

Ability to unify: the chairperson should work to bring all parish groups and factions together in harmony.

Knowledge: An understanding of the nature of church and an openness to learning are essential.

Leadership: The ability to motivate people to do their parish council tasks is vital.[12]

Much of the chairperson's work is done outside of the actual meeting. As part of this extra-meeting activity, he or she should:

1) Maintain regular contact with the pastor to ensure open communication.

2) Be in frequent communication with the pastoral team, committee chairpersons and other appropriate council members, encouraging them in their activities and obtaining feedback and status reports on programs and projects; motivating committees between meetings is an important aspect of the chairperson's function.

3) See that council members make use of available resources and training programs.

4) Insure that the executive committee meets and fulfills its functions.

5) Communicate with the other officers and encourage them in the fulfillment of their tasks.

6) Be personally available to parishioners to receive their input and feedback.[13]

As soon as the meeting begins the chairperson becomes the main facilitator of the council's process. He or she has to resist the temptation to give speeches or to teach the council. The chairperson has to present proposals for discussion in an objective manner, and doesn't give his or her own opinion until all the other members, especially the timid, have been heard. L. H. Mouat gives the following advice to chairpersons: (1) follow agenda; (2) bring out pertinent matter; (3) encourage participation; (4) discourage disruption; (5) try to resolve differences; (6) bring out agreements; (7) don't waste time; (8) summarize from time to time.[14]

As the meeting progresses, the chairperson may be performing five distinct functions:

1) *Initiating:* Keeping the group action moving or getting it going. This may be done by reviewing progress to date, posing a problem, pointing out a goal, clarifying an issue, or proposing a procedure. The chairperson should avoid prematurely shutting off discussion.

2) *Moderating:* Influencing the tempo and flow of the group's work. This can be done by summarizing discussion, pointing out time limits, and restating goals. The chairperson walks a tightrope between controlling the group and allowing the meeting to be come too loose and unorganized. In general, when a person is argumentative, off the subject, rambling, or too dominant, the discussion should be returned to the whole council.

3) *Informing:* Bringing information or authoritative opinion to the group. This should be done to be helpful, but not to prejudice the questions.

4) *Encouraging:* Creating a climate that holds the group together and makes it easier for members to contribute to work on the task. In attempting to harmonize group activities and relieve tensions, the chairperson should: *listen* with interest and show respect for all members and all opinions without judging them; *encourage* ideas and allow members to change their minds gracefully; provide breaks for prayer and refreshment to relieve tension or tiredness.

5) *Evaluating:* Helping the group to evaluate its decision, goals or procedures. The parish council chairperson should seek to become familiar and comfortable with the procedures of consensus decision-making, and with discernment.[15]

Council meetings will, of course, bring together a wide variety of personalities. The chairperson will have to learn to deal with all of them—from the aggressive autocrat to the timid nonassertive. There are no magic formulas. The chairperson will learn and develop leadership skills in the crucible of experience during the council meetings. In dealing with the council's personalities, she or he needs to be aware that there is a distinction between a meeting called to conduct the official business of the parish and one called primarily for social purposes. Without becoming too rigid or formal, the chairperson needs to use the agenda to keep the meeting on the right track. Councilors who wish to socialize can, of course, do so after the meeting.

The chairperson also needs to be conscious of time. Meetings generally should not last longer than two to two and one-half hours, including the time for prayer and reflection on the Scriptures. If they go on longer than that, something is probably wrong with the council process: inadequate committee work, no individual preparation, lack of trust, (with consequent nitpicking), poor communication, poor group dynamics. The chairperson will not be the actual leader at every moment of the council meeting. Leadership may, in varying degrees, pass from one councilor to another depending both on the topic being discussed and on the leadership skill of the individual councilor. For this reason, every member of the council will have an opportunity to exercise some kind of leadership.

Naturally, that leadership will be more effective if the councilor is aware of his or her leadership style. The management experts have identified five of the most typical leadership styles. It may be helpful to describe each of them briefly.

1) *Authoritative:* The leader identifies a problem, considers alternative solutions, chooses one of them and then tells the followers what they are to do. The leader may or may not consider what the group members will think or feel about the decision, but they clearly do not participate directly in the decision making. Coercion may or may not be used or implied.

2) *Persuasive:* The leader, as before, makes the decision without consulting the group. Instead of simply announcing the decision, however, she or he tries to persuade the group members to accept it. The leader points out how he or she has considered organization goals and the interests of group members and states how the members will benefit from carrying out the decision.

3) *Evaluative:* The leader identifies a problem and proposes a tentative solution. Before finalizing it, however, he or she gets reactions of those who will implement it. The leader says, in effect, "I'd like your frank reaction to this proposal and I

will then make the final decision."

4) *Participative:* The leader here gives the group members a chance to influence the decision from the beginning. She or he presents a problem and relevant background information, then asks the members for their ideas on how to solve it. In effect, the group is invited to increase the number of alternative actions to be considered. The leader then selects the solution he or she regards as most promising.

5) *Laissez-faire:* The leader here participates in the discussions as "just another member," and agrees in advance to carry out whatever decision the group makes. The only limits placed on the group are those given to the leader by his or her superiors. (Many research and development teams make decisions this way.)[16]

There may be someone in the parish who is skilled at facilitating meetings; should the elected chairperson wish to do so, she or he may assign this task to the facilitator.

As parish councils gain more experience their meetings will surely become more efficient and satisfying. They will develop their own style, character, and personalities. Each meeting will at least be another step on the way to becoming a unique experience of the life, love, and truth, which is the heart of a genuine Christian community. While no printed page can guarantee the perfect meeting, maybe it can be a helping hand in that direction. Once councilors have learned to conduct satisfying meetings, they will be ready to develop a pastoral plan for the parish. But that too requires skill and know-how. The next chapter, therefore, will discuss some of the essential steps in the planning process.

Notes

1. Norbert Lambert, *Managing Church Groups* (Dayton, Ohio: Pflaum Pub. 1975), p. 72.

2. Joel David Welty, "From Conflict to Consensus." *Today's Parish,* January 1986.

3. Wm. J. Rademacher, *Working with Parish Councils* (Canfield, Ohio: Alba books, 1976) pp. 123-124.

4. Mary Benet McKinney, OSB, *Sharing Wisdom* (Valencia, Calif.: Tabor Publishing), 1987, p. 73.

5. Thomas H. Green, S.J., *Weeds Among the Wheat. Discernment:Where Prayer and Action Meet* (Ave Maria Press, 1984), p. 180.

6. *Ibid.* p. 181.

7. Adapted from *Weeds Among the Wheat*, p. 180.

8. Thomas Gordon, *T.E.T. Teacher Effectiveness Training* (New York: Peter Wyden Publisher, 1974), pp. 228-233.

9. F. J. Bacchus, *The Catholic Encyclopedia* (New York: The Encyclopedia Press, 1913, Vol. XII), p. 220.

10. Unpublished paper (February 1973), p. 36.

11. *Managing Church Groups. op. cit.* 22.

12. *Parish Council Guidelines.* (Archdiocese of Newark, N. J.), p. 36.

13. *Ibid.*

14. *Planning and Running Meetings* (San Jose, Cal.: The Sanford Publishing Co.) p. 5.

15. Adapted from *Parish Council Guidelines*, Newark, N. J., *op. cit.*, p. 37.

16. For more information on the various leadership styles, see Norman Lambert, *Managing Church Groups.* Dayton, *op. cit.*

Sharing

1. How does our council feel about making decisions by consensus rather than Robert's Rules?

2. What can our council do to work toward an authentic discernment process?

3. What steps can our council take to build community among the members as a foundation for discernment?

CHAPTER 11

PASTORAL PLANNING

"Where there is no vision, the people perish." That's right out of the Good Book (Prov. 29,18)(KJV). It's a bit of biblical wisdom parishes and their councils could well take to heart. The pilgrim church will come to a halt, or exhaust itself in aimless talk if the pilgrims don't know where they are going. If councils are going to exercise leadership in the parish, they themselves need a clear sense of direction. That means they have to get involved in pastoral planning.

Before we get into the various methods for pastoral planning we need to review some of our assumptions. The parish is a group of people who are together because they have been called together by God and because they have chosen to be together. They are together for a purpose. In the church we describe that purpose as ministry or mission. We assume further that the people of the parish are empowered or equipped by the Spirit (Eph. 4:11) to accomplish that mission through the various ministries. So, the people have the energy, the ability and the resources to act.

Another assumption is that every parish:
Has the responsibility to try to discern its God-given ministry and mission; to identify present and available resources for that ministry and mission, and to organize those resources to be about its task.

This is church planning. We can expect to be guided by the Holy Spirit, but that does not alter our responsibility to be intentional about our actions as well. To be intentional means to plan, to organize, and to work out ways together in which congregational life can be ever more fruitful.[1]

Without pastoral planning the parish will be characterized by drifting. It will be controlled by external forces rather than being charged by an inner sense of direction and purpose. It may be carried away by fads and gimmicks. Councils may shop around in the open market, looking for that magic plan that they hope will give them the sense of direction they lack. Of course, there are no magic plans out there. Pastoral planning grows from an inner conviction that a baptized community needs to accept the responsibility and the challenge of taking charge of its own mission.

Pastoral planning will focus the energies of many people toward a common mission. It will excite people with a common vision. It will enable the parish to hold itself accountable because it can measure and evaluate itself. Once it knows where it is going, it can measure its progress. It will know what ministries it needs to accomplish its goals. At the same time, it will avoid that crisis mentality that can drain the energies of the parish.

The key to pastoral planning is vision. Councils can show a lack of vision in at least three ways: (1) by perpetuating a "churchy" parochialism by concentrating all their energies on *their* own parish, *their* own needs, *their* own church world; (2) by concentrating on buildings, such as *their* school, *their* church hall, *their* parking lot; (3) by constantly focusing on *one* issue, however important, such as finances, abortion, a good education for their children. A "one issue" council is actually *un*catholic. Besides, it's as boring as an uncle who never talks about anything but fishing. It is not that such councils have no feelings for the hungry masses of the third world. It's just that that other world never comes into the purview of their vision.

There are of course different ways of talking about vision. But the best word to describe the vision is "dream." Martin Luther King, Jr., in a 1963 speech at the Lincoln Memorial, kindled the energies of a nation with his dream of racial justice in America:

I have a dream that one day in the red hills of Georgia the sons of former slaves and sons of former slave owners will be able to sit down together at the table of brotherhood. I have a dream that one day even the state of Mississippi, a desert state sweltering with the heat of injustice and oppression, will be transformed into an oasis of freedom and justice. I have a dream that my four children will one day live in a nation where they will not be judged by the color of their skin but by the content of their character. I have a dream...of that day when all of God's children, black men and white men, Jews and Gentiles, Protestants and Catholics, will be able to join hands and sing in the words of the old Negro spiritual, "Free at last! Free at last! Thank God almighty, we are free at last!"[2]

A vision is a clear picture of what a group sees itself being and doing. A group could have a vision of health where there is sickness; a vision of knowledge where there is ignorance; a vision of freedom where there is oppression; a vision of love where there is hatred.[3]

Of course, having a vision is not enough. Many people have a vision but nothing ever happens. There has to be a commitment to act on the vision. Once a group has a shared commitment the vision can become a mission. Members of the group can assume various roles or ministries to carry out the mission. Then they need a program based on the mission; otherwise, the vision will fall back into mere wishful thinking. It will be a rocking chair dream and nothing more.

This present chapter is concerned with the means or the technique for implementing a broad Christian vision in a concrete way at the parish level. It assumes that each parish council, through its own process, has to internalize, concretize, and implement a new Christian vision. The members have to translate their vision into a mission and then into ministry. Since both the membership of the council and the needs of the parish and society change constantly, pastoral planning has to become a regular event in the parish council experience. Otherwise, the council will soon be off the track. It will run the risk of becoming an inward-turning, self-serving clique. It will be unstable and unaccountable, simply reacting to one crisis after another.

Now how does a council go about the business of pastoral planning? By way of introduction, councils need to be convinced that it is possible, in a Christian community, to arrive at a consensus on certain goals that truly flow out of the Christian tradition. Naturally, councils may not canonize or absolutize these goals. Nevertheless, it is possible, by the grace of discernment, to chart a fairly clear direction for the Christian pilgrimage.

Right off, it has to be said that pastoral planning is not an easy task. Usually the process takes a full weekend or its equivalent. Naturally, a weekend experience away from the parish (at a retreat house) is ideal.

Fortunately, there are many good methods available for pastoral planning. More and more books are being published every year to help the church planners.[4] A fairly simple method is called "Dream Planning," described by Charles Keating. A more complicated, but very effective method is called "Force Field Planning," also described by Keating. The best method is the one that works the best for the particular council doing the actual planning. Many methods, in one form or another, incorporate the following seven steps, not necessarily in the same order:

1) Arriving at a consensus on a common vision of the parish community; writing a *mission statement*
2) Discernment of needs, problems or deficiencies
3) Discernment of gifts, strengths, and resources
4) Consensus-decision on goals
5) Consensus-decision on objectives
6) Consensus-decision on strategies (in appropriate committees)
7) Determination of a system for evaluating the achievement or nonachievement of objectives.

Now before going any further, let's get our terms straight. A *vision* is expressed in a broad mission statement. Every parish is an organic member of the church universal, which gets its mission from the Lord through its own discernment process. Neither the church at large nor any of its parishes exists for itself.

No parish exists apart from the church's universal mission.
Without repeating Chapter 7, the mission of the church includes the following five functions:
1) to proclaim the Good News of Jesus Christ
2) to build up a community of love
3) to celebrate the liturgies of praise and thanksgiving
4) to serve others, in the name of Jesus Christ[5]
5) to enable all the members to grow in their relationship   with
God and with one another.

Each individual parish, however, needs to internalize and
express its own mission in a concrete form. Since the parish
council is a policy-making body, it is responsible for defining
the mission of the parish. It does this by preparing a Mission
Statement,which is simply a *broad statement of the overall direction and purpose of the parish*. It states why the parish as a
unique group exists. This mission statement

> must be clear enough so that its intent is obvious, yet not
> so detailed that it becomes burdensome.... Though the
> statement should be flexible enough to allow for interpre-
> tation according to current conditions and needs, it should
> not try to cover every conceivable situation that may arise.
> The mission statement must be short, clear, and understand-
> able to all who are part of the parish organization.[6]

Since the preparation of the mission statement is the first and,
by far, the most important step in the total parish planning process, it may be helpful to present a model process for preparing it.
A parish is always in the process of *becoming*. Recognizing this
condition of continuous growth, parish leaders try to express,
through a mission statement, *who* the parish is to become, its
identity or personality, and *why* it exists: to proclaim the Word?
To form parish members in their faith? To be of service? To work
for justice? To celebrate together? To form a community of love
and justice? The words in the mission statement must reach and
make sense to people while expressing the parish's unique mission. The mission statement should enable people to identify
with, to own, to discover and rediscover the mission. The language, therefore, must be simple, clear, and understandable.

The following process can be adapted to meet each parish's needs; the council first of all settles on a way to involve the larger parish.

Steps in the Process

First Month—Step 1: Orientation of the Parish

The parish is informed of the mission statement process and the parishioners' participation. The homily at the liturgies centers on the parish mission and its challenge. Parishioners are asked to pray for God's enlightenment as the process unfolds. A flyer with the reflection questions to be used at the parish meetings is distributed so that parishioners may be thinking about them.

Second Month—Step 2: Training of Facilitators

The parish council, along with committee chairpersons, staff, and small-group leaders, engaged in a session to plan and train themselves for a series of information-gathering meetings, in which all parishioners are asked to participate in developing a mission statement. Parish leaders will form teams to facilitate the all-parish meetings.

Third Month—Step 3 Holding Dialogue/Information-gathering Meetings

During this month, a series of dialogue and information gathering meetings for parishioners are held to provide input for the mission statement. The number of meetings depends on the size of the parish. The sessions are facilitated by teams of parish leaders and follow this format:

1) Prayer and reflection on Scripture (Begin with Acts 2: 42-47)

2) Explanation of the reasons for a mission statement and the process for developing one. Questions the mission statement will address: Who are we? What do we believe? What are we called to do? Whom do we serve? The *criteria* to be kept in mind in the following process are: the statement must be *brief* and *understandable:* it must be expressive of the *spiritual* nature of the parish; it must be *continuing* in nature; it should be *inspiring* so as to motivate and challenge people; it must be *local*, reflecting the parish's individuality, loca-

tion, composition, relationships, and accountability.

3) Beginning with the people's own experience, participants are asked to reflect (in small groups, if the number is large) on questions such as these:

•What is your idea or concept of a spiritually successful parish?
•What is your most spiritually enriching experience of parish activity? (Since this is a brainstorming activity, no dialogue is allowed and questions are for clarification only. All suggestions are pasted on newsprint or large cards for arrangement later.)
•How is the parish called to serve others?

4) The team of facilitators from the council/staff/ committees reviews this above experience, noting any developing profile of the parish. This leads into a presentation on parish mission, with scriptural references. Basically, the presentation will cover the parish mission of: worship, proclamation, service/works of justice, and community, as it flows from the mission of Jesus expressed in the gospel and the church tradition. The mission statement will help the parish focus its energies, acquire a sense of direction, develop a stewardship emphasis, and set the tone for parish life.

5) Break: During the break, the team of facilitators rearranges the cards with the responses from the reflection into the four categories of the parish mission.

6) The participants reassemble into small groups and the facilitators lead them through an evaluation of the parish's experience, based on the rearranged responses. What are the parish's strengths and what needs developing? The team of facilitators moves the dialogue forward, if necessary, with questions like: What needs of persons in our parish should we minister to? What concerns of our community (neighborhood, town, rural area) should our parish address? What world/ societal issues should our parish be concerned about? How are we evangelizing? Developing shared responsibility? Practicing good stewardship of resources?

Each small group then tries to come to a consensus on what the parish mission should be in each area, and submits it to the facilitating team.

7) Closing prayer of thanksgiving.

Fourth Month—Step 4: Refining and Writing the Mission Statement

The parish councilors/staff/committee chairpersons/small group leaders meet to refine input from the above process. (If needed, a smaller ad hoc committee can be assigned to this task.) A first draft of the mission statement is written and submitted to the council for evaluation. This process continues until the statement meets council approval.

Fifth Month—Step 5: Implementing the Mission Statement, Ratification, and Celebration

The mission statement is published for the whole parish and ratification is requested. (Since the parish has provided input and been informed right through the process, this should not be a problem. Any additional suggestions are given consideration, however, and a final draft is prepared for implementation.) The mission statement is made a part of parish life in the following ways:

•It becomes the preamble to the council's constitution.

•Copies of the final draft are made available to all parishioners for their reflection (a prepared form works well).

•It is given to all newcomers to the parish.

•It is given to each committee and organization with the request that their goals be based on the mission statement. (Committees might also receive the input from the parish meetings in Step 3, which could be valuable assets.)

•Prayer services could be created based on the mission statement for all the parish groups to use.

•The parish celebrates the mission statement in a special liturgy of commitment to parish mission.

•The council begins its planning process, basing its priorities, goals, and objectives on the mission statement.

Evaluation: Every 2-3 years, the council reevaluates the mission statement and asks the parish at large for its suggestions for updating.

When the mission statement has been completed the council is ready to move on to the next step—goal setting. At this point the process may meet some resistance. Often councilors begin to feel uneasy at this point, because they do not do any goal setting in their personal lives. Those who have a static view of their own lives are not used to this kind of reflective process. They do not see personal growth as a goal of their own lives. They may be afraid of that kind of soul-searching because "personal growth involves changes in attitudes and behaviors that are related to our self-concept and to our needs."[7] We are comfortable with our self-concept and get nervous about the need to change it.

John Haggai lists four common fears of goal setting: (1) the fear of imperfect goals; (2) the fear of defeat; (3) the fear of ridicule; and (4) the fear of considering goalsetting presumptuous.[8] Councilors need an inner conviction and a strong faith to overcome these fears. At the same time they need to deal with their own feelings of powerlessness. Frequently, the poor, who have been victims of a nameless system for many years, do not believe they can take charge of their own direction. For them goal setting may seem like an exercise in futility. They do not believe they can have any influence either on the system or on their own future. They feel their future will be shaped by forces beyond their control. It would be helpful, at the beginning of a goal setting process, to invite all participants to freely express their feelings about such a process.

As councilors begin their pastoral planning process they might once again pause to arrive at a clear understanding of terms. A *goal* is a clear statement of desired direction or activity in broad, general terms. It is the desired end result to be obtained when planning is complete. It can be a desired end state, a desired future condition, or a desired norm. A goal can be defined as *long* term (5 years) or *short* term (1 or 2 years).

A goal statement has seven main characteristics:
1) It is a guide to action—stated as a desired outcome, a result, a desired condition or state of affairs.
2) It is general in its direction.
3) It is challenging, exciting, and inspiring to its participants.
4) It calls for investment and involvement by the participants.

5) It may provide a time target (2 or 5 years).

6) It is directly tied to the purpose and goals of higher units in the organization (example: diocese).

7) It can be attained through a series of objectives and strategies.[9]

Here are a few examples of *lead* words for writing goals: to discuss, to understand, to appreciate, to assure, to believe, to co-ordinate, to know, to improve. Examples of goal statements: 1) To accept responsibility as unified Christian leaders; 2) To motivate parishioners to a new awareness of their spiritual relationship with God so they may better their own condition as well as that of their fellowmen and women; 3) To involve parishioners in all decision-making through varying media/methods; 4) To establish and foster more effective means of communication among all facets of parish life.[10]

An *objective* is a specific, time-oriented, and realistic statement of *what* the council is going to do, *who* is going to do it, for *whom, when,* and *for how much.* Objectives are the main *intermediate results* needed to obtain a goal. A good objective has eight main characteristics:

1) It begins with the word "to" and is followed by an *action verb.*

2) It produces a *single key result* when accomplished.

3) It specifies *for* or *with whom* an action is done.

4) It has a *specific target date* for accomplishment (from three months to one year from planning date).

5) It is *quantifiable and measurable*—how much is to be done. It can be evaluated.

6) It is *clear and understandable* for all those participants in the action.

7) It is *realistic and attainable*—considers present and anticipated resources.

8) It helps the council achieve one or more of its stated goals.[11]

Here are a few examples of *lead* words for writing objectives: to advise, to compare, to eliminate, to write, to establish, to approve, to identify, to design.

A *strategy* is one step or one specific action needed to attain an objective. A group of strategies is a plan of action spelling out how an objective will be reached. Strategies are usually planned in committees, not in the full council. It is in a strategy session that the individual members of the committees commit themselves to take one or more of the specific steps needed to achieve an objective. For example, if a council committee is planning a weekend retreat to develop deeper spirituality (objective) then someone has to commit himself or herself to taking care of transportation. Someone else has to make reservations at a retreat house (dates, meals, lodging, etc.). These are strategies to achieve an objective.

Now that we have defined our terms, let's get into the pastoral planning workshop itself. A typical schedule for a planning workshop may go something like this:

First Session: review of mission statement

This session assumes the council has already been involved in a process for preparing a mission statement as a separate activity. If the council involved the whole parish in a process for developing a mission statement as outlined above, then this first session is simply a reflection on the meaning of that mission statement. Once everyone on the council clearly understands that mission statement, the members are ready to move on to the next session.

Second Session: discernment of needs, problems, deficiencies

Sometimes the needs to be discerned are divided into internal and external. The internal needs pertain to the human dynamics of the council itself. What internal factors, dynamics, hinder the council in achieving its goals and objectives? It may be mistrust, conflict, lack of unity, lack of sufficient education, spiritual formation, etc. External needs grow out of the unique situation of the parish itself, as it responds, or does not respond, to its mission in a specific time and place, in a specific community. For instance, the parish may have very poor liturgy, a poor religious education program, or no ecumenical activities.

In this assessment of needs, the council has to keep an eye on its mission statement. For discernment of needs, it's not simply a question of counting up the *felt* needs of the councilors. For instance, the gospel, with all its tough demands, needs to be proclaimed, even if, and especially if, no one experiences that as a *felt* need. If members depart too far from their mission statement, the final list of needs will have a heavy emphasis on merely parochial or maintenance needs. It' s not that these are not very real. They are real and they need to be considered. If the council focuses too much on these *felt* needs, however, it may lose contact with its mission statement and with the sometimes painful call of the gospel.

The discernment of needs can be a lot of fun. Everybody can "play." It's a good time to use the brainstorm system, which works best when the participants observe the following rules:

1) Everyone is encouraged to think up as wild ideas as possible. If wild ideas are not forthcoming in a brainstorm session, it's a sign that participants are censoring their own ideas. They are thinking twice before they express an idea for fear that they may come up with a silly one and sound foolish.

2) No evaluation of any kind is allowed. If members judge and evaluate ideas as they are thought up, people tend to become more concerned with defending their ideas than thinking up new and better ones. Ideas do not have to be justified.

3) Quantity of ideas must be encouraged. When a great number of ideas come pouring out in rapid succession, evaluation is generally impossible. The participants then feel free to give their imaginations wide range and then good ideas will result.

4) Everyone is encouraged to build upon, or to modify the ideas of others. Combining or modifying previously suggested ideas often leads to new ideas that are superior to those that sparked them.[12]

The brainstorm system works best in small groups. The silent and timid members become more active. When each small group has come up with its list of needs, it reduces its total number to five or ten. It does this by arranging the needs in an order of priority and retaining only the most important ones. Priorities can be quickly determined by dividing needs into: Got-to-dos; Ought-to-dos: Nice-to-dos.[13] Of course, some needs have to be eliminated entirely because the council doesn' t have the time, the authority, or the competence to deal with them. For instance, the council can't abolish the infallibility of the pope. There' s no sense in listing impossible needs and raising unrealistic expectations.

When the individual groups have reduced their lists of needs to five, they come back together in a large group to arrive at a consensus on a master list of needs, problems, or deficiencies. Part of such a list might look like this:

1) No close feeling of community at Sunday Liturgy
2) No one visiting the sick at the local convalescent home
3) No one doing anything for those on welfare in the parish
4) The parish school board is fighting with the religious education committee
5) No programs for the senior citizens in the parish.

When a consensus has been reached, the master list of needs remains on display on newsprint next to the mission statement.

Third Session: discernment of strengths and resources

The first purpose of this session is to discover the gifts, charisms, and ministries that the Spirit has given to the parish community. These gifts or resources will generally fall under the following headings: (1) the gospel; (2) the liturgy and the sacramental system; (3) gifted people; (4) time; (5) buildings; (6) relationships; (7) money. The second purpose of this session is to make the council aware that, in many cases, it has more than enough resources to respond to the needs discerned in the second session.

The process of this session is the same as the second, that is, small groups, then large group. A partial list of resources might look something like this:

1) an up-to-date census with listing of talents and interests of all the parishioners
2) a social worker who is willing to offer free services
3) a competent public school teacher
4) an accountant
5) widows/widowers with cars to provide transportation for elderly.

Fourth Session: consensus on goals

During this session councilors might first reflect on their relationship to the diocesan church. If the diocese, through its diocesan pastoral council, has achieved a consensus regarding diocesan goal statements, the parish council should consider these diocesan goals before it prepares its own goals. In this way, the parish council can reflect on how it will fulfill its responsibility in helping the diocesan church achieve its goals. Some of the parish goal statements may very well flow directly from diocesan goal statements.

After reflecting on the diocesan goals, the councilors take another look at their own Mission Statement, their list of needs, and their list of resources. Then they go into small groups to write goal statements that flow from their Mission Statement and that at the same time, *match the resources to their needs.* After achieving a consensus on goal statements in their small groups, they assemble in a large group to reach a consensus on a master list of goals. Again, they may arrange these goals, like the list of needs, in any order of priority. They may also wish to label them as *long* or *short* range. This list of goals will then remain on display next to the list of resources.

Fifth Session: consensus decision on objectives

During this session each small group selects one goal and breaks it up into objectives. While remembering the definition of a good objective and using the consensus system, each small group formulates objectives designed to effect the accomplishment of its chosen goal.

When the small groups have completed their tasks, they reconvene in a large group to obtain a consensus on a master list of objectives that have been prepared for each goal. At this point it becomes very important that whatever persons or committees are expected to accept responsibility for carrying out an objective actually agree that the objective is clear and understandable, realistic and obtainable. They have to assume *ownership* of the objective. At the same time, they have to be sufficiently motivated and committed to invest their energies in working for the achievement of the objectives they accept.

Sixth Session: strategies

After objectives come strategies. As mentioned earlier, the

decisions regarding the types of strategies needed to implement an objective should be left to the discretion of the various committees. When the council itself gets into strategies, it gets bogged down in endless details. It's the task of the council to give full responsibility to the committees and then hold them accountable. For this reason, strategies are not really a part of a pastoral planning workshop.

Seventh Session: evaluation

During this session, the council draws up a schedule for receiving the reports of the various committees that will work on the objectives. It determines *who* will be accountable to *whom* for *what* by *what date.* It prepares a master list to be duplicated and distributed to all the council members and their committees. This list also becomes part of the council's minutes. Reports from the committees will be on the council agenda according to dates listed on the schedule. If the objectives have been prepared correctly, this session will merely be a summation of the workshop. It is simply a way of building into the workshop a system whereby achievement of goals and objectives will be evaluated according to a mutually agreeable timetable.

Usually this kind of workshop concludes with the celebration of the liturgy. The readings and prayers are chosen for the occasion. The emphasis is on ministry and commitment. The council' s liturgy committee is responsible for preparing this special liturgy.

When the workshop is over, the council faces its toughest job—getting the word out to the rest of the parish. The purpose of a goal-setting workshop is to chart a direction for the *whole* parish, not just for the council. For this reason the council will have to spend some time figuring out how to get the whole parish committed to working toward the attainment of the *parish* goals. Goals may look fine on paper, but they are useless unless the people of the parish bend their energies to make these goals a reality in the actual life of the parish and community. Councilors may be in for a real letdown when they return home to confront the hard facts of parish life. The rest of the parishioners will be slow to change. Apathy will continue. The parish at large will not commit itself to the council's goals and objectives just because they were all published in the bulletin. The chairperson's phone will not be rung off the hook by parishioners volunteering their services. Councilors need to be zealous, committed, and enthusiastic. But they also need to be realistic. They might do well, especially after a goal-setting workshop, to reflect on the principles of change and group behavior. Dr. Charles Sheffieck has outlined both the degree of difficulty and the amount of time involved in bringing about a change in group behavior:

> Parish council members have been charged with the responsibility to work in a collegial mode to develop the local parish. In the few years that any one member might be on the parish council, the amount of change that will take place could be viewed as minimal. The task of bringing about desired change is not only complex, but it also requires time. The following diagram on the base, or horizontal axis, shows the amount of time needed for each type of change, and on the vertical axis, the amount of difficulty involved in achieving this change.

To bring about a change in *knowledge*, the difficulty is basically low, and the amount of time can be measured in hours or days.

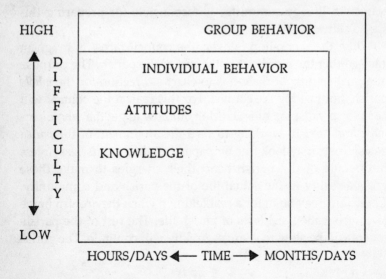

To change an *attitude* of an individual is more difficult and requires more time, maybe weeks or months. When it comes to changing individual *behavior*, again the amount of time increases and so does the difficulty. The most difficult change to bring about is that of a group behavior, and, accordingly, it requires the greatest amount of time, usually years. Parish councils, by their very nature, are groups that are responsible for bringing about changes in group behavior. The task of the parish council, therefore, requires considerable time and is extremely complex.[14]

Of course, Dr. Sheffieck's chart doesn't include the prayer factor. No doubt the Spirit is always at work to bring about the conversion and inner renewal of God's people. Through the power of grace, even the poorest human efforts can and do bring about unexpected results. The Spirit, fortunately, is not limited to the laws of human behavior. At the same time, councilors need to remember that they themselves may not see the results of their work in their own lifetime. They will plant. Someone else will water. And God will give the growth in God' s own time (1 Cor. 3:6). Besides, it's often the case that the work of the prophet doesn't yield its fruit until after the prophet's death. When councilors have finished setting the goals of the parish, they may feel a bit overwhelmed by the task ahead. It is especially at this time that councilors sense the need for spiritual renewal. The next chapter, therefore, will show how the Lord's holiness, working in and through the councilors, will help the council achieve its goals.

Notes

1. *Church Planning: A Manual for Use in the United Church of Christ* (St. Louis: Office for Church Life and Leadership, 1976), p. A-1.

2. Quoted by John Haggai in *Lead On* (Waco, Texas: Word Books, 1987), p. 11.

3. *Ibid.*, p. 12.

4. See especially: *Church Planning* (St. Louis: Office for Church Life and Leadership, 1976); *Pastoral Planning Book* by Charles Keating (New York: Paulist Press, 1981); *Who Are We and Where Are We Going?* by William Harms (New York: Sadlier, 1981); *Hip Pocket Guide* by Dorothy Craig (San Diego, Calif.:

University Associates, Inc., 1978).

5. *Parish Council Philosophy and Guidelines* (Denver, Colorado: Archdiocese of Denver, n.d.), pp. 7-8.

6. Norman Lambert, *Managing Church Groups* (Dayton, Ohio: Pflaum Publishing Co., 1975), p. 28.

7. George Ford and Gordon Lippitt, *Planning Your Future* (San Diego, Calif.: University Associates, Inc., 1972), p. iii.

8. *Lead On!* (Waco, Texas: Word Books, 1986), pp. 39-40.

9. *Denver Guidelines*, p. 20.

10. *Ibid.*

11. *Ibid.*, with adaptation.

12. Adapted from Simon, Howe and Kirschenbaum, *Values Clarification* (New York: Hart Publishing Co., Inc., 1972), pp. 204-205.

13. *Managing Church Groups*, p. 37.

14. *Planning for Parish Development*, p. 13.

Sharing
1. Can you share any experiences in pastoral planning?
2. How does vision relate to pastoral planning?
3. How do you react to the process suggested for the preparation of a mission statement?
4. Which part of the process will present the greatest challenge?
5. Are you aware of any fears of goal setting?
6. Do you feel you have enough resources in your own parish to do pastoral planning?
7. Do you feel it is possible to get the whole parish involved in pastoral planning? How?
8. Do you regularly set goals in your own personal life?

CHAPTER 12

OPEN TO ME THE GATES OF HOLINESS

"Open to me the gates of holiness:
I will enter and give thanks.
This is the Lord's own gate
Where the just may enter." (Psalm 118)

I did not want to write this chapter. I kept looking for an expert in holiness—someone in the unitive way, or someone with a Ph.D. in holiness, or a saint, or a Thomas Merton, who could reveal to the rest of us the secrets of growing in holiness. I wondered why I could not just advise the readers to find a good book on holiness or go to their spiritual director to be tutored to the heights of mystical union with God.

I kept searching for excuses. Part of me was simply overwhelmed by my own inadequacy. After all, I just trudge along in this pilgrim journey, putting one clay foot before the other, hoping I am getting closer to the Lord. The journey has its valleys and its dark nights. What can I possibly write that will be of value to the ministers on parish councils? Sometimes the best I can do is to pray with Thomas Merton:

My Lord God, I have no idea where I am going. I do not see the road ahead of me. I cannot know for certain where it will end. Nor do I really know myself, and the fact that I think that I am following your will does not mean that I am actually doing so.

But I believe that the desire to please you does in fact please you. And I hope that I will never do anything apart from that desire. And I know that if I do this you will lead me by the right road though I may know nothing about it. Therefore will I trust you always though I may seem to be lost and in the shadow of death. I will not fear, for you are ever with me, and you will never leave me to face my perils alone.[1]

On the other hand, part of me feels that even I may have some "utterance of wisdom" (1 Cor. 12:8) to share with my fellow ministers on this pilgrimage. I recall a line from James Fenhagen: "The greatest gift a pastor has to give to another is not the right answer but the authenticity of his or her own search."[2] He then quotes Henri Nouwen: "The minister is the one who can make this search for authenticity possible, not by standing on the side as a neutral screen or an impartial observer, but as an articulate witness of Christ, who puts his own search at the disposal of others."[3] That is the best I can hope to do—place my search at the disposal of my fellow pilgrims in the ministry of parish councils. If readers are expecting answers from an expert I would suggest they skip this chapter and climb the mountain where the expert is found. Then let them come back and share those answers with the rest of us.

For those who are still with me, we need to be absolutely convinced, both intellectually and emotionally, that the main business of this earthly journey is to grow in holiness. That is true of all the baptized, but even more so for those in the ministries of the church. We can, of course, rejoice at the explosion of ministries in the postconciliar church. But we can also get nervous about the serious implications for the church. We can certainly identify with the comments of Fr. Frans van Beeck:

> Watching the student populations of various summer institutes in religious education and pastoral ministry is certainly very exhilarating, but it can also send shudders down one's spine. If all these perceptive, motivated, generous women and men should be frustrated, that would amount to a tragic failure on the part of the Catholic com-

munity to welcome the grace offered to it towards its own growth and development in faith.[4]

As church we have a long way to go in providing a spiritually supportive environment for those who minister within it. Karl Rahner was writing primarily for the German church, but his words can also be applied to the U.S. church:

If we are honest, we must admit that we are to a terrifying extent a spiritually lifeless church. Living spirituali-ty...has withdrawn in a singular way from the public life of the church...and has hidden in small conventicles of the remaining pious people. The church's public life even today...is dominated to a terrifying extent by ritualism, legalism, administration, and a boring and resigned spiritual mediocrity continuing along familiar lines.[5]

Unless we, as church, pay serious attention to the ministers' need for spiritual growth, the danger of frustration with any kind of ministry in the church is a very real probability. So we need to reflect for a moment on some of the very real problems new parish councilors will meet as they offer their ministering gifts to their parish and to their church.

As they begin their ministry on their councils, new members soon begin to see the human side of the church at closer range. They see the warts on the face of holy "mother" church, the people of God. They see bias, conflict, apathy, selfishness, manipulation, narrow vision, and power plays. They discover that some of their fellow ministers, including priests and sisters, can be rigid, insensitive, closed-minded, and authoritarian—more inclined to deal in personalities than with issues. They experience in a new way, an aspect of the mystery of evil, which is the common burden of the pilgrim church, "until he comes."

Then, too, getting beyond the personal, they get a deeper appreciation of the complexity of many of the problems involved in change, renewal, and pastoral leadership in the modern Roman Catholic church. They see that it is not easy to deal with pluralism, shared decision making and the tensions between hierarchic and collegial styles of leadership. They see, finally, that there's more involved in serving on the council than merely taking care of the material things so "Father can take care of the spiritual."

Besides the unique problems growing out of the parish council experience, there are others that are simply part of the growth toward maturity in the spiritual life of ministering Christians. Ernest Larsen mentions the following three obstacles to renewal: lack of courage, personal problems, and refusal to follow the Spirit.[6] Both the courage to be and the courage to become are often lacking in many of us. We are afraid to take any bold new steps in the spiritual life because we are afraid to venture out from our safe, familiar patterns of behavior. We don't know where the Spirit will lead us or to what frightening responsibilities the Spirit may call us. Besides, we feel so inadequate in the face of the tasks ahead. Better to do nothing than to fail.

Then, too, most of us have some personal problems. We often carry the burden of these problems alone because we can't muster the courage to share them with someone else. We are afraid of that kind of intimacy. We concentrate so much of our attention on these problems that we have little time or energy to pay attention to God, to prayer, and to the needs of others. These unshared, and therefore unresolved, problems give birth to anger, impatience, and frustration. We don't own our dependence on the Christian community, so we don't get help from it either.

Also, we do find it hard, as Larsen reminds us, to listen to, and to obey, the Spirit. That's just too slippery for us. We are so used to getting our directions from the law that we look to the law to say it all—clearly, directly, and finally. We just can't stand the freedom of living under the voice of the Spirit. Some of us would still rather live a spiritual life in a neat framework of confessions, communions, novenas, and simple obedience to law. The spiritual life is, of course, not reducible to a neat set of rules. It's not like buying a frozen food package, with clear directions guaranteeing a delightful dish. The Spirit, after all, continues to breathe where and how the Spirit wills. That's the difficulty. But that's also the challenge and the excitement. And Catholics have been responding to that challenge in different ways for many centuries.

Some Pitfalls on the Road

Before we discuss what holiness is, it may be helpful to reflect on some of the pitfalls that can show up on the road to holiness. If we learn to recognize counterfeit holiness, we may be better prepared to recognize the real thing. Many Catholics and saints have been on this road before us. We can learn from their journey.

No doubt the monastic tradition has brought countless riches to the church. Many monks from the time of St. Benedict have attained a high degree of holiness in the monasteries of their choice. Through them the church through the centuries has witnessed to the importance of the evangelical counsels of poverty, chastity, and obedience. It has also witnessed to the importance of the Liturgy of the Hours and to the virtue of hospitality, welcoming the stranger on the road.

1) The first pitfall is that the emphasis on the monastic style of life also had some harmful effects. It implied that the way to holiness required a flight from the world. It seemed to "judge" the world as evil, as an insurmountable obstacle to holiness. Jean Leclercq describes the effects this monastic model had on the laypeople of the twelfth century:

There is a spontaneous desire in men to escape from a world whose vileness they see and feel and that they are powerless to remedy. Thus the same cause, and sometimes the same disappointments, that provoked the movements just discussed (Catharist) drove certain laymen to make the experiment of seeking holiness alone, outside the ordinary conventual setting, or at least within the sphere of influence of a monastery or church.[7]

There is a sense in which flight from an "evil" world as a condition for holiness shows a lack of faith in the power of the risen Lord to overcome the evil of the world. Paul, confronting the evil world of Rome and Corinth, did not hesitate to proclaim: "But where sin increased, grace abounded all the more" (Rom. 5:20). In the evil world of Corinth Paul announced the victory of the cross: "Death is swallowed up in victory. O death, where is thy victory? O death, where is thy sting?" (1 Cor.15:55). As we shall see later, the holy God created the world holy. And Jesus' redemption of that world is a new and holy creation.

While we acknowledge the riches of the monastic tradition, we need to own the historical fact that the monasteries were "white, male, celibate, single-sex communities."[8] We need to own the very real limitations of a long monastic tradition that has left its mark on the Catholic understanding of spirituality even to this day. Elements of monastic spirituality have been and continue to be imposed on the laity: "forms of prayer, styles of penance, negative approach to matter, anti-sexual bias, and a form of obedience to their pastors that resembled the obedience of religious to their superiors."[9] "Our spiritualities and our understanding of holiness will mature only when we begin to include the ways in which God touches persons in a variety of historical circumstances."[10]

2) The second pitfall is the false assumption that the three vows of poverty, chastity, and obedience will be the normal gateway to holiness. Here too the religious orders, modeled on the monastic tradition, have tended to narrow the way to holiness. The emphasis on the vows implied that the way to holiness was not open to married people living in the world. Vatican II, in *The Constitution on the Church*, does not link holiness to the three vows. Instead the chapter on "The Call to Holiness" states that the Holy Spirit produces in the faithful the fruits of grace whereby they may practice the evangelical counsels of poverty, chastity and obedience:

> This practice of the counsels prompted by the holy Spirit, undertaken by many Christians whether privately or in a form or state sanctioned by the church, gives and should give a striking witness and example of that holiness.[11]

Of course, the three vows have been and continue to be the vocation to holiness for many of our fellow pilgrims. But they are not the only way and they ought not to dominate the methods for growth in holiness offered to the faithful.

3) The third pitfall might well be called the danger of elitism. Already in the twelfth century we see this tendency toward a caste of the elite. Dom Francois Vandenbroucke writes:

Men's aspirations to live according to the Gospel in its purity had one consequence that was far from being in the spirit of Christ. They tended to create among those who pursued them a real sense of caste. The "pure," the "holy," the "true Christians," the "true poor men," the "humiliati" too often set themselves above the rest of mankind. The Gospel, after all is not addressed to the "elect" especially not to those who are conscious of being so; it is offered to all, including those least favored by nature or by grace.[12]

The knights, including their armor for war, were blessed during a religious ceremony that was similar to the consecration of virgins and the coronation of kings. Presided over by bishops, this ritual produced a caste of "the pure." Theoretically knighthood was open to everyone. But gradually it became a privilege reserved only to the sons of knights.

We simply do not become holy by entering a caste of "the holy." In fact we ought to be suspicious of any special language or special garb or special place that implies that only the elite, the chosen ones, can enter here. It is helpful to remember that Jesus chose some sinners and zealots to become his disciples. And the church has raised some "bums" to the altar of sainthood.

4) We ought to be on guard against the mere multiplication of pious exercises as a surefire way to holiness. Piling up novenas, pilgrimages, rosaries, and visits to shrines purporting miracles does not necessarily add up to holiness. It may be an indication that holiness is placed in externals, in performing works "to be seen" (Matt. 23:5). Vatican II's *Constitution on the Church* gives us a sober warning: "Let us teach the faithful, therefore, that the authentic cult of the saints does not consist so much in a multiplicity of external acts, but rather in a more intense practice of our love...."[13] Growth in holiness is not the result of human effort or some kind of spiritual aerobics, like climbing the holy stairs. Maybe it is time to get rid of Ignatius's phrase, "the Spiritual Exercises."

5) We need to be on guard lest in our American culture we begin to believe that growth in holiness is a human achievement.

It is true that Catholics have much to learn from humanistic psychology and from the human potential movement as practiced at Esalen, California. These movements often do a better job in affirming the human than Catholics who are in an unreal flight into supernaturalism. Such movements often provide a healing environment for the wounded human condition. They offer a hospitable space for the expression of the emotional side of the human person. They empathize with psychic pain without the quick moralistic judgments of religious. Thus they encourage the honest dialogue that can become a prayerful conversation with God. In practice they often have a high regard for the Thomistic axiom that grace builds on nature. They may be reminding us that the church does not have a monopoly either on grace or the reign of God.

On the other hand, we need to own the real limitations of the human, merely psychological sciences in our effort to grow in holiness. The practitioners of these sciences are not free from the semi-pelagianism that says we can grow toward wholeness and toward God by a mere act of the will. They often imply that we do not need help from God. "Go for it," is the operating principle. "Acquire the skills for winning at life, love, and work." "Break the habits that rule your life." The assumption is that we are all naturally good and that we humans really can "have it all" and do it all—by ourselves. What we call evil is nothing more than a human defect that can be healed by human therapy. Numerous self-help books, with a heavy emphasis on the power of the will, proclaim the message that salvation is the result of a human process very much at our disposal. One can easily agree with Fr. van Beeck that faith-development

> has been mainly approached from the point of view of developmental psychology so far, by thinkers like Erik Erikson, James Fowler, Sam Keen, William Rogers and John McDargh. While the approach is obviously fruitful, it sometimes creates the impression that growth in the spirit is a function of human perfection.[14]

Growing in holiness requires a spiritual sensitivity to the reality of evil in oneself, in the church and in the world. Geofrey Williams, quoting Hannah Arendt, points out that

the Nazi horror which almost obliterated a people and destroyed a culture was established, operated and maintained by normal people—people like you and I—who had milk for breakfast in the morning, liked holidays in the country, Mozart, meals with friends; people who worried about their children' s education, had upset stomachs, made love, cried, slept. People just like you or I! And yet they were evil, destructive.[15]

It is not an accident that throughout the history of the church evil has been depicted with a spiritual quality and symbolized by demons. That means that we cannot wrestle evil to the ground with our bare hands. Overcoming evil is not a mere human achievement. We will definitely need the help of the victorious risen Lord to gain victory over evil. Besides, evil is rightly called a mystery. And that means that we need the Spirit's gifts of wisdom and discernment even to recognize it. It is of course unchristian to have such a pessimistic view of human nature that one sees evil everywhere. But it is an absolute disaster to underestimate the power, the many forms of evil in our world.

While we own the reality of evil in the human condition, we need to be careful we do not take flight into angelism and supernaturalism. It is not enough to just pray and hope that all obstacles will vanish. It is presumptuous to expect a miraculous intervention at every turn in the road. History is a witness that supernaturalism moves easily into magic and superstition. Writing the history of third century Christianity, Jaroslav Pelikan, quoting Shirley Jackson Case, reports:

Traffic was heavy on the highway between heaven and earth. Gods and spirits thickly populated the upper air, where they stood in readiness to intervene at any moment in the affairs of mortals....All nature was alive—alive with supernatural forces.[16]

The continuing popularity of alleged visions and apparitions such as those in Bayside, N. Y., are testimony that the dangers of supernaturalism are still with us. Many people still look for magic and miracle. The church, of course, looks for virtue.

Another pitfall is the danger of individualism. Elizabeth Dreyer is certainly correct: "...The spirituality we have inherited is markedly individualistic."[17] With the compilation of the list of sins in the medieval Irish Penitentials private confession became the norm. Private Masses also became common. Catholics entered a period of spirituality known as "Jesus and I." Until Vatican II it was quite common for Catholics to go to Mass to fulfill their personal obligation and recite their personal prayers to Jesus while the priest said "his" Mass facing the wall.

In the U.S. individualism in the practice of religion is a special danger. Robert Bellah, in his popular *Habits of the Heart*, devotes a whole chapter to individualism in the American culture. He offers considerable evidence for his thesis:

Individualism lies at the very core of American culture.... We believe in the dignity, indeed the sacredness, of the individual. Anything that would violate our right to think for ourselves, judge for ourselves, make our own decisions, live our lives as we see fit, is not only morally wrong, it is sacrilegious. Our highest and noblest aspirations, not only for ourselves, but for those we care about, for our society and for our world, are closely linked to our individualism.[18]

This American individualism shapes our religious behavior. We just do not "talk religion." Religion is a private and very personal matter. We are also affluent enough that we do not need each other very often. We drive our own cars to work. We can afford the luxury of being independent. We no longer need a cup of sugar from the neighbors. We become individuals practicing a private religion with a private, very individualistic spirituality.

A final pitfall is the tendency toward a dualistic mentality that "includes a positive valuation of spirit, heaven, soul, and maleness while in significant ways disvaluing body, earth, nature, flesh, and femaleness."[19] This dualism often takes the form

of an anti-worldly preoccupation. It draws a sharp line between
the sacred and the profane, between matter and spirit. Many
modern spiritual writers, such as Matthew Fox, are trying hard
to move spirituality away from this false dualism. Nevertheless, this dualism remains a real problem, especially for the laity who of necessity are in the sweat and blood of the world.

Growing in Holiness

Now that we have red-flagged just a few of the pitfalls along
the road, we can move toward a positive description of our journey toward holiness. A brief history of spirituality may help.
Once we know where we are coming from we have a better
chance of knowing where we are going.

The history of spirituality has been well summarized by
Leonard Doohan.[20] He describes the three main trends influencing the development of spirituality from the New Testament to
the time of St. Francis de Sales (1608). The first trend was toward dualism; the second was the development of monasticism;
the third was the development of the clerical dimensions of
the church. Of the three trends monasticism had the greatest
influence.

After the long dominance of monastic spirituality it was refreshing to see the arrival of St. Francis with his declaration in
The Introduction to the Devout Life: "My intention is to write
[for] those who have to live in the world and who, according to
their state, to all outward appearances have to lead an ordinary life."[21] After the death of Francis, spirituality was very
much influenced by Illuminism, Jansenism, Quietism, and Mod-
ernism. In the twentieth century we have seen the influence of
writers like Frank Duff, Frank Sheed, Jacques Maritain, Dorothy Day, and Jean Vanier.[22]

Vatican II (1962-65) brought about a renewal of spirituality
in many ways. It eliminated the vocabulary of "States of Perfection." There are no longer levels of holiness, but only one
state of holiness. The evangelical counsels are no longer limited
to three (poverty, chastity and obedience) because there are
many more than three. It speaks instead of the "observance of

the manifold counsels proposed in the gospel by our Lord to his disciples."[23] It attributes growth in holiness to the Lord Jesus: "He himself stands as the Author and Finisher of this holiness of life."[24]

Thus Vatican II tried to steer away from the semi-pelagianism implied in the multiplication of exercises. Now all are called to a holiness based not on unusual asceticism but on charity and the sacrament of baptism. Vatican II tried to deal with at least some of the pitfalls mentioned earlier.

Leonard Doohan has noted four trends in the development of spirituality since Vatican II: (1) ecclesial, (2) incarnational, (3) service-oriented, and (4) liberational.[25] The ecclesial trend can be seen in the growth of parish-based renewal programs and in the new emphasis on family spirituality. The incarnational trend is shown in the church's more positive view of the world and in the growing number of Catholics who commit themselves to a renewal of the temporal order through their presence. The service-oriented trend can be seen in the many Christians who commit themselves to work toward world peace and who are actively engaged, in the sense of ministry, in the fields of politics, finance, education, or administration.[26] The liberational trend can be seen in the growing emphasis on healing ministries and on the prophetic challenge many ministers, including the American bishops, are offering to the unjust structures of our modern society. No doubt these trends will continue to grow as spirituality becomes less monastic, less clerical, and less dualistic.

Some Characteristics of Holiness

Holiness consists in union with the all-holy God. That is the ultimate goal no matter what methods are employed. But saying so is not a great deal of help to the average baptized person. We need to recognize holiness if we are going to orient our lives toward it. One way to identify holiness, at least on this earthly journey, is to be aware of certain marks or characteristics. Without pretending to be exhaustive or to indicate any degrees of importance, we can reflect on some of the broad outlines of growth toward holiness.

We can now work for an M.A. Degree in Creation Spirituality. From the viewpoint of theology this movement toward a more creation-centered spirituality is most welcome.[27] With the help of Matthew Fox and a growing number of spiritual directors this movement will, no doubt, continue in the years ahead. In the past the overemphasis on original sin often produced an understanding of human nature and of creation itself as essentially flawed. In the process we lost the profound meaning of the often repeated phrase "how good it was" in the Genesis creation account. The all-holy God could not, in fact, create anything that was not holy. The fact that humankind's sinful acts have left unholy fingerprints on God's masterpiece does not change the fact that creation, including human nature, is still God's holy artistry. Any growth in holiness needs to honor that most important truth of our faith.

1) As noted above, one characteristic of growth toward holiness will be an emphasis on the incarnation. That emphasis will have a twofold meaning: first, that in Christ an all-holy God lovingly embraced the human condition and became part of it and, second, that he did so unconditionally while that human condition was very much in a sinful state. God's loving embrace confirmed the truth that the human race was in fact God's creation and remained so even after a long history of sinful acts. That embrace was also a transforming embrace. For no one ever remains the same after falling into the hands of the living God.

At the same time, the incarnation teaches us that God became our partner, entered our history, while we were indeed sinful. The New Testament reveals the social sins of discrimination, slavery, sexism, and patriarchism. And Paul's letters add other sins to that list. But God did not wait until we were worthy of divine love, until we had our act together. God's love went out to us precisely because we did *not* have our act together and were in desperate need of God's help. We learn from the scriptures that God's transforming love was efficacious, for after the Lord' s resurrection we are now on the way to "new heavens and a new earth"(2 Peter 3:13).

The incarnation means that in Christ God entered into the

nitty-gritty of our human existence: into Paul's tent-making shop, into Peter's fishing boat, into the pain and loneliness of the lepers, into the near death of the woman caught in adultery. God carried a share of the burdens of a crushing Roman tax structure, suffered the ignominy of a subjugated people, shed tears over the imminent destruction of beloved Jerusalem. Our spinning earth is marked by the blood-stained footprints of the incarnate God on the way to the cross. God was a partner in our tears.

But in Christ God was also a partner in the joy and laughter of the human pilgrimage. God celebrated the wedding feast of Cana with wine and dancing. God went to the mountain top to gaze in awe and wonder at the beauty of the setting sun. God enjoyed the company of Mary Magdalen and the anointing of his feet. No doubt God had a lot of fun playing with the children (Luke 18:16). And God was certainly a partner in the music and dancing at that grand party for the Prodigal Son (Luke 15:24).

The incarnation/resurrection means that Christ continues to enter into the nitty-gritty of our human existence: into the factories, the offices, the schools, the farms, the prisons, the airports, the governments. He is a partner in the struggles of the poor, in the pain and loneliness of the AIDS patient, in the emptiness of the loveless marriage, in the fear of murder in the city, in the despair of those languishing in the dark pit of depression. He continues to be a partner in our tears. If not, the mystery of the incarnation/resurrection is a cruel hoax.

In Christ God also continues to be our partner in our eating, our drinking, our love-making, our celebrating. God's heart beats with ours when we gaze in awe and reverence at the beauties of holy creation. God is our partner in the joy of peace, reconciliation, and the return of those who are lost. God is present in our song, our music, our laughter.

Holiness has the mark of the incarnation when it embraces God as partner in the blood and agony of this world's pilgrimage. They who pursue holiness by placing themselves at God's disposal offer God a canvas on which the master artist will paint yet another masterpiece. This lived holiness is a daily witness to the truth that no matter what the time and place, holy grace does, in fact, overcome evil and transform it. It frees the pilgrim from slavery to drugs, alcohol, sex, etc. But it does more—it brings the creature ever closer to that complete and final union with the holy creator.

2) A second characteristic of growth toward holiness is self-knowledge. Elizabeth Dreyer rightly calls this "the 'first base' of the spiritual life."[28] This self-knowledge proceeds from a humble recognition "that we are creatures and sinners, and second, that we are made in the image and likeness of God."[29] Awareness of our sinfulness helps us constantly to own our dependence on God. It keeps our feet firmly planted on this earth. Awareness of being created in God' s image reminds us of our high destiny to return to the fullness of that image in God.

True self-knowledge helps us to trust our experience of God. While humbly aware of the mystery of evil still at work in us, it is very important to learn to trust what a loving God is doing in our lives. There can be no doubt that God wants to lead us to sanctity. But it is not always easy to trust the different ways in which God is writing God's story in our lives. It takes a lot of courage to be truly open to God' s way of doing things, to be clay in the hands of the divine potter (Is. 64:7). This is especially true when God, fashioning us according to a divine, mysterious blueprint, leads us into our own dark night. But learning to trust our own experience is part of the journey toward holiness.

The growing body of psychological knowledge can be great help in gaining insight into the self. More and more directors of individual retreats use the Enneagram or the Meyers-Briggs Type Indicator to guide retreatants toward a deeper understanding of their own unique path toward holiness. Such instruments, in spite of their limitations, can be a great help in reflecting on our reactions and responses to our experience. They teach us how to "include" the emotional side of our personality in our prayers and meditations. Our experience has its own unique side. It is valuable all by itself, before it is weighed against some one else's experience. The more we know about ourselves, the more secure we will feel in trusting our experience.

3) Another characteristic is the community dimension. Vati-

can II' s *Constitution on the Church* begins its chapter on "The People of God" with the clear statement that God has "willed to make men holy and save them, not as individuals without any bond or link between them, but rather to make them into a people who might acknowledge him and serve him in holiness."[30] Of course, there are many kinds of community—family, professional, religious, and ecclesial. Since the *Constitution on the Church* places the people of God before hierarchy, it has become easier to affirm the primacy of the community of the baptized, whatever the historical form that community may take. Those who hold office in the church are first of all believers and members of the community of believers. And community remains the first ecclesial reality. The truth is that after we are baptized into a community there is no going it alone on the road to holiness. We become holy together or we do not become holy at all.

The ministry of building a Christian community is more important in our contemporary society than ever before. Fr. Jerome O' Connor describes our situation well:

> Loneliness is endemic. The legitimate fear of being used or abused produces a fear of involvement. People can be robbed on the streets in broad daylight and no one will go to their assistance. People refuse to make friends with the people in the next house or apartment because there may be demands that they do not wish to meet. Doors are always locked....[31]

It is of course impossible to think about growth toward holiness without being sensitive to the loneliness and alienation in today' s world.

The Christian community, anointed by the Spirit in baptism, is actually the "sacrament" that sanctifies. "The Christian community preexists the members who belong to it, and it is the community which makes them what they are by empowering them to move from "death" to "life."[32] The holiness, enfleshed in the community, nourishes the individual cells of the members. Just as an individual cell cannot live apart from the body, so an individual simply cannot grow apart from the believing community. To attempt to grow in holiness apart from the body is the worst kind of folly.

It may help to view the Christian community as a community of the priesthood of all believers. Then we can ask, what is the content of that priesthood of the believers? We would have to answer that this common priesthood includes an empowerment for:

1) direct access to God without the need for priestly mediation; 2) offering and sacrifice of one' s self in loving worship to God in the world, in the midst of everyday life; ...3) performance of, and full participation in, baptism, the Lord' s supper, and forgiveness of sins; and 4) sharing in the mediating work of Christ between God and the world by revealing the hidden works of God and making effective his acts of power, and between the world and God by prayer for and service of one's fellow human beings.[33]

4) A fourth characteristic of growth toward holiness is a reverence for its diverse expressions or incarnations. The church has always believed in different spiritualities. In the treasury of our tradition we find Cistercian, Franciscan, Benedictine, Dominican, and Jesuit spiritualities. And within these religious orders we find different, individual forms of each order' s spiritual tradition. The church, in the celebration of its saints, gratefully remembers the active, contemplative, and mystical expressions of holiness. As there are many different stars in the heavens reflecting the same light, so there are many different spiritualities reflecting the one holiness of Christ.

Different authors have discussed the possibility that there is indeed one kind of spirituality for clerics and another for lay persons. Fr. John Staudenmaier, reflecting on the relationship between faith and technology, has been presented as favoring a distinct lay spirituality. However, as we move away from the clerical caste system, more and more laity will find themselves agreeing with Leonard Doohan: "If there is no such thing as spirituality of the priest or the religious—and it seems we are in practice arriving at that conclusion—then certainly there is no such thing as a spirituality of the laity."[34] After discussing the arguments pro and con, Elizabeth Dreyer concludes "that we need a lay spirituality for the present time, but that we look forward to the time when this would not longer be necessary."[35] Dreyer believes that the hierarchical structure of the church may create this need for a distinct lay spirituality; lay people still need to maintain their own identity and guard against an artificial clericalization. I suspect that many lay people agree that spirituality is not yet free from the heavy influence of the centuries of dominance of monastic and clerical models.

5) As growth toward holiness moves into ministry, there will be a greater need for a fifth characteristic: compassion. As we pursue holiness we become more aware of the distance between the broken human condition and the wholeness to which all are called. Jesus had compassion on the multitudes. His heart went out in pity for the people—the blind, the crippled, the hungry. Holiness will begin to feel the hurt and pain of the human pilgrimage. But this compassion is not merely a question of suffering with those who are wounded and burdened by the evils of this world. The compassion of holiness includes a vision of wholeness:

> Compassion as a form of innermost vision not only perceives and interprets wholeness, but it creatively breathes wholeness. In this sense, the mystical tradition is leading us to say that compassion acts as the contemplative breath of apostolic spirituality! Compassion brings a vision that breathes, speaks, moves and embraces personhood. Truly, it becomes the vitality for journeying with all who suffer![36]

When compassion springs from a vision of wholeness it will provide a real healing context. It will inspire hope where there is despair. It will also avoid the danger of falling into pity.

While spirituality has many diverse expressions, we can, nevertheless, identify certain norms common to all its various forms and incarnations. In practice it is not easy to distinguish a *norm* from a *characteristic*. But norms serve as a foundation for holiness whereas characteristics begin to identify its outward expression. Without pretending to be exhaustive, I feel we can highlight at least four norms or principles for growth in the spiritual life.

1) The first norm is the *centrality of the Christ event* in the church and in our personal lives. In this norm Paul is our unfailing model: "...Christ will be honored in my body, whether by life or by death. For to me to live is Christ, and to die is gain" (Phil. 1:20-21). "And he died for all, that those who live, might live no longer for themselves but for him who for their sake died and was raised" (2 Cor. 5:15). "For while we live we are always being given up to death for Jesus sake, so that the life of Jesus may be manifested in our mortal flesh. So death is at work in us, but life in you" (2 Cor.4:11-12).

There can be no growth in holiness, no ministry in the church, that does not get its life, its strength, its inspiration from Christ Jesus. Whatever is separated from him becomes mere activism, pragmatism, or Pelagianism. Growth in the spiritual life will forever remain growth in the Lord. Anything else is nothing more than a grinding of wheels. We say it every Sunday in the third eucharistic prayer: "All life, all holiness, comes from you, through your son, Jesus Christ our Lord, by the working of the Holy Spirit."

To take the Christ event seriously is to believe that he is ready to work in us to overcome evil, whatever its form. It is to believe wholeheartedly in his transforming power. It is to lean on him utterly. It is to offer ourselves as his servants and then to see with his eyes, to speak with his tongue, and to serve with his hands. That may sound a little unreal, even mystical. But the Scriptures tell us "that' s where it's at" in this business of growing in holiness.

2) But before we can "put on Christ," we have to have a *metanoia,* a conversion, a change of heart. And that is the second norm of the spiritual life: *to be disposed to an ongoing conversion.* It's the law of the Gospel: "...The kingdom of God is at hand: repent...," that is, change your mind, your heart, your attitude (Mark 1:15). The first step in the spiritual life is not to set up a neat system of spiritual exercises, like a physical fitness program. The first step is an inner change of heart that opens the door to Christ and lets him take over. It is an honest to good-

ness admission of our own frailty and sinfulness and of our utter impoverishment without him. Again, Paul is our model: "...for three days he was without sight...and immediately something like scales fell from his eyes and he regained his sight" (Acts 9:9 and 18). Then he became the Lord's chosen instrument.

3) The third norm of the spiritual life is *vision*. It means to have the mind of Christ, to have a picture of the whole—the past, the present, and the future. Especially the future. It is this vision of the future that engenders hope. And hope is optimistic. It is contagious. It kindles energy in the hearts of all those who begin to share the Christian vision. Nobody has said it better than Paul:

> ...We rejoice in our hope of sharing the glory of God. More than that, we rejoice in our sufferings, knowing that suffering produces endurance, and endurance produces character, and character produces hope, and hope does not disappoint us, because God' s love has been poured into our hearts through the Holy Spirit who has been given to us (Rom. 5:2-5).

Christians never forget that it is by God's great mercy that they have "been born anew to a living hope through the resurrection of Jesus Christ from the dead..." (1 Peter 1:3). It is because Christians cling to a firm hope that the future belongs to God that they are able to "bring samples of the ultimate future into the pain of the present."[37] For this reason too, they can "proclaim and pioneer the future of the world within the horizon of faith in God' s coming kingdom."[38]

4) The fourth norm is *prayer*. Husband and wife will not grow in love and knowledge unless they communicate with each other. So, too, the Christian will not grow in love of Christ without constant dialogue with him. It is a dialogue that speaks, listens, and shares in a very intimate way. It is a dialogue that brings about change and growth. Because prayer is an expression of the mystery of the human person, it takes many forms. Now it will be a shout of praise and joy; then it will be tears of sorrow and repentance. Now it will be a song of love and thanksgiving; then it will be a cry of demand and petition.

In the Catholic church, of course, all prayer reaches its fulfillment and its earthly perfection in the celebration of the community liturgy. As noted earlier, there is no Lone Ranger holiness. Christians will grow in holiness only insofar as they are an organic part of a worshiping Christian community. They grow in a living partnership with a specific community or they will soon not grow at all. Vatican II restated the normativeness of the liturgy:

> ...the liturgy is the summit toward which the activity of the church is directed; it is also the fount from which all her power flows. For the goal of apostolic endeavor is that all who are sons of God by faith and baptism should take part in the sacrifice and eat the Lord's Supper.[39]

Just as husband and wife discover their identity as husband and wife in communion and conversation with each other, so we discover our identity as Christians in our communion and conversation with Christ and with our worshiping community. This worshiping community is a channel of the Lord's holiness to us. Even though holiness remains the Lord's holiness, the worshiping community, as already mentioned, is a vehicle or sacrament of that holiness.

Participating in the liturgy is not the only way to holiness, but it is by far the most important one. We're used to instant rice and instant coffee, so we often expect instant holiness. However, growth in the spiritual life, just like growth in human and vegetable life, will be slow and gradual. It will take many years filled with new starts and half-starts, stumblings, failings, successes, and half-successes. In fact, growth in holiness will not be complete until the coming of the Kingdom of God in fullness. Then, and only then, will there be a "new heaven and a new earth." "And night shall be no more; they need no light of lamp or sun, for the Lord God will be their light, and they shall reign for ever and ever" (Rv. 22:5).

Some Practical Applications

Before leaving this chapter, I would like to offer some practical suggestions for those serving in the various ministries on the parish council. First, seek out a spiritual director and go to her or him on a regular basis. We simply cannot afford to ignore the wisdom of centuries of experience in this regard. While spiritual writers may disagree on various points and various methods proposed for growth in holiness, we find universal agreement about the need for spiritual direction. It is a real tragedy that many lay persons still feel spiritual direction is reserved to clerics or religious. Fortunately, more and more religious women are offering spiritual direction to lay persons. But we have a long way to go.

Selecting a spiritual director requires prayer and discernment. Not everyone has that gift. Spiritual direction is different from the ordinary human process by which people guide others. It has been carefully defined by Rev. John Sheets:

Spiritual direction, then, is the way that a person or institution fosters the life and the direction of the Holy Spirit, bringing the various aspects of a person's life into a convergence, freeing us from whatever gets in the way of the direction of the Spirit in our lives. All spiritual direction, then, in the human sense, lives in a kind of apprenticeship to the Holy Spirit. "We are God's work of art" (Eph. 2:10), as Paul puts it. Human spiritual directors are in some way instruments, or disciples, of the main artist, who is the Holy Spirit. Like some of the famous painters who have a school of disciples, the Holy Spirit has many disciples who are engaged in the one work of art, which is to change us into the image of Christ.[40]

The foundation of good spiritual direction will always be the truth. Knowledge of sound doctrine and sound teaching should be an important criterion for selection of a director. There is no substitute for the wisdom handed down to us through the gospel and the teaching of the church. Good intentions, however pious, are not enough. Spiritual direction is a ministry and the church does not let just anyone, without the necessary qualifications, minister to the people of God. Just as we do not entrust our physical health to just anyone, so too we cannot entrust our spiritual welfare to just anyone.

Each person serving as a parish councilor is responsible for formulating a personal spirituality that includes both private and communal prayer, reflection on the word of God, and participation in the sacramental life of the parish. Unless councilors are serious about efforts to grow in holiness, they will not be able to see the importance of providing many opportunities for faith development for the rest of the parish; nor will they contribute to the development of a council spirituality. Fortunately, as a result of the RENEW program (and other spiritual renewal programs), which many dioceses have experienced over the last few years, a large number of Catholics have become interested in their own faith development and that of others.

As noted in Chapter 7, councils have to recognize their need for shared prayer and reflection, based on Scripture, at every meeting. The Archdiocese of Milwaukee recommends that their councils spend at least one-half hour of each meeting in this prayer and formation, not only to help council members themselves grow in holiness, but also to create a strong spiritual foundation for choosing directions for the parish that are consistent with God's will for the Christian community.

Shared prayer is sometimes difficult for Catholics, so the council may want to take advantage of the many fine resources available. (See list at the end of this book.) Each council member could take turns preparing and leading shared prayer.

Councilors also need faith formation and development through a deeper knowledge of Scripture and some study of the Vatican II documents (especially the *Constitution on the Church* and the *Church in the Modern World)* as well as the more recent documents such as *Economic Justice for All*, the U.S. Bishops' pastoral on the economy. They need a renewed appreciation for the Catholic tradition and teaching in its fullness.

The parish council, as a partnership in the Lord, will grow in holiness only when time and effort are devoted to this growth on a regular basis. For this reason, councilors would do well to celebrate the liturgy together now and then. This will be a time for healing whatever hurts and misunderstandings develop during the council discussions. But it is also a time to celebrate the real feeling of community that grows up among councilors because they share and minister together. The spirit of community and the spirit of the celebrations will spill over into the whole parish. The council's witness will be the spark that kindles renewal.

At least once a year, a council serious about its spiritual growth will schedule a day of reflection and prayer or overnight retreat, preferably away from the parish and its interruptions. (See the appendix for a retreat outline.)

Once councilors have made spiritual growth part of their council's permanent agenda, it is time for the council to assume responsibility for its growth in all areas. And that means that the council will, as a matter of course, constantly evaluate itself and recognize its accountability to the broader parish, the diocese, and the civic community. The next chapter will offer some pointers to help the council sharpen its evaluative skills. But first, let's take along a poem-prayer for holiness from *The Seafarer*: [41]

Let us determine where our homeland might be,
And let us think how we might travel there;
And let us try to make that journey
To the lasting joys of eternity,
Where life is lived in the love of God,
The bliss of Heaven. Wherefore thank the Holy One For
that he glorified us, Eternal God,
Lord of wonder, world without end. Amen.

Notes

1. Quoted by David O'Brien in *The Renewal of American Catholicism* (New York: Oxford University Press, 1972), frontispiece.

2. *Mutual Ministry* (New York: Seabury Press, 1977), p. 105.

3. *Ibid.*, pp. 105-06.

4. *Catholic Identity after Vatican II* (Chicago: Loyola University Press, 1985), pp. 35-36.

5. *The Shape of the Church to Come* (New York: Seabury Press, 1974) p. 82.

6. *The Renewed Parish in Today' s Church* (Liguori, Mo.: Liguori Publications,

1976), pp. 17-19.

7. *The Spirituality of the Middle Ages* (New York: Desclee,1968), p. 274.

8. Elizabeth Dreyer, "Tradition and Lay Spirituality: Problems and Possibilities," *Spirituality Today* 39 (Autumn 1987), p. 204.

9. Leonard Doohan, *The Lay-Centered Church* (Minneapolis, Minn.: Winston Press, 1984), p. 98.

10. Elizabeth Dreyer, "Tradition and Lay Spirituality," *Spirituality Today* 39 (Autumn, 1987), p. 204.

11. *Vatican II* (Northport, N.Y.:Costello, 1975), Austin Flannery, ed., p. 396.

12. *The Spirituality of the Middle Ages, op. cit.* p. 273.

13. *Vatican II, op. cit.* p. 412.

14. *Catholic Identity After Vatican II, op. cit.* p. 80.

15. "Prayer, Pain and Community," *Review for Religious*, 46, No. 1 (January-February 1987), p. 78.

16. *The Emergence of the Catholic Tradition* (Chicago: Chicago University Press, 1971), p. 132.

17. "Tradition and Lay Spirituality," *Spirituality Today*, 39, no. 3, (Autumn, 1987), p.205.

18. (Los Angeles, California: University of California Press, 1985), p. 142.

19. Elizabeth Dreyer, "Tradition and Lay Spirituality: Problems and Possibilities," *Spirituality Today*, 39, no. 3, (Autumn 1987) pp. 201-02.

20. *The Lay-Centered Church* (Minneapolis, Minn.: Winston, 1984), pp.92-102.

21. Quoted by Leonard Doohan in *The Lay-Centered Church, op. cit.* p. 100.

22. *Ibid.*, p. 101.

23. *Constitution on the Church, op. cit.* p. 401.

24. *The Constitution on the Church, The Documents of Vatican II* (New York: Herder and Herder, 1966), p. 66.

25. *The Lay-Centered Church, op. cit.* pp. 105-11.

26. *Ibid.*, p. 109.

27. For a very helpful comparison between Fall/Redemption and Creation-Centered spirituality, see Matthew Fox, *Original Blessing* (Santa Fe, New Mexico: Bear & Company, 1983), p. 316.

28. "Tradition and Lay Spirituality," *Spirituality Today* 39, No. 3, (Autumn 19, p. 204.

29. *Ibid.*, p. 204.

30. *Vatican II, op.cit.* p. 359.

31. *Becoming Human Together* (Wilmington, Delaware: Michael Glazier, Inc.

1977), p.139.

32. *Ibid.*, p. 197.

33. Thomas Myott, "The Ecclesial Base for Lay Spirituality," *Spirituality Today*, 32, no. 3, (Sept., 1980), p. 200.

34. *Op. cit.* p. 23.

35. "Spirituality for Laity," *Spirituality Today* 38, (Autumn, 1986), p. 207.

36. Sister Gerald Mary Harrison, "Compassion: Vision of Wholeness," *Review for Religious* 46, no. 5 (Sept.-Oct., 1987), p. 749.

37. Carl Braaten, *The Future of God* (New York: Harper & Row, 1969), p. 119.

38. *Ibid.*, p. 109.

39. *The Constitution on the Sacred Liturgy*, Austin Flannery, O.P., ed. (Northport, New York: Costello Publishing Co.), p.6.

40. "Spiritual Direction in the Church," *Review for Religious* 46 No. 4, (July-August 1987), pp. 507-08.

41. *The American Benedictine Review*, 38 (June 1987), p.126.

Sharing

1. Do you agree with Karl Rahner that we are "to a terrifying extent a spiritually lifeless church"? Why or why not?
2. How do you react to your own experience of the "warts" on the face of holy "mother" church?
3. Are any of the pitfalls to holiness listed in this chapter still evident in your own life?
4. Are you aware of any indications in your parish or your life that growth in holiness is a human achievement?
5. What is meant by "a flight into supernaturalism?"
6. Do you believe there is a distinct lay spirituality?
7. How do you react to Doohan's four trends in spirituality?
8. What is the role of community in your spiritual growth?
9. How do you apply the incarnation to your spirituality?
10. How do you feel about seeking out your own spiritual director?

CHAPTER 13

ACCOUNTABILITY AND EVALUATION

"This is how one should regard us, as servants of Christ and stewards of the mysteries of God. Moreover, it is required of stewards that they be found trustworthy" (1 Cor. 4:1-2). If councilors are truly ministers (Chapter 3), then they are accountable for the quality of their ministry. The ministers must render an account of their stewardship. At election time politicians are held accountable by the public for their public service. At the end of the school year, teachers are evaluated for their teaching. Before the renewal of their contracts, civil service employees are rated by efficiency reports. The assumption is that the public has a right to receive quality service from its public servants.

In the church, when we assemble for the sacrament of reconciliation, we examine our conscience. When we gather together to celebrate the liturgy, we confess publicly "to almighty God and to our brothers and sisters that we have sinned...in what we have done and in what we have failed to do." As Catholics, we are quite comfortable in admitting before the church and the world that our ministry isn't perfect, that it's still flawed by the mystery of evil. It should come as no surprise, then, that councilors should be held accountable for their ministry. Since parish pastoral councils serve within a system of relationships, it makes sense that they should be held accountable within that system. Councilors, therefore, are accountable to the Lord, to the diocesan church, to the parish, to the civic community, and, finally, to one another.

1) *Councilors are accountable to the Lord.* They are called to be faithful disciples. In baptism they have vowed themselves to their Lord. If they are not faithful to that commitment, their service to the church will be just about useless.

2) *As discussed in Chapter 6, councilors are accountable to the diocesan church.* The parish lives as one cell within the larger body of the diocesan church. It lives in communion with that body through the life-giving bonds of faith, morals, liturgy, and law. It expresses its union with the diocesan church by sharing the same Lord, the same word, the same bread, the same cup, the same baptism. It needs to nourish and foster that unity both for its own life and for that of the diocesan church. Unity is not automatic.

The parish, as a smaller cell within the larger body, has a twofold responsibility to the diocesan church. First, it has to be open to receive from the diocesan church guidance and the gifts of discernment, which are the fruits of its larger faith experience. The diocesan church, in the normal course of events, just has more to share. If it is really in touch with the faith of all its parishes, it has a broader faith experience to share with each individual parish. If it is really in touch with its own tradition, it has a longer experience to share. For its own good, the parish needs to own its dependence on the life of the larger diocesan church. And for some American parishes, that is not easy to do. Often they suffer from a narrow parochial attitude.

The parish also needs to do its share in building up the diocesan church. It needs to share with the diocesan church the fruits of its preaching, the fruits of its sacramental life, the fruits of its own discernment. Therefore, the parish needs to be present at diocesan workshops, conferences, and assemblies to witness to its own unique faith experience; it needs to report to the chancery office and to diocesan offices and departments by writing letters regarding the strengths and weaknesses of diocesan programs; it needs to share with the diocesan church the many gifts and ministries the Spirit has given to it in response to its faith; it needs to take the pulse of the grassroots and report its findings to the diocesan church.

Councils are not showing accountability to the diocesan church when they take up a petition to keep their pastor when the diocesan church needs his unique ministry elsewhere. The priest is ordained for the diocese, not for the parish. No congregation acquires ownership over the ministering gifts given to it. They remain the Spirit' s gifts to be used where they build up the church most. If Paul' s first congregation (Seleucia) had taken up a petition to keep him, he would never have been able to evangelize the rest of the Gentile world. His congregations were, of course, founded on Jesus Christ (1 Cor. 3,11), not on himself. The parish council builds up the diocesan church by offering responsible criticism, by reading the signs of the times, and by discerning the changing pastoral needs. Councils will not always find it easy to offer feedback to the diocesan church. Some dioceses may not be disposed to receive upbuilding input "from below."

3) Councilors are accountable as servants to their fellow parishioners, the "brothers and sisters." The council does not exist for itself, but for the whole parish. It is called to touch, to engage the faith of all the parishioners and then to challenge them to become holier and more responsive to the Spirit. Councilors show themselves accountable to the parishioners when they serve as models for them, when they keep in touch with their opinions and when they report back to them. The relationship of council to parish is expressed rather well in the Guidelines for the Archdiocese of Detroit:

As a group of Christian leaders, the parish council should be a witness to the parish that barriers can be broken and separation healed by men and women of patience and good will. As members become a warm, loving, caring group themselves, they are a model of what the parish might be. By their unity with one another, as well as by their decisions, they gradually influence the people of the parish to make worship and service to people a priority in their individual lives, as well as the goal of the entire community of faith....

It is important that the council members know what the people are thinking and feeling on the issues of their lives and of their parish. The effort to remain informed and in touch with the people must be a continuous one, because in a fast-moving society, the opinions and feelings of parishioners are also changing quickly....

...The parish council as a leadership group cannot be limited in its action to the present views of parishioners. Neither, however, can they afford to become an elite group passing decisions down from on high, with little or no regard for the feelings and views of the parishioners. The basic characteristic of leadership in a Christian community is not power but service.... Every effort must be made to involve parishioners in the decisions that affect their own growth.[1]

So long as the councilors make no effort to invite parishioners to internalize the decisions of the council, they run the risk of becoming an elite power group. They may be using the parishioners (especially their money) to achieve their own hidden agendas. They may engage in political maneuvering to gain their own ends, but they are no longer ministering to build up the faith of the community they are called to serve. They may consider many issues and fund all kinds of programs, but they have lost the parishioners. Councilors also need to be accountable to the parish staff. They need to work collaboratively with the education director, business manager, liturgist, pastor, and associate pastor. If the councilors' ministry is going to advance the mission of the parish, it will have to be carried out in relationship to all the full-time ministries. Effective coordination of the parish ministries is everyone's responsibility.

4) *Councilors are accountable to the civic community.* The church exists for the world, not for itself. Therefore, the world can demand that the church's actions conform to the church's words, especially *the* Word. In practice, the council becomes accountable to the world by being accountable to the civic community. If the council professes ecumenism, it needs to relate to the other churches in its community. If it professes to feed the hungry, to clothe the naked, etc., then it must do these in its own

community. If it professes to minister to the civic community, then it must listen and respond to the city council, the United Way, the public school board, etc. The council does this by being present at their meetings, by writing letters to the newspaper regarding current civic issues, etc. That's one of many ways the council renders an account of its stewardship under the gospel.

The council, as leaders of the parish, must also be accountable to the civil law prevailing in the community.

5) *The council members are accountable to one another.* They need to support one another in their mutual ministry. They (and not just the chairperson) need to hold one another accountable for commitments they have made to meetings, programs, and committees. They need to be prompt at meetings and do their homework. They need to call absentees to offer help when they are sick, to offer rides when they need one, to visit them when they become discouraged. They need to agree never to do alone what can be done with another. By personal example, they have to encourage openness, honesty, and trust in all of the council's activities. They also need to be accountable to one another for growth in faith and holiness. If council members have no concern for the growth of all, the council will soon become static, sterile, dead. To relate to a living cell in the body of Christ is to accept some responsibility for its growth. For this reason, council members need to ask hard questions about both the process and the content of meetings; otherwise the council will drift into stagnation.

Removals and Resignations

It is to be hoped that in a Christian community, concerned for the growth of all, it would be rare to need to remove a person from membership on the council. However, councilors are not exempt from human frailty. If a councilor promotes factionalism, divides the council, or otherwise obstructs its purpose, it is only fair to both the parish and the other council members to consider removal. "Just cause" should be cited, i.e., missing several consecutive council meetings without excuse, physical or mental incapacity, losing good reputation, etc. Usually, the member whose removal is proposed is given the opportunity for a hearing at a closed session of the council. A two-thirds vote of the total council membership is generally required for removal.

It is also wise to provide in a council document a procedure for resignations. A council member may resign by filing a written resignation with the secretary or chairperson. Vacancies on the council are usually filled for the unexpired term by the presently eligible person who received the next highest number of votes.

Reconsideration and Appeal

In spite of all efforts to come to a prayerful discernment on an issue at council meetings, there may be a time when the pastor and the other members of the council reach an impasse. In such cases, many councils follow a process of reconsideration and appeal. The pastor withholds ratification and asks the council to reconsider its decision, giving them the reasons. The action is suspended until the next regular monthly meeting. If at that time, no agreement can be reached, an appeal is made to the diocese, which will determine the disposition of the matter. Either the pastor or the council members may present such an appeal. The Diocese of Harrisburg makes this process explicit:

Whenever the pastor cannot accept or implement an action, policy or program approved by the council, he may appeal to the bishop of the diocese for conciliation on the issue. Whenever the pastor chooses (for reasons other than conflict with church doctrine, church law, or diocesan policy) not to implement an action, policy or program approved by a two-thirds majority vote of the parish council, this same majority may appeal to the bishop of the diocese for conciliation of the issue.

A parish council of mature Christians, however, should be able to determine when mediation by the bishop is a real need. It obviously should be a matter of widespread pastoral concern, and not on the level of personality clashes or church decor. Additionally, when a council decides to seek diocesan mediation, it should be able to do so without fear that such action will harm its future growth.

The ultimate goal should be not to know who is right, but what is best for the parish and its people.[2]
Full and frank communication between the pastor and the council is essential. An appeal to the diocese (usually the bishop) should be used only as a last resort; every effort should be made to resolve the conflict on a parish level through mediation process.

Developing Council Guidelines

One of the ways the parish council expresses its own uniqueness, as well as its accountability to the diocesan church, is to develop a document (guidelines or a constitution and by-laws) that sets forth the purpose of the council and the way it will function in the service to parish life.

There is no such thing as a constitution or guidelines designed to fit all parishes with their diverse size, needs, culture, and history. In fact, it might be good pastoral practice for councils to operate with simple general guidelines or understanding until they have gained some experience. In this way, they would not be bound by rigid or artificial provisions that don't really serve their particular needs. Whatever document then emerges would truly be the fruit of a unique discernment process and the actual pastoral experience of the council and parish.

Insofar as constitutions reflect a continuity with the overall mission of the church universal and the norms or policies of the diocese, and insofar as they flow from the larger cultural experience, they will be the same. Insofar as they reflect a unique incarnation of a church in a specific place with its own particular needs, they will be different. It is quite important that councils be able to own and internalize their own constitution/guidelines. It is even more important that they evaluate them regularly and that they feel free enough to amend them when they no longer serve the gospel and the changing needs of the parish. Constitutions are not ends in themselves, but only means to an end. Therefore, they should not hinder, but actively build up the parish community as it carries out the church's mission.

Let's look at the parts of a council document and the information that might be included:[3]

Mission Statement: How do we understand parish as a faith community? Who are we? What is our mission as parish? How do we localize that mission? Where are we going as a parish? What is unique about how we live out our mission?

Name: By what name is the council to be known? Where is the parish located?

Purposes: What are the basic purposes of the council, as representative of the parish, and consistent with the mission of the church? What does the parish want to do by means of the council?

Scope: What kinds of policy decisions does the council make on behalf of the parish? What is the scope of its authority and mission? How will the council handle reconsideration and appeal?

Membership: What members will the council have? What is the term of office? What are the requirements and preparation for service? Who may vote for cuncil members? How will vacancies and removals be handled?

Officers: What officers will the council have? What term will they serve? How will they be chosen by the council? What are their duties?

Orientation/Nomination/Election: What orientation procedure for nominees will be followed? When, how and by whom are elective members to be nominated and elected? What are the eligibility requirements for nominees?

Relationship of Pastor to Council: How will the pastor preside at the council?

Meetings and Quorum: When and where will the council met (regular and special meetings)? How many members constitute a quorum?

Operating Method: What method will the council use to make decisions?

Committees: What standing committees will be established by the council? What will their purpose, scope, and responsibilities be? How will members be selected and approved by the council? How will chairpersons or liaisons be chosen? What will the term of service be?

Evaluation and Amendments: When will the constitution be evaluated? How will the constitution be amended by the parish? Approved by the diocese?

Date: Date of ratification or amendment.

Some dioceses approve or certify such documents periodically (every 3 to 5 years is usual) following the evaluation of the council itself. Others require a "charter of accountability" to be filed with the diocese. Certification or approval by the diocese can be a very positive experience. It could mean that the bishop makes a firm commitment to support the parish council. It could mean that the council would not be dissolved upon a pastor's whim or when he moves on to another parish. Certification by the diocese, therefore, can be a positive commitment to the continuity of the council. In this way, council members will feel better about investing themselves in the council. Certification or approval should be a flexible process, however, looking more to the spirit than to the letter of the law. It ought to allow for a certain diversity of council structure, but also a unity with the mission and priorities of the diocesan church. The diocese can rightly expect a core committee system, for example, education/ formation, spiritual life and worship, Christian service, administrative services. Certification or approval can also build a more positive linkage with the diocesan church and so deliver the council from its often parochial and congregationalist tendencies. The diocese thus becomes a support system for the council in a very real sense. While the document (constitution, guidelines, or charter) is essentially the *council's* document, it is a good idea to submit it to all the parishioners for ratification and when amendments are necessary, both to educate them and to build up a two-way relationship of responsibility with them. It is through the council that they express their voice in parish affairs. Rather than simply voting on it, however, it might be worthwhile to have an open parish meeting to offer the parishioners ample opportunity to discuss and to react to its provisions. Approval might take a little longer that way, but because of improved parish understanding and cooperation, it would be worth it in the long run.

Parish ratification could also be handled in somewhat the same manner as a council election. It could be given out to those attending the liturgies on one or two designated Sundays with the provision that input and approval be expressed within two weeks. The importance of the matter may be emphasized in the homilies on those Sundays and in the parish bulletin.

Evaluation

If council members are going to render an account of their ministry, they have to get in the habit of evaluating their own services. They have to measure their behavior and their activities against certain criteria they have agreed to apply to themselves. The first criterion is the council's document (constitution/guidelines) with its mission statement, which has already been discussed. A second set of evaluation criteria could come from any goal-setting process in which the council engages. These could be applied to the council and its committees.

After the council has reflected honestly on these criteria, it might examine its conscience regarding some of the more common faults of parish councils, such as:

• power/status seeking
• putting personal desires before parish needs and goals
• a lack of accountability to the parishioners
• a lack of honesty and personal support among the members
• not doing the homework before doing the talking
• inadequate grasp of gospel values
• poor relationship with the staff or committees.

A parish council might evaluate itself during a celebration of the sacrament of reconciliation. It might also take some time at the end of a meeting to reflect on some of the following questions, either individually or as a group:

• How do we relate to the neighboring Catholic parishes? to the civic community? to the churches of other faiths? to the diocesan church?

• What are we doing to build up unity between our parish and our diocese?

- Do we foster and encourage a positive attitude toward the diocesan church?
- Have we groused about the past rather than looking to and planning for the future?
- In our reports, do we give credit to those who help in parish council projects?
- Have we tried to become ministers with a broad vision?
- Are we content with treading water when we should be swimming faster and farther and deeper every year?
- Are we a Pentecost people or are we only bookkeepers?
- Have we considered an open parish forum? Or are we satisfied with a comfortable isolation in which our fellow parishioners almost never share?
- Do we take the initiative or do we simply sit back and wait for marching orders?
- Are we really going about the business of pastoral planning? If not, why not?[4]

A thorough self-evaluation will reveal both strengths and deficiencies in various aspects of the council's life. A maturing council will, of course, accept the challenge and deal with the deficiencies as part of its own continuing program of renewal. It may even design and administer its own evaluative instruments.[5] Self-examination and fraternal correction have been part of the Catholic tradition for centuries.

Notes

1. *Directives and Guidelines for Parish Councils* (Archdiocese of Detroit), p. 9, 10.
2. *Called to Serve: Parish Council Policy and Guidelines* (Dioc. of Harrisburg).
3. Adapted from guidelines of dioceses of Milwaukee and Nashville.
4. The last six questions have been adapted from Robert G. Howes "Parish Councils: Do We Care?" *America* (November 27, 1976), pp. 371-72.
5. See appendix for council and committee evaluation forms.

Sharing:
1. What kind of document would be best for our council? Why?
2. Use some of the above questions at each council meeting during the year. How can the council improve in these ways?

POSTSCRIPT

Now more than twenty years beyond Vatican II, we are in a sort of "between times" of church existence. What will happen to parishes and to councils in the next decade? Into the twenty-first century?

The parish, no doubt, will continue to be important in the lives of people for spiritual nurturance, faith challenges, and belonging. Whether it will become more or less relevant to people's daily lives depends on how well it grapples with their life issues and with the major traumas of our times: hunger, unemployment, violence, the alienation of people (especially young people) from an active life of faith, the disintegration of the family, etc. The parish will also need to address such developments as the decrease in clergy; the increase of lay ministry, especially that of women; the formation of active grass-roots faith and action groups that promise to transform the parish radically; the continued need for collaboration in parish life and more effective stewardship of the gifts people offer to the church.

What kind of council will be needed for the future parish? How will the structure and style of leadership change as the parish changes and grows? It's possible that a future council will be made up of leaders from small groups ("base communities") as is the case in the church of Africa. We invite your insights and ideas. There are exciting and challenging times ahead as we continue to work together for the coming of the Kingdom. God's presence in our activity reassures us and calls us forth into the future.

(Read Paul's prayer to his readers: Phil. 1:3-6 and 9-11.)

RESOURCES FOR
PARISH PASTORAL COUNCILS

Books

Leadership in a Successful Parish, Thomas Sweetser, S.J. and Carol Holden Wisniewski, Harper & Row, 1987.

Successful Parishes, Thomas Sweetser, S.J., Winston, 1986.

The Emerging Laity: Returning Leadership to the Community of Faith, James and Evelyn Whitehead, Doubleday, 1987.

Sharing Wisdom, Mary Benet McKinney, O.S.B., Tabor Publishing, 1986.

Volunteers and Ministry, William J. Bannon and Suzanne Donovan, Paulist, 1983.

Vatican Council II: Conciliar and Post Conciliar Documents,. edited by Austin Flannery, O.P., Costello Publishing.

Servant Leadership, Robert K. Greenleaf, Paulist, 1977.

Church Meetings That Matter, Philip A. Anderson, Pilgrim Press, 1987.

How To Make Meetings Work, Michael Doyle and David Straus, Jove, 1982.

How to Mobilize Church Volunteers, Marlene Wilson, Augsburg Publishing, 1983.

Catholic Contributions: Sociology and Policy, Andrew Greeley and William McManus, Thomas More, 1987.

Answers for Parish Councillors, William Rademacher, Twenty-Third Publications, 1981.

Ecumenism: Striving for Unity Amid Diversity, Twenty-Third Publications, with Archdiocese of Milwaukee, 1985.

Pilgrim Church, William J. Bausch, Twenty-Third Publications, 1977 and 1981.

The Christian Parish: Whispers of the Risen Christ, William J. Bausch, Twenty-Third Publications, 1981.

The Holy Use of Money: Personal Finances in Light of Christian Faith, John C. Haughey, S.J., Doubleday, 1986.

Community of Faith: Models and Strategies for Developing Christian Communities, James and Evelyn Whitehead, Seabury, 1982.

Prayer Services for Parish Meetings and *Gathering Prayers*, Debra Hintz, Twenty-Third Publications, 1983 and 1986.

Weeds Among the Wheat, Discernment: Where Prayer and Action Meet, Thomas H. Green, S.J., Ave Maria, 1984.

Psalms Anew, Nancy Schrech, OSF and Maureen Leach, OSF, St. Mary Press, 1987.

Catholic Identity After Vatican II, Frans Jozef von Beeck, S.J., Loyola Univ. Press, 1985.

The American Catholic People: Their Beliefs, Practices and Values, George Gallup, Jr. and Jim Castelli, Doubleday, 1987.

The Evangelizing Parish: Theologies and Strategies for Renewal, Patrick J. Brennan, Tabor, 1987.

The Emerging Parish, Joseph Gremillion and James Costello, Harper & Row, 1987.

Periodicals

Church, National Pastoral Life Center (quarterly), 299 Elizabeth St., New York, NY 10012.

Action Information, Alban Institute (monthly), 4125 Nebraska Ave., NW, Washington, DC 20016.

Today's Parish, Twenty-Third Publications, P.O. Box 180, Mystic, CT 06355.

Praying, NCR Publishing (bi-monthly), 115 E. Armour Blvd., P.O. Box 410335, Kansas City, MO 64141-0335.

Audiovisual Resources

The Parish: A People, A Mission, A Structure, slide presentation with discussion guide, Franciscan Publications, 1229 S. Santee, Los Angeles, CA 90015 (14 minutes).

The Ministry of the Parish Council, with Richard T. Lawrence, Archdiocese of Baltimore, Avis Media Services, 2813 N. Calvert St.,

Baltimore, MD 21218 (Videotape, VHS, one hour).

Parish Councils: Do We Need a New Approach?, National Pastoral Life Center (videotape, VHS [two hours]).

SCILS (Serving Christians in Leadership Series)—series of videotapes (VHS) designed to be used during the formation part of a council/ committee meeting to help members learn a skill; 20-35 minutes in length; materials for process outlined on the tapes are included. Topics covered: spiritual formation and leadership; making group decisions through a discernment process; the parish council as change agent; developing a parish mission statement; planning with committees; effective meetings; learning a conflict management strategy; creating an environment for consensus. Other videotapes are also available. Contact: Office for Stewardship and Lay Leadership, Archdiocese of Milwaukee, P.O. Box 2018, Milwaukee, WI 53201.

RESOURCES FOR COUNCIL COMMITTEES

The Parish Committee Member, Jack Buchner, Pastoral Arts Associates, Florida, 1986 (booklet).

Education Committees

To Teach as Jesus Did, A Pastoral Message on Catholic Education, N.C.C.B., 1972.

Sourcebook for Modern Catechetics, edited by Michael Warren, St. Mary Press, Winona, MN.

Sharing the Light of Faith, The National Catechetical Directory for Catholics of the U.S., U.S.C.C. Dept. of Education, Washington, D.C., 1979.

Leadership for Youth Ministry, Zeni Fox, Marisa Guerin, Brian Reynolds, John Roberto, St. Mary Press, Christian Bros. Publications.

Youth Ministry Alive: It Can Happen in Your Church, six-segment program by Brian Reynolds and John Roberto. A guide to planning a total youth ministry program based on the needs of the young people in your parish.

Catechist (periodical), Peter Li, Inc.

The Religion Teacher's Journal (periodical), Twenty-Third Publications.

Administrative Services - Financial Stewardship Committees

Improving Parish Management, George M. Williams, Twenty-Third Publications, 1983.

Creative Church Administration, Thomas Campbell and Gary Reierson, Westminster.

Stewardship: A Response to the Gift of Creation, Richard Waddell, Alban Institute, 1986.

Stewardship of Money: A Manual for Parishes, National Catholic Stewardship Council, 1 Columbia Pl., Albany, NY 12207.

Total Stewardship: The Christian Celebration of Life, 204 page manual outlining a 2-1/2 year program on stewardship of time, talent and treasure, National Catholic Conference for Total Stewardship, 3112 7th St., N.E., Washington, DC 20017.

Sharing Treasure, Time and Talent, A Parish Manual for Sacrificial Giving or Tithing, Joseph M. Champlin, Collegeville, Minn.: Liturgical Press, 1982.

The Center for Parish Development, 1448 E. 53 St., Chicago, IL 60615, offers resources and processes for parish stewardship development.

Parish Life and Evangelization Committees

How to Reach Out to Inactive Catholics, Rev. William McKee, C.SS.R., Liguori Publications, 1982.

Evangelization in the Modern World, popular summary of *Evangelii Nuntiandi*, available from Paulist Catholic Evangelization Center, 3031 Fourth St., N.E., Washington, DC 20017.

RCIA Resources: *Made, Not Born* and *A Journey in Faith* by Rev. Raymond Kemp, and *New Wine, New Wineskins* and *Exploring the RCIA* by Rev. James Dunning, Sadlier Series.

Ministries: Sharing God's Gifts, James B. Dunning, St. Mary's Press.

Many Hands: Making Volunteer Ministry Work, Cyndi Thero (3 audiocassettes #AA1678; 3-1/4 hours), Credence Cassettes, 115 E. Armour Blvd., P.O. Box 414291, Kansas City, MO 64141-4291.

National Council for Catholic Evangelization, P.O. Box 10525, Chicago, IL 60610-0525 (organization)—provides helpful evangelization resources for parishes and publishes a regular newsletter.

Spiritual Life and Worship Committees

Miryam of Nazareth, Ann Johnson, Ave Maria, 1984; *Miryam of Judah*, Ann Johnson, Ave Maria, 1987.

Prayers for the Domestic Church and *Pray Always*, Edward Hayes, Forest of Peace Books, 1981.

Preparing for Liturgy: A Theology and Spirituality, Austin Fleming,

Pastoral Press, 1985.

The Liturgy Documents: A Parish Resource, edited by Mary Ann Simcoe, Liturgy Training Publications, 1985 (includes many of the important documents on liturgy).

Liturgy Committee Basics: A No-Nonsense Guide, Thomas Baker and Frank Ferrone, Pastoral Press, 1985.

Christ Living Among His People: A Guide to Understanding and Celebrating the Liturgical Year, Robert L. Tuzik, FDLC, Washington, DC, 1984.

Goal Setting for Liturgy Committees, Stephanie Certain, Marty Mayer, Liturgy Training Publications, 1981.

How to Form a Parish Liturgy Board, Yvonne Cassa, Joanne Sanders, Liturgy Training Publications, 1987.

Wellsprings: A Book of Spiritual Exercises, Image Books (Doubleday), 1986.

Catechesis for Liturgy, Gilbert Ostdiek, Pastoral Press, Washington, DC, 1986.

Modern Liturgy Planning Guide, Resource Publications, San Jose, CA 1987.

Celebration, N.C.R. Publishing, P.O. Box 4093, Kansas City, MO 64141-4293 (periodical).

Weavings: A Journal of the Christian Spiritual Life, P.O. Box 189, Nashville, TN 37202 (periodical).

Pastoral Music, 225 Sheridan St., N.W. Washington, D.C. 20011 (periodical).

North American Liturgy Resources, 10802 N. 23 Ave., Phoenix, AZ 85029 and Pastoral Arts Associates, 642 N. Grandview Ave., Daytona Beach, FL 32018, produce excellent liturgical resources.

Social Ministry Committees

Thy Kingdom Come, Mary Elizabeth Clark, S.S.J., Paulist, 1986 (24-page prayer/reflection sessions for social concerns groups).

Works of Mercy, John B. Martin and Catherine Martin, Paulist with Archdiocese of Newark, 1984 (prayer and action suggestions).

Activism That Makes Sense: Congregations and Community Organization, Gregory F. Pierce, Paulist, 1984.

The Prophetic Parish, A Center for Peace and Justice, Dennis J. Geaney.

Confident and Competent: A Challenge for the Lay Church, William J.

Droel and Gregory F.A. Pierce, Ave Maria, 1987.

Economic Justice for All. Catholic Social Teaching and the U.S. Economy, U.S. Bishops' Pastoral, 1986—Office of Implementation, USCC.

Campaign for Human Development, USCC, 1312 Massachusetts Ave., N.W., Washington, DC 20005-4104—education materials.

What Should I Know About Economic Justice for All?—study/ reflection guide, English and Spanish, 1987.

To Campaign for Justice—study of the 1971 synod statement, "Justice in the World," 1982.

Religion in Politics: Church and Society, Bryan Hehir, 12 pp., 1985.

Poverty Profile, USA: In the Eighties, 51 pp.

Salt —10 times a year, 205 W. Monroe St., Chicago, IL 60606, Claretian, $10 (periodical).

Network, 806 Rhode Island Ave., N.E., Washington, D.C. 20018—membership in this organization gives access to excellent materials; publishes a fine handbook for legislative advocacy.

Bread for the World, 802 Rhode Island Ave., N.E., Washington, DC 20018—advocacy organization on hunger issues; publishes good congregational materials and a political action newsletter.

Center of Concern, 3700 13th St., N.E., Washington, D.C. 20017—organization for social analysis of peace and social justice issues; publishes helpful peace resources.

Pax Christi USA, 6337 W. Cornelia Ave., Chicago, IL 60634—Catholic peace organization.

Sojourners, P.O. Box 29272, Washington, D.C. 20017 (periodical)—monthly, book service.

Institute for Peace and Justice, 4144 Lindell Blvd., #400, St. Louis, MO 63108—publishes helpful materials on peace and justice such as *Parenting for Peace and Justice* and *Educating for Peace and Justice.*

Planning Committees

Handbook for Parish Evaluation, edited by Thomas P. Walters, Paulist/Archdiocese of Detroit, 1984.

How to Grow a Better Parish: From Insight to Impact, Robert G. Howes, Alba House Communications, 1986 (planning book and audiotape).

The Leadership Book, Charles J. Keating, Paulist Press, 1982.

The Parish: A People, A Mission, A Structure (vision statement) and *The Parish Self Study Guide,* National Conference of Catholic

Bishops (NCCB), 1981.

Pastoral Planning Book, Charles J. Keating, Paulist Press, 1981.

Who Are We and Where Are We Going?, William C. Harms, Sadlier, 1981.

Transforming People, Mission and Structure: The Parish Planning Manual, Mark C. Kemmeter, Archdiocese of Milwaukee, 1987.

The Archdiocese of Milwaukee has extensive resources for parish councils. Included are *Living the Spirit: A Parish Council Manual;* Parish Council Committee Packet; Parish Council Self-Evaluation Packet, Orientation/Nomination/Election booklet; *Growth in Discipleship: Spiritual Resources for Parish Councils.* A series of videotapes are also available. Contact: Office of Stewardship and Lay Leadership, Archdiocese of Milwaukee, P.O. Box 2018, Milwaukee, WI 53201.

The CALL Process, a series of renewal workbooks for parish councils that contain materials for 8 sessions of scriptural reflection and prayer, dialogue/group process; action goals, journaling and background reading. CALL I reflects on seven important aspects of council ministry; CALL II concentrates on the relationship of the council to the parish. Contact: Parish Leadership Services, 2163 N. 61 St., Wauwatosa, WI 53213. (CALL III to be available in 1989.)

PADICON (Parish and Diocesan Council Network), the national organization for councils, is an excellent source of parish council and committee resources. Contact S. Luanne Smits, P.O. Box 1825, Green Bay, WI 53405-5826 for their resource directory or Mrs. Eileen Tabert, P.O. Box 191, Metuchen, NJ 08840, for membership and newsletter information.

APPENDICES

A Retreat for a Parish Pastoral Council

A parish council needs to spend a day at least annually away from the parish to pray, reflect, and vision together. Such an experience can have several results: deeper faith development, building community and relationships among council members, and a strong spiritual foundation for discerning decisions. The council's committee members could also be invited to participate.

An outside facilitator for the retreat is desirable (inquire at your diocesan office or a nearby religious community) but a team of two-three council or committee members could also do a creditable job with adequate planning and preparation. Retreat facilities are often scarce, so it would be wise to reserve a place well in advance.

The retreat could take place on a Saturday (from approximately 9:30 a.m. to 3:00 p.m., with the first half-hour for gathering time and opening prayer) or during an evening, using only three of the segments.

Preparation: Who will the team members be? How will council members be invited? Where will the retreat be held and at what times? Who will be responsible for such matters as set-up, coffee, lunch, hymnals, Bible, and "prayer candle." Assign roles for each hour of the retreat; several persons could prepare brief presentations during the "input" portion of each segment, if desired. Be sure to let the parish know that the council will be on retreat and ask them to pray for council members.

The following outline for a council retreat is based on Chapter 2 of this book: "Councils and the People of God." (It would be good for councilors to read this chapter beforehand.) Each councilor needs a journal notebook in which to write some personal input. If the council is large, it could form several smaller sharing groups (4-5 persons is ideal).

The theme of the retreat is: The Parish Council as a Community of Disciples:

- becoming a community of disciples
- becoming a prayerful community
- gifted in the Spirit
- called to service and ministry.

The council gathers in a circle; the "prayer candle" is lit. A suitable hymn is sung. ("Here I Am ,Lord" is a good choice.) The council prays a psalm together (#40, 67, or 96).

First Hour: Becoming a community of disciples

Input: "The people of God are all called to be a communion of disciples in the Lord. They are called to follow him in laying down their lives for others. To follow the Lord as a disciple is to become totally identified with his mission in today's world....All councilors, therefore, when they gather around the table for their monthly meeting, are first called to be faithful disciples of the Lord."

Scripture for reflection: John 13:2-17 and Luke 9:57-62. Allow a period of silence following the reading.

Sharing in small groups

1) What does it mean to be a faithful disciple of the Lord?
2) How do council members discern God's call to be a community of disciples?
3) Why must discipleship result in service to be true discipleship?
4) In what ways does the council help the parish become more mission-centered?

Large group process: List on newsprint all the ways the parish can become more mission-centered, as discerned in the small group sharing. Which of the ideas seem most important and feasible? List these for dialogue and discernment during a future council meeting.

Journaling: A sign of discipleship in my own life is...

Prayer: After a few moments of silent reflection, council members share an insight or concern about the parish community or about the meaning of discipleship, each followed by a group response; Lord, grant us wisdom and understanding. A sign of peace and love is then shared.

Brief break.

Second Hour: Becoming a prayerful community

Input: "It means that the council is called to rely more on faith, prayer, and the Spirit than on its bylaws and constitution.... Every meeting is meant to be an experience in faith and in community."

Scripture for reflection: Romans 8:26-27 and Luke 11:1-13. Allow a period of silence following the readings.

Sharing in small groups: What is my personal experience of Jesus Christ? Of prayer? Are our council meetings an experience in faith and community? If not, why not? How can we help our council to be more prayerful, especially as part of our decision-making process? (Decide on one or two practical ways—shared prayer during meetings; occasional liturgy together, etc.).

Large group process: Share the practical ways the council can be more prayerful; try to come to consensus on one or two.

Journaling: One way I can become a more prayerful person is....

Prayer: During a few moments of silence, each council member personally asks for the presence of the Holy Spirit; together, they then offer spontaneous prayers of praise and thanksgiving. An amen is sung.

Brief break or lunch period.

Third Hour: Gifted in the Spirit

Input: "The Spirit equips the people of God for the work of the ministry. The gifts are allotted according to the measure of faith, as the Spirit wills. The Spirit makes the people of God fit and ready to undertake various tasks and offices for the renewal and upbuilding of the church. This means that the Spirit is constantly active in every believing Christian, acting on the Spirit's terms, not theirs.... Most parishes probably have more gifts and talents than they need. These gifts may still need to be discovered, trained, and then supported by the people of God. They may also need to be submitted to a process of prayerful discernment to determine if they are truly of the Spirit."

Scripture for reflection: 1 Cor. 12:4-11. Allow a period of silence following the reading.

Sharing in small groups:

(Note: Identifying the gifts of the laity on page 226 may be used in this segment.)

1) What gift has each of us been given by the Spirit? Share your gift and how you are using it on the council. Record the gifts.

2) What can we do as a council to help parishioners discern their gifts for service and ministry?

3) The gifts of the Spirit are given to build up the community of faith, and also to make an impact on the larger community— how can we support those who exercise their gifts in the larger community?

Large group process: Using the input from the small groups, develop an action plan to identify and support the giftedness of people in the parish. (The plan can be fleshed out at a later council meeting.)

Journaling: A gift I can offer the parish council is...

Prayer: Each member shares one of the gifts he or she has; the group prays in thanksgiving for the gifts present in the council and closes with this litany:

Response: We are the body of Christ:

In one spirit, all of us were baptized into Christ...

The body is not one member, but many...

If all the members were alike, where would the body be?

When all members are concerned for one another...

When the gift of each member is deemed indispensable...

When all suffer with one member who is suffering...

When all are honored when one member is honored...

In council meetings, as we try to establish goals...

In all of our council deliberations and planning...

As we steward the gifts of the Spirit for ministry and service...

Amen!

Brief break.

Fourth Hour: Called to service and ministry.

Input: "God calls us constantly...to new responsibility and new service."

Scripture for reflection: Matthew 5:3-11 and 14-16; Matthew 13:53-58. Allow a period of silence after the readings.

Sharing in small groups:

1) How does the council carry out its call to service and ministry in the church? In the world?

2) When committees are formed to develop and sustain ministries, how can the council help them to be effective?

3) What are some of the "new responsibilities" to which the council may be called? (e.g., more just attitudes, an emphasis on peace issues, etc.).

Large group process: Using the input from the small group sharing, decide how the council will more effectively carry out its call to service and ministry. In what ways will the council live out these "new responsibilities"?

Journaling: When I review the ministry or service in the parish in which I am engaged...

Prayer: The council members are invited to form a circle. After a few silent moments to place themselves in God's presence, they join in prayer:

We will sing your praises forever, Lord, for your goodness endures even to our generation. Though pressure and confusion daily surround us, Lord, your promise of strength is our comfort and refuge. When through our folly, personal and national relationships are broken, you lift us from despair with the hope of reconciliation for all peoples. We will give thanks to you with rejoicing, for even in our imperfect lives you continue to bless us. Your prophets speak to us, O Lord, and servant hearts still respond to your Word.

Council members are asked to share a hope for the future of the council and the parish. The closing prayer is the Our Father.

Appendix–Chapter 3

Identifying the Gifts of the Laity

Introduction: In helping laypeople to gain a vision of their universal calling to ministry in the world, there are several psychological barriers that must be overcome. Two of these barriers have to do with one's talents or "gifts."

The first attitude frequently expressed by laypeople is that

God's work has always been done by "giants of the faith." Too frequently we have so romanticized these "giants" that they have taken on the aura of super people. A careful reading of both the Old and New Testament will confirm that, throughout history, God has done uncommon things through very common people. Our so-called Bible heroes frequently were reluctant, doubting, frightened people possessing no outstanding talents. It was the power of God working through them that made the difference. Lay people need to recognize this, and thereby recognize their own potential.

The second attitude has to do with our understanding of humility. While it is a virtue to be humble, too many Christian laypeople carry their concept of humility to the point of denying their own God-given talents. Despite the fact that Paul highlights the importance of our gifts in Chapter 12 of Romans, Chapter 12 of 1 Corinthians, and elsewhere, too many laypeople depreciate their own gifts through a distorted sense of humility.

In an effort to help laypeople recognize their gifts and consider their potential for ministry, we frequently allocate a period of time for "Gift identification." While there are a number of methods for helping people to identify their gifts, ...the following self-study is especially useful....For best use, Steps One, Two, and Three should be presented on one sheet of paper, while the talent list and Step Four should be on a second sheet. This is to prevent the talent list from influencing decisions made in the first three steps.

Identification of Gifts

Step One: Write down a list of things you have done in your life that you value or enjoyed doing, no matter how small or insignificant you think they might appear to others. Try not to be influenced by what you think others would call valuable. This is what *you* value or enjoy. Go back in your childhood as far as you can. Try to list at least 30 things.

Step Two: From your large list select the five you value or enjoy the most and list them below.

Step Three: Think about this list as five accomplishments.

Starting with number 1, recall step-by-step what you did. Refer to the following list of talents and put one small checkmark next to each talent you used in doing or making that accomplishment. If a talent comes to mind that isn't listed, add it to the list and check it. When you have done this, go back over the list of checkmarks and determine which talent was the *most* important for the accomplishment, and put two more checkmarks on the line beside it. For the *second most important* talent put one additional checkmark on the line beside it.

Repeat the process for each of the five accomplishments.

A Talent List for the Identification of Gifts

Advise, counsel	Interpret
Arrange	Lead
Artistic presentation	Learn
Audit, bookkeeping	Listen
Caretaking	Love
Classify	Maintain
Collect	Manage
Communicate	Make from instructions
Compare	Motivate, inspire
Commit myself	Negotiate
Compile	Observe
Compute	Organize
Construct, build	Perform
Coordinate	Persuade
Conceptualize	Read
Copy, record	Repair
Create	Research, investigate
Demonstrate	Search for
Design, invent	Sell
Display	Serve, wait on others
Drive	Supervise
Do precision work	Support
Encourage	Talk
Envision	Use hands
Evaluate	Use tools
Facilitate	Write
Instruct, teach	Other

Step Four: Now add up the total number of checkmarks for each talent used. Identify your most frequently used talent on a sheet. List the second most frequently used talent, the third, fourth and fifth. You have just identified your God-given gifts.

(The above article by William E. Diehl originally appeared in *Laity Exchange*, copyright 1980, and may be reproduced as desired with acknowledgment.)

Appendix–Chapter 8

Sample Agenda for First Committee Meeting

1) *Introductions:* Invite every member, whether new or experienced, to introduce himself or herself and to complete the statement: I have become involved in the work of this committee because.... Encourage some storytelling in this regard so that all will gain new insights into the life, circumstances, interests, and motivations of others.

2) *Reflection time:* Invite each person to reflect silently on the following statements and to complete a statement of feeling that is most true for him or her at this time:

This evening, I feel
- hopeful
- somewhat anxious or fearful
- somewhat uncertain or confused
- happy
- sad

because....

3) *Group sharing:* Invite each person to turn to share his or her response with the group. All should listen without comment. Participation should be entirely voluntary.

4) *Affirmation of Individuals:* Invite those who wish to respond to a particular person or persons to do so. The purpose is not to question the validity of the person's feelings but to affirm them. Appropriate comments might be:

- I can identify with that feeling because...
- You made me aware that...

•I want to hear more about...

5) *Supplementary Activity:* If time permits, the process may be repeated with members completing the following statements. When this year ends, I will feel a sense of accomplishment:

•If I have...

•If we have...

•If the parish has...

6) *Orientation for Action:* Depending on the nature of the committee and the stage of its development, any of the following might be an appropriate first step toward accomplishment of chosen goals:

•Review goals of committee, roles of individual members

•Review work of past year

•Name particular events/programs for which group will be responsible during the weeks/months to come.

•Plan for orientation/enrichment of group members

•Assign tasks to individuals or subcommittees

•Set agenda for next meeting

Reprinted with permission from *Today's Parish*, September 1985.

Checklist for Committee Chairpersons

Am I fully aware of the committee's purpose and responsibilities?

•areas of responsibility

•competency and limits of committee's action

•parish priorities/goals

Am I willing to give the time to familiarize myself and the committee with those things that make for informed action by the committee?

•council bylaws

•consensus decision making

•planning and budgeting process

•diocesan guidelines

•diocesan resources

•what makes for effective leadership/membership in a group

Do I know some how-to's for effective leadership?
- plan a meeting
- involve other parishioners
- recruit talent to assist in areas in which I am weak
- share leadership
- write reports and publicize activities, etc.

Do I recognize the importance of the following:
- regular prayer and reflection
- attending council meetings
- communicating with council and other committees
- personal commitment
- promoting and taking advantage of diocesan opportunities for ongoing education
- working as a team

Reprinted with permission from *Called to Serve With Vision: Handbook for Parish Pastoral Councils*, Diocese of Nashville.

Appendix –Chapter 9

Rite of Nomination

The following rite may be used in place of the penitential rite on Nomination Sunday:

Presider: Let us pray for the Spirit of God to help us nominate leaders for our parish community.

All: Lord, you have consecrated us and called us to be your holy people. We ask that you send us your Holy Spirit—so that in wisdom we will choose people whom you have marked with leadership and who will want only to serve you. Help us to hear whom you are calling. Help them to say yes.

Presider: Spirit of God, among us there are those whom you have gifted for leadership.

Lector: Because we need leaders who have the vision to see the parish as our community and respond to its needs, we pray....

All: Help us to recognize them and call them by name
            to leadership in our parish.
Presider: Let us bow our heads and pray in silence.
Lector: Spirit of God, you have gifted those among us
            with creative imagination, tenacious faith and fi-
            delity to the Gospel, we pray....
All: Help us to recognize them and call them by name
            to leadership.
Presider: Let us bow our heads and pray in silence.
Lector: Spirit of God, you have gifted those young people
            who have a loving enthusiasm, a hope-filled vi-
            sion and commitment to their peers, we pray...
All: Help us to recognize them and call them by name
            to leadership.
Presider: Let us bow our heads and pray...
All: Lord God, whenever we ask, you gift us with your
            Spirit. May your Spirit continue to be with us in
            calling and choosing the leaders of our parish
            community, so that we may grow together in unity
            of faith, hope, and love through Christ our Lord.

(This prayer service was developed by St. Alphonsus Parish,
Greendale, Wisconsin.)

Formation for Discipleship: An Orientation Program for Parish Council Nominees

Parish councils are often ineffective because they do not understand the meaning and goals of leadership in the contemporary
church. The following outline of a two-session program may be
helpful. Session I concentrates on parish council identity and a
clarifying of roles and relationships within parish leadership.
Session II addresses the issues and concerns that should be the
focus in the individual parish. The facilitator of the sessions
should be someone with broad parish council and committee experience, and with an ability to guide discussion. The sessions
should involve prayer and reflection.

Session I: The Parish Council as Leadership Ministry

Purpose: to clarify the identity, scope, role and relationships, as well as the mission of the parish council and its committees.

Identity: Who are we as a parish council? Discuss why the council exists: not just to handle the "business" of the parish but to be catalyst for parish renewal, and to coordinate the gifts and talents poured out by the Spirit on the parish. Discuss the role of the council as leaders of the parish in implementing the mission of the church. Does the council understand that it is not a board of directors or an organization of organizations and that its mission is broader than the parish? Discuss the importance of planning for the future rather than just reacting to crises, and the importance of assuring that the views of the parishioners are heard. How does the council practice good stewardship of parish resources?

Scope: The council discerns policy for the parish. Its decisions must reflect the Gospel and the mission of the church, and not just be a matter of democratic vote. It must also take into account civil law, canon law, and archdiocesan guidelines. Discuss the process through which council decisions are made—consensus, discernment, majority vote, or a combination of these. Why is *Robert's Rules* unsuitable for council decision-making?

Roles and relationships: In order to be effective, the relationship between the council (policy-formulating) and the staff (administrative), especially the pastor, must be clarified. If a parish is a corporation with lay trustees, what is their relationship to the council? Discuss the committees as the implementing and recommending arms of the council and the principle of subsidiarity. Do all parish leaders work as partners? What skills do they need to learn? Discuss how council membership must be both functional and representative.

Spiritual formation: The council is not a decision-making body that happens to pray, but a praying body that makes decisions: prayer and reflection are an integral part of each meeting in order to set the tone for a discernment of issues facing the council. The councilors are also expected to participate in an annual day of spiritual renewal.

Session II: Knowing our Parish Council

Purpose: to cover the past history and practical details of our parish council.

After a welcome and introduction of the nominees (or new councilors, if this is the case), the following agenda may be used:

History of the council in our parish: Discuss how past experience affects the manner in which the council functions and some of the issues handled in the past. Review and explain the parish council constitution and bylaws, and the parish mission statement. Review the council's relationship with the diocese. How are officers of the council chosen?

Goals: Review the goals the council has set for the next year as well as any long-range goals. What time commitments will be required of each councilor to meet these goals?

Council committees: Review the standing committees of the council. How they relate to the council and their responsibilities and functions. Encourage the use of each person's gifts on a committee. Review how committee chairpersons are chosen. How do parish organizations fit in?

Meetings: Describe the specific way decisions are made on the council and explain how the council will pray, reflect, and study together. Stress the importance of listening so that the needs of the parish and the community may be discerned. How will agendas and minutes reach the councilor?

The sessions may be completed with a prayerful period during which the nominees may discern whether or not they wish to be candidates for council, and a social time.

Prayer Service

Leader:	And now, my friends, we want to invite you to pray and reflect with us on the challenge which the Lord Jesus has offered to us: "Come and follow me."
First reading:	John 15:5-11
All:	Response: Lord, you have called us to be hearers of the Word: open our minds to what you have to say to us.
Second	#11, *Church in the Modern World* (first two para.).

All: Response: Lord, you have called us to be doers of the Word—open our hearts to the needs around us. (*silent meditation*)

Leader: Lord God, after reflecting upon your great love for each of us shown in the creation of the world and our own gift of life, we offer you our petitions: (Respond: Lord, we pray; make us your disciples.).

That through our union with Christ in baptism and our growth in confirmation, we may attain a full maturity in a spirit of charity and responsibility...

That we may share our talents and resources for the building up of our parish community...

That we may be open to making a commitment to parish council service...

That we may ever believe in God's love for us...

All: We thank you, Lord, for the gift of your Holy Spirit. Help us to use the Spirit's gifts in love for each other and to encourage the people of our parishes to offer their talents gladly to build up the body of Christ, which is the church. Grant zeal, courage, and caring to all our councils and committees. May your name be blessed now and forever.

Amen.

(The above orientation program and prayer service were adapted from the Orientation/Nomination/Election Process booklet, Archdiocese of Milwaukee.)

Commissioning Service and Appreciation Service for New and Retiring ParishPastoral Council Members

(*Follows the homily in the Liturgy of the Word.*)

Pastor: Let those who have been chosen for service to _____ Parish as members of the parish pastoral council now come forward.

(*Deacon or other assisting minister reads names of the council as they come forward.*)

Pastor: Each of you has been called out of the parish community to render a special service of leadership to
us, the believers in the Body of Christ of the parish of _____. Do you accept the responsibilities of parish leadership we are placing upon you?

Members: I do.

Pastor: Will you work to build up our parish community of
faith by your generous gift of personal talents,
time, and energy in the spirit of Christ-like love?

Members: I will.

Pastor: Each of you has gifts to enable you to render this
ministry of service for which you have been cho-
sen, and the generosity with which you have accepted this responsibility is encouraging to all of
us. We ask you now to step forward and receive a
burning candle lighted from the Easter Candle.
This is a sign that you have determined in a special way to spread the light of Christ in this parish community by your actions, counsel, and decisions on the parish pastoral council.

*Each member steps up to receive the light from the pastor. All
then turn and face the congregation and say together.)*

Members: We humbly accept your confidence in us. We ask
your prayerful support, encouragement, and honest
criticism as we attempt to carry out this leadership service according to the spirit of the prayer
of St. Francis of Assisi. We ask you to join us in
singing (*or saying*) that prayer.

(All pray the Prayer of St. Francis.)

Pastor :   (*to congregation):*Let us show our support for this
leadership council. (*applause*)

(Invite members to return to their seats.)

Pastor: I invite those who have served on our parish pastoral council for the past _____ years now to come
forward.

*(Deacon or other assisting minister reads the names of the out-
going parish pastoral council members.)*

Pastor: On behalf of the entire parish, I would like to present you with this token of our appreciation. May you continue to carry out your baptismal and confirmational call to ministry by ever being of service to others.

(Pastor hands each person some gift [a plaque, certificate, etc.]).

Pastor: Let us show our appreciation of the service given by the former council members. *(applause)*

(All are invited to return to their seats.)

The prayers of the faithful that follow should contain a prayer for the council, their families, and for the grace of leadership. They should contain a prayer of thanks for the work of the outgoing council members.

(Reprinted with permission from *Called to Serve with Vision*, Diocese of Nashville.)

Appendix–Chapter 10

Resolving Conflict

Conflict is inevitable and even valuable in human experience. The question is not to avoid conflict but to deal with it constructively. By understanding the following principles, we can learn to recognize: (1) When a person needs help, (2) What we do that is harmful, and (3) What we do that is helpful.

I. Our "success" as people is dependent upon our ability to resolve conflict.

  A. Conflict means: to be at variance; two or more opposing viewpoints; to clash.

    1) Conflict of perspective

    2) Conflict of values

  B. There are two kinds of conflicts:

    1) Internal (person against self)

    2) External (person against person)

  C. Resolution of conflict produces growth.

    1) Conflict is not bad and to be avoided, but rather good and to be resolved.

2) The success of all of us is dependent upon our ability to handle internal and external conflict.

II. We often resolve conflict in three ways that do us great harm.

A. Fighting (symptoms: physically fighting, gossiping, arguing, blaming, excusing, defending, bragging, lecturing, etc.).

B. Running (symptoms: physically running, crying, pitying, attacking oneself, becoming silent, etc.).

C. Ignoring (symptoms: "intellectualizing," remaining apathetic, acting unaffected).

III. These methods of resolving conflict do us great long-term damage.

A. We develop a lifestyle built around one of them.

B. We concede control of our lives.

1) We fail to solve the real problem

2) We fail to control our feelings

3) We fail to grow.

IV. Leaders, with helpful intentions, often perpetuate poor conflict resolution.

A. Fighting evokes obedience (so we give in); resentment (so we ignore); anger (so we fight).

B. Running evokes guilt (so we play up to); resentment (so we ignore; pity (so we moralize).

C. Ignoring evokes envy (so we pull back); anger (so we attack).

V. There is a constructive means of dealing with conflict: "leveling."

A. The key to leveling is developing an awareness of one's honest feelings.

1) One must *recognize* his or her feelings: the hurt; the fear; the anger; the threat; the inferiority

2) One must *admit* his or her feelings (verbally and physically): "I feel hurt" "I feel angry" "I feel threatened" "I feel unappreciated"

3) One must *accept* these feelings as a part of oneself: "I feel hurt and yet I cherish myself" "I feel unloved and yet I like myself"

4) One must *concede* the feelings of others

5) We must *concentrate* on problem-solving behavior

B) That awareness grows into two personal concepts which are essential in order to resolve conflict constructively.

1) I am responsible for what I am and for what I become. "I can blame (run, ignore) but what will it accomplish?" "I have to take control and solve the problem if it is to be solved."

2) I am valuable. "I can defend (run, cry, ignore) but it won't change what I am. I love myself despite these conflicts."

VI. Leaders can set the "leveling" climate so that councilors can resolve conflict constructively.

A. Recognize the methods being used by a councilor to resolve his or her conflict (fighting, running or ignoring)

B. Change the method to that of "leveling"

1) By communicating: You are responsible. You are worthwhile.

2) By communicating: You are valuable. (I trust you even if you make mistakes.)

Dealing With Types of Personalities

How to deal with the autocrat:

1) Maintain a strong personal emotional stability.

2) Clarify and purify your own objectives and attitudes.

3) Assume the responsibility of being the one who understands.

4) Listen.

5) Monitor your own verbal, non-verbal and extra verbal behavior.

6) Find a point of agreement.

7) Tell how you feel, what you can see—not what you think.

8) Avoid "yes but" phrases.

9) Avoid apologetic and whiny tones of voice—speak with strength.

10) Stand erect.

11) Ask for clarification of points.

12) Consider detailed "jargon" if necessary.

13) As an absolute *final* attempt—be equally direct and assertive.

14) Remember—we are more emotional than rational.
15) Clarify your objective.
16) Develop a personal dominance.
17) Keep "selling" tools sharp—help visualize.
18) Be persistent.
19) Accept reality—sometimes improbable if not impossible.
How to deal with the non-assertive:
1) Avoid being "hooked" into being the opposite (manipulative, aggressive).
2) Recognize their sensitivity to directness.
3) Realize their vulnerability to intimidation.
4) Respect their ability to counterattack with passive aggressiveness.
5) Listen—"with the third ear."
6) Tell them how you feel, what you see and not what you think.
7) Monitor their feelings and responses continually.
8) Strive to build their self-esteem.
9) Be sincere in praise—praise often—be specific.
10) Build a bank account of good will.
11) Be patient.
12) Believe in them.
13) Be sensitive to their self-criticism.
14) Understand their needs.
15) Help them experience achievement.
16) Avoid having your prejudices stimulated or activated.
(The above material is from the Archdiocese of Denver.)

Prayer to Be a Better Listener

"We do not really listen to each other, God, at least not all the time. Instead of true dialogue, we carry on two parallel monologues. I talk. My companion talks. But what we are really concentrating on is how to sound good, how to make our points strongly, how to outshine the person with whom we are talking. Teach us to listen as your Son listened to everyone who spoke with him. Remind us that, somehow, you are trying to reach us through the conversation. Your truth, your love, your goodness are seeking us out in the truth, love, and goodness of being communicated. When our words are harsh, hostile, angry, we convey the very opposite of these qualities. Teach us to be still, Lord, that we may truly hear our brothers and sisters and in them, you. Amen." (The Christophers).

Appendix - Chapter 11

A PLANNING COVENANT

Between_____ Parish and _____ (diocese).

By resolution of this parish on _____ (date), we have agreed to participate in the Parish Planning Process.

We approach this planning process with the explicit understanding that:

• our parish leadership is totally committed to this planning; process;
• we understand that some changes will be made in our parish;
• we are dedicated to taking the time to plan well.

Our parish recognizes that planning does not work perfectly and we are committed to learning from our efforts.

Our parish has prepared for this process by:

• establishing a planning committee
• assembling a parish profile
• discussing the contents of this profile.

The diocese will provide the following assistance to our planning team: _____

We fully understand and support our parish's participation in this planning process and agree to this covenant as a sign of our willingness to work together to effectively plan for our common future.

Date_____

_____
Parish/Administrator

Date _____

_____

Parish Council Chairperson

("A Planning Covenant" is reprinted from Transforming People, Mission & STructure: A Planning Manual, by Mark Kemmeter, Archdiocese of Milwaukee.)

Appendix - Chapter 13

Building a Foundation for More Effective Parish Councils

Evaluate how you feel your parish council functions. If unsure of your response, mark with a 2.

Score the following as general indicators:

3 - Good (or very good)

2 - Adequate, would work on this if enough time.

1 - Less than adequate, top need for improvement.

SPIRITUAL

☐ Membership on this council has provided a climate for our spiritual growth.

☐ Community prayer has been authentic and valued.

☐ We make time as a council to reflect about our Christian direction and responsibility to each other.

ORIENTATION

☐ Adequacy of council orientation, including

    Purpose of the parish council

    Getting acquainted

    Expectations and limitations of the council

    Meeting dates and meeting information

    List of council members

    Budget and financial report

      Committee functions, membership

      Relationship to the parish

      Relationship of the parish to the diocese

☐ Written material reinforcing orientation is available.

☐ There is opportunity for ongoing clarification of basic information.

TEAM BUILDING

☐ Council members, pastor, and staff know each other well enough to work effectively as a group.

☐ Individual values are explored.

☐ There is enough trust within the council that members feel free to express their feelings.

COUNCIL/STAFF ROLES, RESPONSIBILITIES

☐ The working roles and functions of council members, pastor, and staff are openly explored and defined.

☐ The council receives adequate information to make decisions based on data.

☐ When a decision is made, it is clear to everyone who is responsible for implementing action.

GROUP PROCESS

☐ Time is well spent on meaningful items.

☐ Decision-making methods are defined and agreed upon; multiple options and solutions are explored in the decision-making process.

☐ The group understands options (consensus, voting) in dealing with conflicts effectively.

PLANNING

☐ The council does long-range planning.

☐ There is involvement of council and staff in writing measurable short-term objectives that can be accomplished in a set time.

☐ Feedback received from evaluation is considered in future planning.

LEADERSHIP

☐ The roles of leadership are explored and understood.

☐ Leaders are supported and given opportunity to grow in their role by council members and staff.

☐ There is an effective plan to develop new leadership.

COMMITTEES

☐ Committee responsibilities and limitations are both appropriate and understood.

☐ The council holds committees accountable for meetings and objectives.

☐ The council respects committee work and recommendations.

BUDGET

☐ The budget reflects the parish program and is understood by all council members.

☐ There is active participation in budget decisions by council members.

☐ Budget decisions serve the goals and objectives of the parish.

COMMUNITY OUTREACH

☐ Effort is made to understand the community served by and affecting the parish.

☐ There is understanding of how the parish is a link with other community groups, other churches, other agencies.

☐ Council membership is representative of the parish community.

EVALUATION

☐ The council evaluates its own functioning as an ongoing process.

☐ The council solicits feedback from the parishioners.

☐ The council is actively involved in program evaluation.

Add total scores in each seection; for example:

PLANNING

3_____

2_____

2_____

Survey Results—Council Needs

From the survey sheets, rank order the 5 areas needing improvement, starting with the lowest totaled score of the eleven categories (e.g. Spiritual, Orientation...)

1. _____
2. _____
3. _____
4. _____
5. _____

As a group, share your ranking. The facilitator will ask:

How many ranked *Orientation* first, second, etc. through the eleven categories.

While these scores are being tabulated, each participant should make a personal decision on what activities, (Orientation, Planning, etc.) he/she feels would be most valuable to the council right *now* in order to improve effectiveness. This list may or may not coincide with the previous list. You may be more skilled in group process than in planning but feel a greater need to work on group process to best increase your effectiveness now. The categories I feel are most important to our council *today* are:

1. _____
2. _____
3. _____

Congratulations!! You've already evaluated your current council experience, identified strengths and growth needs, and prioritized learning goals.

If you've verified you're doing a great job...*Great*!

Or, do you need future sessions to help your council become even more effective? The decision is based on the council's need to spend time on tasks that need to be done *balanced* by time devoted to increasing skills. Greater effectiveness may save time. And do view this model as a foundation for ongoing exploration of needs, feeding back results, planning, and implementation!

Assumptions Worksheet

This exercise is designed for your use to help you evaluate your parish council's current climate. In your opinion, would your parish council generally agree with these *Assumptions*?

1) The purpose of the parish council is agreed upon by the group and seen as important.

2) Each council member has the right to experience personal growth and to feel that time is well used.

3) Individual differences of members (due to different life experiences, values, and length of time with the council) are accepted.

4) Council members who are experienced in group process aid others on the council by their examples.

5) Council members assume responsibility in determining needs and planning group activities.

6) The council is willing to explore ways of improving its effectiveness, even though time is limited (meeting once a month, many tasks to accomplish).

7) Council members are aware of what is needed to increase effectiveness.

8) Time will be made for growth activities, if needs are identified and requested by the council. (Shared prayer, spiritual or social activities).

9) As much as possible, the total council membership would participate in growth activities.

10) Effectiveness could increase without working on all identified ares of weakness.

Complete the bar graph below. Count the number of "yes" responses and fill in two squares for each "yes" answer; for each "unsure" answer fill in one square. Start from the left, and move sequentially to the right. When completed, the chart will give you some measure of your parish council's openness to exploring and improving effectiveness.

start here   Ready to *go* and *grow!*

We have a slow start and meet resistance.

INDEX